UNCOMMON
THERAPY

ALSO BY JAY HALEY

UNCOMMON THERAPY

THE PSYCHIATRIC TECHNIQUES OF MILTON H. ERICKSON, M.D.

JAY HALEY

W·W·NORTON & COMPANY

New York · London

W. W. Norton & Company, Inc. is also the publisher of the
works of Erik H. Erikson, Otto Fenichel, Karen Horney, Harry Stack
Sullivan, and The Standard Edition of the Complete Psychological
Works of Sigmund Freud.

Library of Congress Cataloging in Publication Data

Haley, Jay.
    Uncommon therapy.

    1. Hypnotism—Therapeutic use.   2. Family
psychotherapy.   3. Erickson, Milton H.   I. Title.
RC495.H34   616.8'9'00924   72-12924

ISBN 0-393-30424-8

W. W. Norton & Company, Inc., 500 Fifth Avenue
New York, N.Y. 10110
W. W. Norton & Company Ltd. 10 Coptic Street
London WC1A 1PU

PRINTED IN THE UNITED STATES OF AMERICA

5 6 7 8 9 0

CONTENTS

PREFACE   9

I.   STRATEGIC THERAPY   17

II.   THE FAMILY LIFE CYCLE   41

III.   THE COURTSHIP PERIOD: CHANGING
       THE YOUNG ADULT   65

IV.   CHARACTER REVISION OF THE YOUNG
       ADULT   111

V.   MARRIAGE AND ITS CONSEQUENCES   149

VI.   CHILDBIRTH AND DEALING WITH THE
       YOUNG   183

VII.   MARRIAGE AND FAMILY DILEMMAS   223

VIII. WEANING PARENTS FROM CHILDREN   265

IX.   THE PAIN OF OLD AGE   297

PREFACE

In an epilogue to this book when it was originally published, I wrote:

> Milton H. Erickson is reaching the final chapter himself. Quite ill and
> confined to a wheel chair, he sees a patient only occasionally. In his later years
> his approach to human problems has a simplicity and efficiency that reminds
> one of the later work of many artists. Picasso achieves more simplicity in his
> drawings, Borges turns to a more elementary way of telling stories, and
> Erickson has mastered an economy of therapeutic style, perhaps compensating
> for his increasing physical weakness, which is like the strokes of a diamond
> cutter. He appears to grasp the fundamentals of a human situation with
> remarkable quickness, and his therapeutic interventions are simple and pre-
> cise, without wasted effort. With old age his wisdom has increased, just at the
> time when he has lost the personal strength to put it into effect, which seems to
> be one of the inevitable ironies of life.

Since Erickson's death in 1980, his strategic approach to therapy has
increased in popularity and is studied and taught everywhere. He has
changed from a controversial figure in the therapy field to a universally
admired one. A book about him appears almost monthly and many
people are giving workshops in Ericksonian therapy. He is assuming the
stature of a cult figure with thousands of admirers attending meetings of
the foundation formed in his honor.

I think Erickson would be pleased that his years of hard work,
innovating new ways to influence people, have resulted in such a
following. He might be less pleased about the cult being built around
him, since he was such a practical man. However, he also liked to create
an aura of mystery about his ways of working. At one time I considered
entitling this book "Sorcery and Common Sense," since both aspects of
him were part of his life.

I was given a rare opportunity in January 1953, when I was employed by Gregory Bateson on his research project to study communication. John Weakland also joined the project at that time, and Bateson
offered us full freedom to investigate whatever we wished as long as we
dealt somehow with the paradoxes that arise in the communicative
process. That first year Milton H. Erickson passed through our area
offering one of his weekend seminars in hypnosis. I said I would like to
attend, and Bateson arranged it. He had known Dr. Erickson from an

earlier period when, with Margaret Mead, he had consulted him about trance films they had made in Bali.

After that seminar my research investigation included the communicative aspects of the hypnotic relationship. John Weakland joined me in this endeavor, and we began to make regular visits to Phoenix, where Dr. Erickson was in private practice. We spent many hours talking with him about the nature of hypnosis and watching him work with subjects. On the road teaching and consulting somewhere in the country several times a month, he was also conducting a busy private practice. Despite his two attacks of polio and his need to walk awkwardly with a cane, he was vigorous and in good health. His office was in his home, a small room just off the dining room, and his living room was his waiting room. Several of his eight children were still small and at home in the 1950s, and so his patients mingled with his family. His home was a modest brick house on a quiet street, and I often wondered what patients from various parts of the country, who expected a leading psychiatrist to have a more pretentious office, must have thought.

After we had studied the hypnosis of Dr. Erickson for a time, our interest shifted to his style of therapy. In the mid-1950s, I began a private practice of psychotherapy, specializing in brief treatment. My task was to get someone over his problem as rapidly as possible, usually using hypnosis. I soon realized that merely hypnotizing people did not cure them; I must do something to bring about change. I sought a consultant in brief-treatment methods, and in those days of long-term, insight therapy there was no one available. Don D. Jackson, who had been supervising the therapy we were doing with schizophrenics in our research project, could be helpful, but his experience with brief therapy was limited. As I cast around for someone to advise me, I found that the only person I knew with special experience in short-term therapy was Dr. Erickson. From our talks on hypnosis, I knew he had a special style of therapy that sometimes involved hypnosis and sometimes did not. I began to visit him to discuss problems about the cases I was treating. It soon became obvious to me that he had an original style of therapy that had never been adequately presented in the field. I attempted to describe his approach in an article on brief therapy, which was later incorporated as a chapter in *Strategies of Psychotherapy.** Over the years I was tempted to present his approach more fully in book form. I hesitated because of the formidable labor of such a work and also because I did not have an appropriate theoretical framework for thinking about and presenting his

---

*Jay Haley, *Strategies of Psychotherapy* (New York: Grune & Stratton, 1963).

methods of therapy. Our research project at that time was investigating a variety of forms of therapy, and we were recording and filming different practitioners. Yet Dr. Erickson stood out as a unique school in himself, and the usual premises of psychiatry and psychology were not adequate to describe him.

During this period a revolution occurred in the field of therapy, with the introduction of the idea of a family orientation. What were once called symptoms, or individual problems, began to be redefined as products of personal relationships. As we explored the newly developing field of family therapy in our research, and as I began to treat couples and families, I found that Dr. Erickson's approach to treatment was especially revealing. It began to seem possible to place his therapy within a framework of family theory. His family orientation was implicit in his work, and talking with him and examining his cases helped me toward a new view of the family as a center of human dilemmas. When I began to think of human problems as inevitable in the way a family develops over time, I realized that Dr. Erickson's therapy was largely based upon that assumption. I had found the framework for describing his work.

The reader of some of these extraordinary cases who is unfamiliar with Dr. Erickson and who might want to know more about him will find in *Advanced Techniques of Hypnosis and Therapy,** Dr. Erickson's collected papers, an introduction giving biographical information about him, as well as an appendix offering a general discussion of his work. There is also in that book a complete bibliography of his writings for those who wish to pursue their interest further.

But a few words about Dr. Erickson's professional background may be useful. He attended the University of Wisconsin and received his medical degree at the Colorado General Hospital, simultaneously receiving his master's degree in psychology. After completing special training at the Colorado Psychopathic Hospital, he became a junior psychiatrist at Rhode Island State Hospital. In 1930 he joined the staff of the Worcester (Massachusetts) State Hospital and became chief psychiatrist of the Research Service. Four years later he went to Eloise, Michigan, as director of psychiatric research and training at Wayne County General Hospital and Infirmary. He was also associate professor of psychiatry at the Wayne State University College of Medicine and professor in the graduate school. Concurrently, he was briefly a visiting professor of clinical psychology at Michigan State University, in East Lansing. In 1948 he settled in Phoenix, Arizona, largely for his health,

*Jay Haley, ed., *Advanced Techniques of Hypnosis and Therapy: The Selected Papers of Milton R. Erickson, M.D.* (New York: Grune & Stratton, 1967).

and entered private practice. He was a Fellow of both the American Psychiatric Association and the American Psychological Association, as well as a Fellow of the American Psychopathological Association. In addition to being an honorary member of numerous societies of medical hypnosis in Europe, Latin America, and Asia, he was the founding president of the American Society for Clinical Hypnosis as well as editor of that society's professional journal. His professional life after 1950 included both a busy private practice in Phoenix and constant traveling to offer seminars and lectures throughout the United States and in many foreign countries.

Despite the collaboration in the ideas presented here, the point of view generally expressed in this work is not necessarily that of Dr. Erickson. It is my own way of describing his approach to therapy. He read and approved of the manuscript, but his own view of his therapy is expressed in his own writings. The case reports I have included are in his words, many of them taken from his articles, but they are edited to emphasize the points I wish to make. This work is only a partial portrait of Erickson's therapy. He wrote over a hundred professional articles, and I had over a hundred recorded hours of conversation with him. This selection of his cases represents only a portion of that vast amount of data on his work. He had a great range of hypnotic techniques that have not been included here, as well as a variety of approaches to individuals and families that have not been explored.

This work also does not offer a critical review of Dr. Erickson and his work. I have not emphasized my disagreements with him but have emphasized as clearly as I could his ideas about what therapy should be. Where I agree with him, I cite cases of my own where I have used his approach, but where I disagree, I have presented his ideas and not my own.

Some readers may be irritated by the continual emphasis upon successful treatment in this work. It is not that Dr. Erickson did not fail with cases or did not have his limitations. Occasionally, failures are mentioned to illustrate a point. But this is a book about successful ways of solving human problems, and therefore the cases included are those in which his approach worked. We have had enough books about methods of psychotherapy that consistently fail, although sometimes the authors emphasize the beauty of the theories and not the poor outcome of the therapy.

Ordinarily, in this technical age, if one is describing a therapist at work he should present films of him with patients, or at least tape recordings, to document the intricate involvements in the therapeutic enterprise. This book is more old-fashioned. It is a casebook based largely upon the therapist's description of what he does. Therefore it has the demerit of being a subjective interpretation of what happened in therapy. All the opportunity of bias arises when a therapist describes his own work. Yet no matter what technical facilities become available to present therapeutic encounters, I think there will always be a place for a description of his work by a therapist. I have described therapists by using audio recordings of them at work, by using videotape and films, by having the therapist comment on such recordings, and by having discussions of theory with the practitioner. The case example in which a therapist describes how he saw a problem and what he did about it will continue to be a valuable way of understanding a therapeutic approach. The kind of casebook offered here allows brief coverage of a vast number of techniques for approaching a wide range of human problems. Each case is discussed briefly to illustrate a few points, but any one of these cases could be a book in itself if presented more fully. Because of the oversimplification of such complex interchanges, this work is really a book of case anecdotes; the summaries are designed to present the crucial incidents in the therapy. Generally, Dr. Erickson described his approach with remarkable clarity, at times adding a touch of drama, since he tended to see the world in that way. Often he liked to present the problem he was faced with as an impossible one and then reveal the solution. What he did in therapy seems so reasonable once one grasps his point of view, that it might be said that if he didn't make these therapeutic interventions, someone should. Over the years I have tried his methods, and so have many other people, and they are effective. One can adapt his approach to one's own style. It was characteristic of Erickson to be intensely involved with a person, and the patient who received his full attention experienced the impact of his personality. Yet other therapists with different personalities and less involvement can use many of his techniques.

As I look over this book for the new edition, I am pleased to find that I do not regret what is said and would not change it. The ideas and theories are still basic and the cases are eternal: it is characteristic of Erickson's work that his therapy is crystallized in each case. I am still pleased with the framework of the family life cycle which I created to describe Erickson's work. That idea is widely used today, and it is taken for granted that there are stages of family life which are relevant to therapy. At the time this work was written that was a new idea.

In the 1960s, when I began the task of writing this book, I was fortunate to have almost a year to work on it full time. I thought that would be sufficient. In fact, it was five long years of effort before the work was finally completed. I had to listen to, and transcribe, audiotapes of conversations with Dr. Erickson which ranged over a seventeen-year period and covered a great variety of topics, ranging from therapy to hypnosis to many kinds of human experimentation.* I also had to describe Erickson's approach in a way that made sense when traditional ideas about therapy were not applicable to his work. It is always difficult to describe the ideas and inventions of another person since one is never certain whether the facts are correct and the ideas would be approved by him as expressed. This is particularly so when they are new ideas still murky and in the process of formulation. What I liked most about the reception of this book was that Erickson was pleased by it as an expression of his work. He ordered many copies of the book and enjoyed passing them out to colleagues and students.

For many of the ideas about Erickson's work I am indebted to John Weakland. We spent years together sharing a common interest in both hypnosis and therapy. Gregory Bateson made his contribution to this work not only by providing ideas but by sheltering the research within his wide-ranging project on communication. In the final stages of the manuscript, conversations with Braulio Montalvo were extremely helpful in clarifying many of the ideas.

Jay Haley, 1986

*A selection of these conversations has been published. Jay Haley, *Conversations with Erickson*, volumes 1, 2, and 3 (Washington, D.C.: Triangle Press, 1985; distributed by W. W. Norton, 500 Fifth Avenue, New York, N.Y. 10110).

UNCOMMON
THERAPY

1 STRATEGIC THERAPY

Therapy can be called strategic if the clinician initiates what happens during therapy and designs a particular approach for each problem. When a therapist and a person with a problem encounter each other, the action that takes place is determined by both of them, but in strategic therapy the initiative is largely taken by the therapist. He must identify solvable problems, set goals, design interventions to achieve those goals, examine the responses he receives to correct his approach, and ultimately examine the outcome of his therapy to see if it has been effective. The therapist must be acutely sensitive and responsive to the patient and his social field, but how he proceeds must be determined by himself.

During the first half of this century, clinicians were trained to avoid planning or initiating what was to happen in therapy and to wait for the patient to say or do something. Only then could the therapist act. Under the influence of psychoanalysis, Rogerian therapy, and psychodynamic therapy generally, the idea developed that the person who does not know what to do and is seeking help should determine what happens in the therapeutic session. The clinician was expected to sit passively and only interpret or reflect back to a patient what he was saying and doing. He could also offer only one approach no matter how different the kinds of people or problems were that came to him. It was considered "manipulative" to focus on a problem, set goals, deliberately intervene in a person's life, or examine the results of such therapy. This passive approach lost for the clinical profession many of the effective therapeutic strategies that were developing before this century.

Strategic therapy is not a particular approach or theory but a name for those types of therapy where the therapist takes responsibility for directly influencing people. In the middle of this century, in the 1950s, a variety of strategic therapeutic approaches began to proliferate. Various types of family therapy and the conditioning therapies developed with the premise that a therapist should plan what to do. For a time there was controversy over whether it was wrong for a therapist to take action to bring about change, but now it seems clear that effective therapy requires that approach, and the disagreements are over how to go about it.

Although therapy has shifted from the passive to the active, there has always been continuity with the past in the procedures of therapists who use hypnosis. It is in the nature of hypnosis that the hypnotist must initiate what is to happen. The influence of hypnosis upon all forms of therapy has not been fully appreciated. It can be argued that most therapeutic approaches have their origins in that art. The conditioning therapies with their different names came from Thorndike through Skinner, but their basic premises derive from Pavlov, who was immersed in hypnotic theories. Behavior therapy in the form of reciprocal inhibition was originated by Joseph Wolpe and came partly from his experience as a hypnotist. Dynamic psychotherapy, particularly in its psychoanalytic form, arose in that great period of hypnotic experimentation at the end of the last century. Freud's method was rooted in hypnosis, and although he shifted from the direct induction of trance to a more indirect approach, his work grew out of a hypnotic orientation. A possible exception to the influence of hypnosis on all forms of therapy may be certain of the family therapies. A family therapist who attempts to change the individuals in a family has carried many ideas from hypnosis into the family field. Other family therapists, however, who focus upon the sequence, or process, of behavior between two or more family members, seem less influenced. An exception to the latter group is Milton H. Erickson, who will change behavior between people with an approach that has developed directly out of a hypnotic orientation.

Erickson can be considered the master in the strategic approach to therapy. He has long been known as the world's leading medical hypnotist, having spent his life doing experimental work and using hypnosis in therapy in an infinite variety of ways. What is less well known is the strategic approach he has developed for individuals, married couples, and families without the formal use of hypnosis. For many years, he has conducted a busy psychiatric practice dealing with every kind of psychological problem and with families at every stage of life. Even when he does not formally use hypnosis, his style of therapy is so based upon the hypnotic orientation that whatever he does appears to have its origins in that art. He has brought to therapy an extraordinary range of hypnotic techniques, and he has also brought to hypnosis an expansion of ideas that have broadened hypnosis beyond a ritual to a special style of communication.

One way to view the strategic therapy of Milton Erickson is as a logical extension of hypnotic technique. Out of hypnotic training comes skill in observing people and the complex ways they communicate, skill in motivating people to follow directives, and skill in using one's own words, intonations, and body movements to influence other people. Also out of hypnosis come a conception of people as changeable, an appreciation of the malleability of space and time, and specific ideas about how to direct another person to become more autonomous. Just as a hypnotist can think of transforming a severe symptom into a milder one, or one of shorter duration, he can think of shifting an interpersonal problem into an advantage. More easily than most therapists, a hypnotically trained person can grasp the idea that subjective feelings and perceptions change with a change in relationship. The strategic way of thinking is central to the hypnotic approach when it is used properly, and Erickson has carried it to its limits. He is both an experimental hypnotist and an experimental therapist transferring ideas from hypnosis into therapeutic procedures where one might not expect to find them. Once found, they can clarify and sharpen the skills of any therapist.

Most people, including many clinically trained professionals, think of hypnosis as a special situation unlike other situations in life. People untrained in hypnosis think of it as a procedure in which a hypnotist says "Relax" and the subject goes to "sleep," and then suggestions are given to him. Or a subject is asked to look at a light or an object and is told that his eyelids will get heavy and he will go to sleep. The naïve person thinks that unless such a ritual is followed, there is no hypnosis. Given the idea that hypnosis is a stereotyped ritual that involves sleep, it is difficult to see its relation to a type of therapy where those words are not said and where a therapist might even be interviewing a whole family group.

As the word "hypnosis" is used here, it does not apply to a ritual but to a type of communication between people. Milton Erickson has explored an almost infinite variety of ways of inducing hypnotic trance. Examining his work and the work of other contemporary hypnotists, one finds it difficult to state clearly what is a hypnotic relationship and what is not. Erickson may use a ritual form of trance induction, but he may also, without ever mentioning the word "hypnosis," merely have a conversation. He can hypnotize one person while talking with another, he can give a lecture and induce a trance in a particular person in the audience by emphasizing certain words, and often he will work with a person who only later, if at all, realizes that he was hypnotized. From this type of exploration, Erickson has redefined hypnotic trance to apply not to the state of one person but to a special type of interchange between two people. Once one grasps that view, it is possible to think of hypnosis in broader terms and to see its presence in a wide variety of situations, particularly in the intense involvements in therapy.

The preconceptions of a clinician about hypnosis can handicap him in his understanding of the use of hypnotic skills. One should keep in mind that what hypnosis *is* can vary with the ideological climate of the time. When therapy was thought of as a religious experience, hypnosis was a mystical ritual. As psychodynamic theory developed, hypnosis was considered a transference phenomenon. (It was also, as part of the politics of therapy, dismissed by psychoanalysts as shallow or supportive therapy, or distorted into that peculiar mutation, hypnoanalysis.) Currently, we are going through a period of an excessive scientific examination of hypnosis. Considerable research is being done to demonstrate that hypnosis doesn't exist, or, rather, that no more can be accomplished in trance than when awake. In a scientific age, hypnosis becomes defined as a rather unspecial situation. Such research is largely irrelevant for clinicians, since hypnosis in research and hypnosis in therapy are two different orders of phenomenon. As a way of creating a working relationship with people with problems, hypnosis will continue to be used, even if laboratory investigations find that there is no such thing as "hypnosis." If hypnosis can survive a religious period, it will survive a scientific one. The next step will probably be to redefine it as a conditioned phenomenon, if the conditioning therapies develop further and become more popular. Learning theory will be applied and trance will be explained within that framework.

One aspect of hypnosis will be the special focus in this work. It will be regarded as a special type of interaction between people, rather than as a religious experience, a transference situation, or a conditioned process. From this point of view, hypnosis is a process between people, a way in which one person communicates with another. Erickson's approach makes it possible to see this mystery within an interpersonal framework.

The relevance of hypnosis to therapy from this point of view can best be illustrated by generalizing what is held in common over and above the specific rituals of either hypnotists or therapists. When hypnosis is used effectively, the approach is strategic, and the strategies are similar to those one finds in different therapeutic approaches. Parallels between hypnosis and therapy can be drawn in terms of goals, procedures, and specific techniques for dealing with resistance.

At the most general level, the goal of a hypnotist is to change the behavior, sensory response, and consciousness of another person. A subsidiary goal is to extend that person's range of experience: to provide him with new ways of thinking, feeling, and behaving. Obviously, these are also the goals of therapy. Both hypnotist and therapist seek through the relationship with a person to introduce variety and extend the range of his abilities.

Looking over the various hypnotic procedures, as well as Erickson's wide variety of methods of induction, one finds that there is a common theme as well as a sequence of steps that are followed despite the diversity of forms. The hypnotist *directs* another person to *spontaneously* change his behavior. Since a person cannot respond spontaneously if he is following a directive, the hypnotic approach is the posing of a paradox. Two levels of message are simultaneously being communicated by the hypnotist: he is saying "Do as I say," and within that framework he is saying "Don't do as I say, behave spontaneously." The way the subject adapts to such a conflicting set of directives is to undergo a change and behave in a way described as trance behavior.

The steps in this paradoxical procedure can be broken down into two types of directives: (a) The hypnotist directs the subject to do something he can *voluntarily* do, such as look at a point, concentrate on a hand, sit in a certain position, think of an image, and so on. (b) Next, the hypnotist directs the subject to respond with *involuntary*, or spontaneous, behavior. He asks for a hand to move without the person's moving it, for a feeling of heaviness of the eyelids, for a relaxation of muscles, for seeing something that isn't there, for different physiological processes to be turned off or on, or for other responses that are not under voluntary control. The same steps are often followed without a formal hypnotic ritual. A person can be asked to make himself comfortable and then be asked to have an idea, to notice a new sensation, to have a different thought, or to experience something else that is involuntary. When a doctor says to a patient, "Take this pill three times a day and you will feel better," he is following these steps of asking for something that can be done voluntarily and then asking for an involuntary change. The hypnotist does not want merely a voluntary response, since he does not want the subject to do what he is told like a robot. He wants him to follow directives but also to participate by responding autonomously.

The various forms of therapy also make use of these two steps in their procedures. The therapist directs a patient to do those things he can voluntarily do, and then requests, or communicates an expectation of, spontaneous change. Different schools of therapy emphasize one or the other aspect of this process. Some minimize the directive aspects and emphasize the spontaneity, while others minimize the spontaneity and emphasize the importance of being directive.

For example, in psychoanalysis the therapist directs the patient to do what he can voluntarily do, such as appear at designated times, pay a certain fee, and lie down on the couch. Then the analyst asks for "involuntary" behavior by asking the patient to say anything that comes to mind and to have spontaneous dreams that can be analyzed. The analyst does not want the patient to do merely what he is told. He wants him to participate by responding autonomously and independently. The emphasis in the ideology is upon the spontaneity, and the directive aspects of the approach are minimized and concealed in the framework of the therapy.

In behavior therapy a similar procedure is followed. The patient is directed to do what he can voluntarily do, such as make a list of his anxiety situations, put them in a hierarchical order, and sit in a certain position. The therapist then directs him to "relax" and to "not become anxious," which cannot be voluntarily done but must just happen. The therapist also sends the patient out to "assert" himself in certain situations. The therapist does not want the patient to do merely what he is told, he wants him to change spontaneously so that he is no longer anxious and is asserting himself without effort.

The positive and negative reinforcement procedures of a conditioning therapist also have these steps. It is assumed that responding to the subject with a correct reinforcement in the therapy situation, which is essentially directing his behavior, will cause the subject to "spontaneously" generalize that kind of behavior to other situations. The conditioner does not want a robot response in perpetuity but only temporarily, so that the subject will later respond independently in the appropriate way. Conditioners tend to emphasize the directive aspects of their procedure and make less mention of the spontaneous change they seek. Sometimes they conceal this change under the word "learning."

There is a further similarity between hypnosis and therapy. Both are usually based upon voluntary relationships; the procedures are imposed not upon an unwilling person but upon someone who seeks out this type of relationship. Yet both subject and patient will often resist the directives offered even though they have volunteered to be in the situation. An essential aspect of both hypnosis and therapy is the need to motivate someone to cooperate fully in following directions, and to deal with resistance when it arises.

Although the relationship is voluntary, both hypnosis and therapy require persuasion, a selling job, at the beginning of the process. The subject or patient must be motivated to cooperate, usually by emphasizing what he has to gain if he cooperates and what he might lose if he does not. But even when motivated, subjects and patients will still resist the benefits offered by the practitioner. In hypnosis, there are two main types of resistance: not being quite cooperative enough, and being too cooperative.

When a subject does not respond quite as he should and so resists, the hypnotist has routine ways of dealing with the problem. Milton Erickson, more than any other hypnotist, has focused upon developing techniques for persuading resistant subjects to achieve their goals. While exploring hypnotic resistance,

Erickson was at the same time developing ways of dealing with human problems in therapy. His approach to people with problems when he is not formally using hypnosis is essentially the same as his approach to resistance in hypnosis. Once one grasps this similarity, many of Erickson's therapeutic techniques follow logically.

When a person has a symptom, by definition he is indicating that he cannot help himself. His behavior is involuntary. The phobic or compulsive or alcoholic or disturbed family continue in ways that bring distress while protesting that they cannot help behaving as they do. In the same way, the subject who volunteers for hypnosis will often not follow a directive. He does not refuse; he merely indicates that he is unable to. Or he will respond in a contrary way, while indicating that he is not causing this to happen. For example, if a subject is asked to place his hand on the arm of the chair, and is then told that it will get lighter and lift, he might not let it lift, or he may say, "It is getting heavier." The art of hypnosis is to deal with this kind of resistance and bring about change, and so too is the art of therapy the effective solution of this kind of problem.

ENCOURAGING RESISTANCE

If a subject is asked to have his hand get lighter and says, "My hand is getting heavier," the hypnotist does not say, "Now cut that out!" Instead, he accepts that response, and even encourages it, by saying, "That's fine, your hand can get heavier yet." This acceptance approach is typical of hypnosis and is also Erickson's fundamental approach to human problems whether or not he is using hypnosis. What happens when one "accepts" the resistance of a subject and even encourages it? The subject is thereby caught in a situation where his attempt to resist is defined as cooperative behavior. He finds himself following the hypnotist's directives no matter what he does, because what he does is defined as cooperation. Once he is cooperating, he can be diverted into new behavior. The analogy Erickson uses is that of a person who wants to change the course of a river. If he opposes the river by trying to block it, the river will merely go over and around him. But if he *accepts* the force of the river and diverts it in a new direction, the force of the river will cut a new channel. For example, if a person seeks help for headaches that have no physical cause, Erickson will "accept" the headache as he might hypnotic resistance. He will focus upon the need for a headache, but its duration, its frequency, or its intensity can vary to the point where the headache disappears.

Examples from Erickson's marital and family therapy show how different therapeutic interventions can be related to their hypnotic origin and particularly to the encouragement of resistance. Generally, with a couple or a family, Erickson uses a sequence approach in which he asks them to do something deliberately, usually what they are already doing, and then either asks for spontaneous change or the change occurs as a consequence of his encouragement of the usual behavior. Rarely does he tell a couple to stop what they are doing. With this "accepting" approach, if a married couple fights continually and resists good advice, he is likely to direct them to have a fight, but he will change the place or the time or some other aspect of it. The response is a "spontaneous" change in behavior.

PROVIDING A WORSE ALTERNATIVE

A therapist prefers that a patient initiate new behavior himself and choose his own direction in life. Yet at the same time, the therapist wants the patient to change within the framework the therapist considers important. A problem in both therapy and hypnosis is how to get the patient or subject to follow directives but also to achieve autonomy in making his own decisions and setting out on new paths.

One procedure Erickson typically uses deals with this problem by directing the patient in one direction in such a way that he is provoked to go in another. If Erickson wants a hypnotic subject to respond in a certain way, he might ask for a response the subject does not care for, and the subject will then choose an alternative in which he participates fully. As an example, if Erickson wishes a subject to respond with amnesia, he may ask the subject to forget something he would prefer to remember. As an alternative, the subject will forget another item more fully and completely because *he* has chosen it.

In discussing this, Erickson says, "With this kind of directive, you establish a class of things for a patient to do, such as the class of 'exercising.' Then you provide one item in that class which is something he isn't going to be very happy to do. You want him to 'spontaneously' find another item in that class. It is a way of inspiring someone to find things he can do that are good for him and that he can enjoy and succeed at."

Although both the therapist and the hypnotist are benevolently motivated, they are often willing to make it hard on the person who does not cooperate. Sometimes this is calculatedly done by offering something the person does not like so that he will choose something else, and sometimes a threat or a procedure is used so that the person will change in order to avoid something worse. For example, a hypnotist might say, "Would you rather go into a trance now or later?" By putting the matter that way, he is avoiding the issue of whether the subject wants to go into a trance or not, but he is also offering him an easy way out. The subject can say "Later," to escape going into a trance right then. Similarly, a hypnotist might say, "You can go into a *deep* trance, or into a *light* one." The subject can grasp at the light trance to avoid the deep one, when he might not have chosen a light trance if something worse had not been offered.

Erickson has a variety of procedures for making it harder on the person with a problem to keep the problem than to give it up. Some of these involve a benevolent ordeal, such as exercises at two in the morning on any day that the symptom occurs more than the patient wishes it to. At other times Erickson will combine "distraction," which is a typical hypnotic technique, with an ordeal to bring about a change.

CAUSING CHANGE BY COMMUNICATING IN METAPHOR

When a subject resists directives, one way to deal with the problem is to communicate in terms of an analogy, or metaphor. If the subject resists A, the hypnotist can talk about B, and when A and B are metaphorically related, the subject will make the connection "spontaneously" and respond appropriately. In the intricacies of hypnotic induction, the analogy can be communicated in verbal or nonverbal ways. Typically, when a hypnotist is suggesting that the subject's hand get lighter and lift, he lifts his head and his voice, indicating metaphorically how the hand is to move. The subject responds to that spatial and vocal shift. If a subject has been previously hypnotized and the hypnotist wants a "spontaneous" trance, he might begin to discuss how *this* room or situation is similar to one the subject was once hypnotized in. The subject will respond to the analogy by producing the same behavior he produced in that other room or situation. Similarly, if one person is being hypnotized in the presence of another, it is possible to speak metaphorically to the other person in such a way that trance is induced in the subject while ostensibly he is not being focused upon at all. The analogic, or metaphoric, approach to hypnosis is particularly effective with resistant subjects, since it is difficult to resist a suggestion one does not know consciously that he is receiving.

Milton Erickson is a master in the field of metaphor. In the way he listens to and observes a subject, as well as in the way he responds, he deals with the multiple metaphoric messages that are constantly communicated between people in their interchange. He functions as easily in metaphor as most people function with conscious, logical communication. His directives to patients are not often simple and straightforward but include a variety of analogies that apply to the patient's problems. The metaphoric approach he uses when not formally using hypnosis is clearly related to his years of experimenting with metaphoric suggestions outside the awareness of the subject.

As a typical example, if Erickson is dealing with a married couple who have a conflict over sexual relations and would rather not discuss it directly, he will approach the problem metaphorically. He will choose some aspect of their lives that is analogous to sexual relations and change that as a way of changing the sexual behavior. He might, for example, talk to them about having dinner together and draw them out on their preferences. He will discuss with them how the wife likes appetizers before dinner, while the husband prefers to dive right into the meat and potatoes. Or the wife might prefer a quiet and leisurely dinner, while the husband, who is quick and direct, just wants the meal over with. If the couple begin to connect what they are saying with sexual relations, Erickson will "drift rapidly" away to other topics, and then he will return to the analogy. He might end such a conversation with a directive that the couple arrange a pleasant dinner on a particular evening that is satisfactory to both of them. When successful, this approach shifts the couple from a more pleasant dinner to more pleasant sexual relations without their being aware that he has deliberately set this goal.

Erickson's willingness to accept working within metaphors applies not only to verbal interchange but even to persons who live a metaphoric life. Such a style of life is typical of schizophrenics, and Erickson assumes that with a schizophrenic the important message is the metaphor. For example, when Erickson was on the staff of Worcester State Hospital, there was a young patient who called himself Jesus. He paraded about as the Messiah, wore a sheet draped around him, and attempted to impose Christianity on people. Erickson approached him on the hospital grounds and said, "I understand you have had experience as a carpenter?" The patient could only reply that he had. Erickson involved the young man in a special project of building a bookcase and shifted him to productive labor.

In another case in that same hospital, Erickson dealt with a competent industrialist who had lost a fortune and become depressed. He spent his time crying and repetitively moving his hands back and forth straight out from his chest. Erickson said to him, "You're a man who has had his ups and downs," and asked him to modify his movement by moving his hands up and down instead of back and forth. Then he took him to the occupational therapist and asked for cooperation. Pointing to the man's up-and-down movement, he said, "Put a piece of sandpaper in each of his hands and fasten a rough board upright between them. That way he can sand and polish the lumber." The man began to do something productive, and he stopped crying. He then began to work in wood and carved chess sets and sold them. He improved so much that he went home on a trial visit, and the first year after he was discharged he made ten thousand dollars in real estate.

Although Erickson communicates with patients in metaphor, what most sharply distinguishes him from other therapists is his unwillingness to "interpret" to people what their metaphors mean. He does not translate "unconscious" communication into conscious form. Whatever the patient says in metaphoric form, Erickson responds in kind. By parables, by interpersonal action, and by directives, he works within the metaphor to bring about change. He seems to feel that the depth and swiftness of that change can be prevented if the person suffers a translation of the communication.

His avoidance of interpretation applies not only to the verbal statements of patients but to their body movements. Erickson is famous for his acute observation of nonverbal behavior, but the information he receives remains nonverbal. For example, a woman patient once said to her therapist, "I'm fond of my husband," and she placed her hand over her mouth while she spoke. The therapist interpreted to her that since she was covering her mouth, she must have some reservations about what she said. He was helping her become aware of her "unconscious" gesture. Erickson would never make such a comment but would accept the woman's gesture as a perfectly valid way of communicating. To translate her message into a different form would be disruptive and discourteous. Worse, it would oversimplify an extraordinarily complex statement. Typically, "insight" interpretations of unconscious communication are absurdly reductionistic, like summarizing a Shakespearean play in a sentence.

Erickson works in metaphor not only in his therapeutic maneuvers but even in the way he gathers information. For example, one day in the presence of a visitor he was talking with a patient who had come to him because of phantom limb pain. The patient, a seventy-one-year-old man, had fallen off a roof and injured his arm so badly that it had to be amputated. He had suffered pain in the vanished limb for months and found no relief in various kinds of treatment. Finally he had traveled to Phoenix to be treated by Erickson. During the conversation, in which the man discussed his recovery, he mentioned two brothers. Later, talking with the visitor, Erickson commented that he had only known about one brother. Perhaps the man had other relatives he hadn't mentioned. Erickson also remarked that the man had used a vague phrase that indicated he might have been married more than once. The visitor inquired why Erickson did not ask the man about his relatives. Erickson replied, "That man made his living for twenty-seven years laying floors. Most men can't last fifteen years at that kind of work, but he lasted almost twice that long. If I really wanted to find out more about his family background, I might start talking about driving in the desert. I would describe driving along the road and rounding a high point rising from the desert floor. Suddenly rounding that high point, I would see a rather lonesome ironwood tree. One of the branches had been broken, probably by the wind smashing around that high point.

"I would use the image of 'ironwood' because of that man's work history. An ironwood tree with a broken branch. Probably from the wind smashing around that high place. Then I'd talk about the mesquite bushes around the tree. I would learn about his relatives, because a tree doesn't stand alone. 'If I should be the last leaf upon the tree.' "

Puzzled by this way of gathering information, the visitor asked why he would not merely ask about the man's relatives. Erickson replied, "Because when I ask you about your sister, brother, parents, you put them into the social frame befitting your education. When I do it in this indirect way, the information is different. There's that broken branch on that lonely ironwood tree." Erickson seemed to enjoy the image, perhaps because, with his herculean struggle over his own physical difficulties, he's rather like an ironwood tree in the desert himself. He went on, "When I mention looking around for low sagebrush, taller mesquite bushes, the man will talk about grandchildren and relatives taller than grandchildren."

ENCOURAGING A RELAPSE

Sometimes when a patient is improving, particularly when he is improving too rapidly, Erickson will direct him to have a relapse. This appears to be an unusual procedure unrelated to most techniques of therapy. Yet when one examines resistance in hypnosis, the approach logically follows.

One of the typical problems in hypnosis is the subject who is too cooperative. Sometimes a subject will too promptly follow all directives—in fact, he will often anticipate them—so that it is unclear who is in charge of what is happening. Often such a subject will stop being cooperative at a certain point, saying, "I don't believe this is working at all." In the wisdom developed in the history of hypnosis, this type of resistance has been dealt with by the "challenge." The hypnotist challenges the subject to resist him, which is a way of asking the subject to try not to cooperate and fail. For example, the hypnotist says, "I want you to try to open your eyes and find that you cannot." In subtle or direct ways, the challenge forces the subject to attempt to resist and concede that he cannot.

With the too cooperative patient who improves too rapidly, psychodynamic therapists are likely to interpret the improvement as resistance, or flight into health. Sometimes they do this because the theory argues that it is not possible to improve rapidly, and so they mistake rapid improvement for overcooperation. At other times the interpretation functions like a challenge.

Erickson often deals with such a situation by using a challenge that is a directive rather than an interpretation. If a patient is too cooperative and seems to be recovering too rapidly, he is likely to relapse and express disappointment with the therapy. To avoid this, Erickson will accept the improvement but direct the patient to have a relapse. The only way the patient can resist is by not relapsing but continuing to improve. With this approach, Erickson uses different explanations to make it reasonable to the patient. One of his more graceful procedures is to say to him, "I want you to go back and feel as badly as you did when you first came in with the problem, because I want you to see if there is anything from that time that you wish to recover and salvage." When done effectively, the directive to relapse prevents a relapse, just as the challenge enforces a hypnotic response.

ENCOURAGING A RESPONSE BY FRUSTRATING IT

Another technique for dealing with resistance and encouraging someone to initiate a response and so make a "spontaneous" contribution is typical of both Erickson's hypnosis and his family work where hypnosis is supposedly not involved. With a hypnotic subject who responds only partially, Erickson has recommended that the hypnotist should inhibit the response. That is, he should direct the subject to behave in a certain way, and as the subject begins to do so, the hypnotist should cut off the response and shift to another area. When he returns to that directive again, the subject will be more responsive because he has developed a readiness to respond but was then frustrated.

Erickson has carried this same procedure into family work. Sometimes, when he is interviewing a whole family, a member of the group does not talk even when encouraged. Formally, this is the same problem as the hypnotic subject who responds less the more he is encouraged to respond. Erickson handles the problem in the family interview by inhibiting the person from talking.

Related to this procedure is the way Erickson will arrange that a husband who has been uncooperative will "spontaneously" decide to come in for treatment with his wife. If the husband refuses to attend the sessions, Erickson will see the wife alone. In each interview he will mention something that he knows the husband will disagree with, and he will say, "I suppose your husband would agree with that," or "I'm not sure how your husband would understand that." Hearing from his wife how the doctor misunderstands him, the husband will exercise his free will and insist that his wife make an appointment for him so he can straighten Erickson out, thereby becoming available for therapy.

THE USE OF SPACE AND POSITION

Another aspect of hypnosis is a concern with spatial orientation. The ability of a subject to be disoriented in relation to place and time teaches a hypnotist to appreciate that space and time are subjective experiences. A subject can sit in one room and believe himself in another, he can sit in one place and see himself there from across the room. He can feel that the time is some other time and the hypnotist some other person. With experience, a hypnotist realizes that people orient themselves in terms of visual and auditory cues and that shifts in those cues can change a person's orientation.

Apparently because of this background, Erickson, when he interviews a family, is conscious of how the behavior of each member toward the others can shift if their spatial orientation is shifted. More than many family therapists, he tends to shift family members about in different chairs as well as in different combinations in the office. As he puts it: "When I see a family, I may deal with them jointly, but I also like to retain the freedom to send the members in and out of the office. While they're in the office, I like to lay down a foundation by happening to mention that father is sitting in that chair, and of course mother is in that other chair, and sister is sitting here and brother sitting over here. Mentioning that in several ways, I define them geographically. Each of them has a spatial position in the interview.

When I talk to them, I talk to that particular space and the others listen. When a person talks to me, the others listen in. That spatial compartmentalization usually prevents the others from barging into the conversation, and it forces the others unmercifully to take a more objective view.

"If I send someone out of the room—for example, the mother and child—I carefully move father from his chair and put him into mother's chair. Or if I send the child out, I might put mother in the child's chair, at least temporarily. Sometimes I comment on this by saying, 'As you sit where your son was sitting, you can think more clearly about him.' Or, 'If you sit where your husband sat, maybe it will give you somewhat of his view about me.' Over a series of interviews with an entire family, I shuffle them about, so that what was originally mother's chair is now where father is sitting. The family grouping remains, and yet that family grouping is being rearranged, which is what you are after when changing a family."

This spatial orientation not only seems generally reminiscent of hypnotic concerns but is quite specifically related to Erickson's hypnotic procedure. The steps he outlines for working with a family are first to define the person in terms of his position, and then to shift his position so that he changes with it. Similarly, when dealing with resistant hypnotic subjects, in various ways he accepts and labels the resistance as located in a geographical position. For example, he will say something like, "You find yourself very resistant sitting in that chair." Then he asks the person to move to another chair, leaving the resistance in the previous place, where it was established.

EMPHASIZING THE POSITIVE

At the end of the nineteenth century, the idea of the "unconscious" appears to have branched into two different streams. Sigmund Freud emphasized that the unconscious was composed of unsavory forces attempting to break through into consciousness. His method of therapy was built upon a distrust of those ideas outside conscious, rational awareness. The other stream was composed largely of hypnotists, who emphasized that the unconscious was a positive force. The unconscious would arrange that the person do what was best for himself. Hypnotists therefore tended to recommend letting the unconscious express itself in a person's life. Erickson inclines toward this latter view, and in both his hypnotic and his family work tends to emphasize what is positive in the behavior of the person. This is based partly upon his assumption that there is a natural desire for growth within a person and partly upon the view that there is greater cooperation from the patient if one emphasizes the positive. Unlike psychodynamically oriented therapists, who make interpretations to bring out negative feelings and hostile behavior, Erickson relabels what people do in a positive way, to encourage change. He does not minimize difficulties, but he will find in the difficulties some aspect of them that can be used to improve the functioning of a person or his family. Rather than assuming there is something hostile in the unconscious that must be brought out, he assumes there are positive forces there that need to be freed for the person's further development. When working with couples or families, he does not focus upon their unfortunate ways of dealing with one another but finds an aspect of their relationship that is worth while and that can be enlarged. This emphasis upon the positive appears to come directly out of his experience with hypnosis.

SEEDING IDEAS

In his hypnotic inductions, Erickson likes to "seed" or establish certain ideas and later build upon them. He will emphasize certain ideas in the beginning of the interchange so that later, if he wants to achieve a certain response, he has already laid the groundwork for that response. Similarly, with families Erickson will introduce, or emphasize, certain ideas at the information-gathering stage. Later he can build upon those ideas if the situation is appropriate. In this way his hypnosis and his therapy have a continuity, in that something new is introduced but always within a framework that connects it with what he has previously done.

AMPLIFYING A DEVIATION

It is characteristic of Erickson's hypnotic work that he attempts to gain a small response and then he builds upon it, amplifying that response until he has achieved the goal. He has often cautioned hypnotists about trying to achieve too much too quickly, rather than accepting what is offered and enlarging that. It is also characteristic of Erickson's family work that he seeks a small change and enlarges upon it. If the change is in a crucial area, what appears small can change the whole system. Sometimes he uses the analogy of a hole in a dam; it does not take a very large hole to lead to a change in the structure of a whole dam.

In the family field there is increasing awareness that a family therapist is focused upon changing a system in which patterns keep repeating and that therefore is stable. Two general approaches are thought of as appropriate: one is to induce a crisis in the family that unstabilizes the system so that the family must reform with different patterns; the other is to choose one aspect of the system and cause it to deviate. This deviation is encouraged and amplified until the system goes into a runaway and must reorganize into a new set of patterns. Erickson is willing to induce crisis to bring about a change, but he is also more willing than most therapists to influence a small deviation and then build upon it until larger changes occur. That approach appears characteristic of the way he learned to enlarge the responses of a hypnotic subject.

AMNESIA AND THE CONTROL OF INFORMATION

Different schools of family therapy have different premises about what causes change, and their procedures follow. It is not uncommon, for example, for a therapist to believe that the expression of affect and the gaining of insight are causal to change. Therefore he will encourage family members to express their feelings to each other and help them understand why they behave as they do in terms of residuals from their past. Often, too, family therapists seek to encourage the open flow of communication among family members so that everything on anyone's mind is said to the others. Erickson's family therapy does not appear to have that orientation. Although in specific cases he might focus upon affect or understanding or encourage open communication, generally he does not. He often sees family members in separate interviews, and when he brings them together he likes to organize what is to be said and how it is to be said so that what happens is directed toward particular goals. Sometimes he will see a wife and give her certain directives and then see the husband and give him different directives. He does not encourage, and might even prevent, their discussing with each other what is happening. Often he gives separate directives that later bring about a coming together of husband and wife and open communication between them at that time. He usually manages to follow what is a fundamental rule in family therapy—not to side consistently with one family member against another or one part of the family against another part. However, when he enters a family system, his input might be directed to various parts of the family, with careful control of how new information is to be distributed among the members.

Since this approach is quite different from that of most family therapists, one can wonder about its origins. I think it grows out of hypnotic technique. Not only does his experience as a hypnotist give him a willingness to take charge, to give directives, and to control what happens, but, like many hypnotists, he has been a specialist in controlling the conscious awareness of subjects. He tends to conceptualize a person in two parts, and he controls the flow of unconscious ideas to conscious awareness. An obvious example is bringing into awareness a past traumatic experience, which is an approach Erickson used in his early hypnotic work. He would train the patient in amnesia and then systematically influence in what way the trauma was recalled. Typically, the experience is recalled or relived, but the subject is awakened with amnesia for the recollection. Then, either bit by bit or in specific ways controlled by Erickson, the information is shifted from an unconscious to a conscious awareness. Sometimes the step will include insight into the situation, which is then rendered amnesic and only later brought forward. To me, this process is formally similar to Erickson's control of information among family members, where he allows some information to be exchanged but not other information, step by step until the goal he is after is attained.

AWAKENING AND DISENGAGEMENT

Erickson, like some other family therapists, focuses as much, if not more, upon the achievement of autonomy of family members as he does upon bringing about togetherness. If there is a child problem, he tends to look for the parent who is too intensely involved with the child and then intervenes to provide more separation and space. If the problem is adolescent schizophrenia, he tends to work toward disengaging the young adult from his pathologically intense involvement with the family and move him out toward a life of his own. This concern with intense dyadic involvement, where two people respond so strongly to each other that they block off others, seems to me to be natural to the hypnotist. A hypnotist focuses upon his subject and seeks to have the subject respond fully to him and not to other stimuli. When a hypnotist watches family members dealing with each other, he would immediately recognize and deal with a dyad where there was too intense an involvement. I would think too that our knowledge of the process by which a hypnotist awakens a subject is relevant to a therapeutic intervention to shift people from an intense to a more casual involvement. Often we think of awakening from a trance as a simple matter of responding to a cue, such as "Wake up" or a count of three. Yet when one observes a hypnotist and his subject together, one sees that the process is more complex than that. The hypnotist not only gives a cue but alters his entire behavior. His body movement changes, his vocal intonation becomes different, and he often turns his interest elsewhere. The subject also makes a shift from trance behavior to a more social interchange. When a subject is reluctant to awaken, he tends to continue with trance-like behavior, and the hypnotist then often exaggerates his non-hypnotic, social behavior, thus requiring the subject to respond to him in a more disengaged, social way. It seems to me that Erickson has drawn upon his vast experience in awakening subjects and brought that to bear upon ways of intervening to shift the behavior of the members of an overintense family dyad.

AVOIDING SELF-EXPLORATION

Erickson's willingness to provide a task to change a relationship is only equaled by his unwillingness to focus upon helping people understand how or why they have been dealing with each other in unfortunate ways. What appears radical in his therapeutic approach is the absence of interpretations about the supposed causes of behavior. Although Erickson might not put it this strongly, implicit in his work is the idea that a therapist who tries to help people understand "why" they behave as they do is preventing real therapeutic change.

The most basic idea about the cause of change in dynamic psychiatry has been the notion that if a person understands himself and his motives he will recover from distressing symptoms. This idea would seem to have been carried over from the nineteenth-century idea of the rational man. Freud decided that men were not so rational, but that if they understood the forces in their unconscious they would become rational. In Freudian theory, repression was considered the basic cause of psychopathology, and the lifting of repressions by conscious insight was the primary focus of therapy. The technique centered upon interpreting what the patient said and did and making him conscious of his transference distortions.

As psychiatry became more interpersonal, the focus of therapy shifted slightly. With Sullivan came the emphasis upon helping the person become aware of his interpersonal difficulties. If the patient could "see" what he was doing, particularly if he could "connect" this with the past, he would be transformed and recover.

Later, when therapists began to interview whole families instead of individuals alone, many of them unthinkingly carried into their work this same idea—that conscious awareness causes change, with experiential or emotional awareness as the occasional variation on the theme. If family members could understand how they were dealing with each other and why, the family system would be transformed. Sometimes the therapist used psychodynamic interpretations to help family members discover their introjected past images. Sometimes the interpretations were more Sullivanian as family members were helped to discover their interpersonal difficulties and provocations. Often the interpretations were about a family member's provocations or transference relationship to the therapist.

In the last decades the conditioning therapists have proposed an alternative theory of change. Reciprocal inhibition procedures and the modification of behavior by designed reinforcements are not based upon the idea that becoming aware of why one behaves as one does is causal to change. It is assumed that changing the reinforcements of behavior will change that behavior. Similarly, a few types of family therapy are based upon the idea that the way a therapist intervenes in a family brings about change, quite independent of the awareness of the participants. Therefore it has become more respectable to suggest that therapeutic change occurs without the person's understanding the meaning or function of his behavior. The change also appears to persist longer than it does when people are helped to understand why they behave as they do.

Yet the average well-trained clinician today still tends to make interpretations, almost as a reflex. He may talk about interpersonal behavior, systems theory, reinforcement, or experiential happenings, but his therapeutic technique leans largely on characterizing how people behave and helping them to understand the causes of their behavior. Most clinicians would feel handicapped if they did not focus upon understanding. Their therapeutic repertoire would be limited to a few unfamiliar conditioning and behavior-modification procedures. Another alternative is the general therapeutic approach of Erickson that is presented in this book.

Milton Erickson was properly trained as a psychiatrist, and yet he went his original way. At the time of his training, Freud's objections to hypnosis had forbidden that art to several generations of young psychiatrists. Yet Erickson learned hypnosis and used it extensively in treatment. Even those clinicians who did use hypnosis worked largely within a Freudian framework. They practiced hypnoanalysis and brought into conscious awareness past traumas and unconscious ideas. Erickson experimented with that approach and abandoned it, developing instead a quite different use of hypnosis. From thinking in terms of helping people become aware of why they did what they did, he shifted to thinking about how to bring about therapeutic change. With that shift he left the traditional approach of psychiatry. He did not do so arbitrarily, but because he examined the results of his therapy and devised new procedures for improving them. His therapeutic approach now represents the effect of thirty years of experimentation with different ways of bringing about therapeutic change.

It is easier to say what Erickson does not do in therapy than to say what he does, except by offering case examples. His style of therapy is not based upon insight into unconscious processes, it does not involve helping people understand their interpersonal difficulties, he makes no transference interpretations, he does not explore a person's motivations, nor does he simply recondition. His theory of change is more complex; it seems to be based upon the interpersonal impact of the therapist outside the patient's awareness, it includes providing directives that cause changes of behavior, and it emphasizes communicating in metaphor.

THE FAMILY LIFE CYCLE

The strategy Erickson has designed for relieving the problems of people is incomplete if one does not consider his goals of therapy. More than any other therapist, he has in mind the "normal" or ordinary processes in the lives of people. He would not treat a newly married couple as he would a couple who had been married for twenty years, nor would he approach a family with young children in the way he would a family with children old enough to leave home. Often the ending of his case reports sounds pat, because his goals are very often simple. At the time of courtship, success is the achievement of marriage. During early marriage, success is the birth of children. Whatever the stage of family life, the transition to the next stage is a crucial step in the development of a person and his family. The outline of this work is in terms of the family life cycle from courtship through old age and death. The strategies used by Erickson to resolve problems at each of these stages are reported in the case examples that follow. His therapy is most understandable if one takes into account family development processes and the points of crisis that arise when people go from stage to stage through the family life cycle.

II

THE FAMILY LIFE CYCLE

Although the arena of human passion is ordinary family life, only recently has this context come under actual observation and been taken seriously. It is becoming more evident that families undergo a developmental process over time, and human distress and psychiatric symptoms appear when this process is disrupted. Yet it has been difficult for a professional in the clinical or social-science field to take these ordinary affairs of life seriously. In psychiatry and psychology, it has seemed to be more profound to focus upon questions of identity, delusional formations, unconscious dynamics, or laws of perception than upon the dilemmas that arise when men and women mate and rear children. Now that we have begun to understand the enormous influence of the intimate social context on the nature of the individual, we find ourselves facing the fact that social contexts change with the passage of time, and that we have only very limited information about that process.

To say that one should use a strategic approach in therapy is to raise the question of the end to which the strategy is planned. We have progressed to an ever wider view of the function of symptoms and other human problems in the last twenty years. Symptoms were once seen as an expression of an individual independent of his social situation. The anxiety attack or the depression was an expression of the state of a person. Next came the idea that symptoms were an expression of a relationship between people and

41

served some tactical purpose between intimates. The question about an anxiety attack was the function it served in the marriage or family, on the job, or in the relationship with a therapist. Now there is a yet wider view, which is implicit in Milton Erickson's therapy. Symptoms appear when there is a dislocation or interruption in the unfolding life cycle of a family or other natural group. The symptom is a signal that a family has difficulty in getting past a stage in the life cycle. For example, an anxiety attack in a mother when she gives birth to a child is an expression of the difficulty of that family in achieving the child-rearing stage of development. While focusing sharply on symptoms, Erickson's therapeutic strategy has as its larger goal the resolution of the problems of the family to get the life cycle moving again. Admiration for his technical virtuosity can lead one to miss the basic assumptions about family life that guide his strategy.

If one accepts the importance of a developmental process in families over time, he discovers at once how little information there is about the life cycle of families. Longitudinal studies based on observation of the family have not been done. Only self-report surveys, in which family members are asked about their lives, are available, and they have proved to be highly unreliable. What other information we have is based upon families entering therapy when they are in trouble, and so we have observed different stages in the family cycle without knowing what came before or what naturally follows. The clinician who wishes to understand the natural development of families in order to guide his strategy finds himself largely ignorant of this process and labors under the burden of myths about how families ought to be rather than how they are.

An additional problem is that what understanding we do have about the development of a family can be quickly outdated as the culture changes and new forms of family life appear. The nuclear family of parents and children living in households separate from their extended kin is a relatively recent development. As we begin to understand the nuclear family, we find that new forms of communal families are appearing, and a therapist dealing with young people can find himself thinking in terms of a conceptual model that is obsolete. A clinician must be tolerant of the diverse ways there are in which to live while at the same time having a grasp of the developmental process of families to serve as a guideline for recognizing crisis stages.

A brief outline of some of the crisis stages in middle-class American families will perhaps provide a background for understanding Erickson's strategic approach, though it is far from comprehensive and ignores differences in class and culture. The extraordinary complexity of a family at any given moment, much less over a lifetime, makes it impossible to attempt more here. It is a rudimentary framework for the later chapters, which present Erickson's ways of resolving problems at different stages of family life.

But before attempting to describe the family cycle, we should perhaps deal with a possible objection to this view of therapy. To say that the goal of therapy is to help people past a crisis to the next stage of family life might lead some clinicians to consider it a way of "adjusting" people to their families or to the society that shapes the family. Such a point of view is naïve, since it overlooks the fact that the freedom and growth of the individual are determined by how successfully he participates in his natural group and its development. One can think of the social isolate as more free than the person participating in love and work, but not if one examines the restrictions on the social isolate.

There are two ways of "adjusting" a person to his situation without producing growthful change. One is to stabilize the person by the use of medication. If a young person has reached the age where the family cannot get past the stage of releasing him, the young person will manifest symptoms. Medication at this point will prevent trouble, but it will also prevent change and make the situation chronic for both young person and family. The other method of adjustment is long-term individual therapy focusing upon helping the person to understand his childhood development and his misperceptions rather than the reality of his present life situation. Many wives, for example, discontented with the narrow pattern of suburban life, have been stabilized for years by intensive analysis. Instead of encouraging them to take action that would lead to a richer and more complex life, the therapy prevents that change by imposing the idea that the problem is within their psyche rather than in their situation.

If one thinks of therapy as the introduction of variety and richness into a person's life, the goal is to free the person from the limitations and restrictions of a social network in difficulty. Symptoms usually appear when a person is in an impossible situation and is trying to break out of it. It was once thought that focusing upon symptoms was "merely" relieving the symptom as the person became adjusted. This view was held by clinicians who did not know how to cure a symptom and so did not realize that, except in rare instances, a symptom cannot be cured without producing a basic change in the person's social situation, which frees him to grow and develop. Anxiety spells, for example, which are a product of a restricted interpersonal situation, cannot be relieved unless the therapist intervenes to help the patient find more alternatives in life.

THE COURTSHIP PERIOD

The systematic study of the human family is quite recent and has coincided with the study of the social systems of other animals. Since the 1950s, human beings as well as the beasts of the field and the birds of the air have been observed in their natural environments. Both similarities and crucial differences between man and other animals, which help us to clarify the nature of human dilemmas, are becoming evident. Men have in common with other creatures the developmental process of courtship, mating, nest building, child rearing and the dislodging of offspring into a life of their own, but because of the more complex social organization of human beings, the problems that arise during the family life cycle are unique to the species.

Every learning animal goes through courtship rituals at the appropriate age, and the range of possible variations is wide. In species that exist in anonymous flocks, at the proper season an individual will mate with whoever happens to be passing at the moment, preferably a member of the opposite sex. In other species the mating is less anonymous; a creature will meet his spouse during the mating season each year, but they will never associate with each other at other times. Many species also select mates who remain lifelong companions and produce offspring regularly over the years. The graylag goose, for example, mates for life, and if the spouse dies the survivor mourns and may not mate again.

The human species, with its complex capabilities, can follow any of the mating habits of other animals. A man can copulate with any woman who passes, the more anonymous the better. Men can also have clandestine affairs, meeting a specific woman only on sexual occasions, and never seeing her at other times. Human beings have also tried out the arrangement of multiple husbands or wives characteristic of some species. Most commonly, men select a single mate for life and remain with her constantly; at least this is the myth of monogamy in middle-class America, which is the focus of this discussion.

A crucial difference between men and all other animals is the fact that man is the only animal with in-laws. Extended kin are involved at every stage of life in the human family, but in other species there is a discontinuity between the generations: parents rear their young, who then go off and select mates without assistance from their elders. A mother bear does not tell her daughter whom to marry or supervise the way she raises her cubs, but human parents screen potential mates for their children and help rear grandchildren. Marriage, then, is not merely a joining of two people but a coming together of two families who exert their influence and create a complex network of subsystems.

This involvement with extended kin is more important in differentiating the human species from other animals than the opposable thumb, the consistent use of tools, or the large brain. In fact, man's large brain may have developed in order to deal with his more complex social network. It is also possible that multiple generation involvement has produced psychiatric problems among human beings not found among other animals. (Neurosis or psychosis in animals seems only to occur when human beings have intervened—not in nature.)

Many of the major dilemmas of human life appear during the period when a young person is making the shift from being a juvenile to becoming a member of the adult community. What happens at that time can have lifelong effects on the individual's place in the social hierarchy. It is one of the major times in life when professional help is called for, and the consequences of this intervention can be more lasting than at any other time.

When human beings, or animals of any species, enter late adolescence, they begin to lose the tolerance given to juveniles as they are integrated into the adult community. There is a certain period, fortunately a relatively long one in the human species, for establishing status in relation to others and for selecting a mate.

Among most animals, those who fail to establish a territory of their own during this crucial period fall to the lowest status in the community and do not mate. They become peripheral animals, wandering about on the edges of the territory of others, and if they attempt to fight to gain space and status, they come up against the rule that the creature who controls space almost invariably wins when fighting on his own ground. These outcasts find that females are disinclined to mate with males who have not achieved status, and females who have not been selected as mates in turn become peripheral creatures, ignored by males and picked on by all females who have acquired mates and therefore status. The peripheral animals of most species are undefended and uncared for. They are nature's discards, and are offered up to predators as part of the protection of the group. Their life is comparatively short, and they do not breed and reproduce their kind.

In the human species, the peripheral discards are offered up to the helping professions: charity, social work, psychology, and psychiatry are applied to them. The helping professions are, by their nature, benevolent helpers and also agents of social control. In their benevolent aspect, they attempt to help the social deviant to obtain a job and a mate and to become a functioning part of the community. As controllers, they attempt to herd the deviant into an institution, where he is kept from being troublesome to those who have won space and achieved status. Sometimes this is also thought to help him.

Although we know less about the courtship behavior of American adolescents than we do about other animals (the courtship of the graylag goose has been studied for half a century), we do know that there is a time factor and a risk factor. There is an age period when young people are all learning to court and participating in this activity, and the longer a child delays this process, the more peripheral he becomes to the social network. The young person who has not had a date until his twenties will be a deviant when dealing with others of his age who have been experiencing courting procedures for years. It is not only that the inexperienced young person has not learned how to deal with the opposite sex or that he cannot trigger the proper physical responses, but his social behavior is not appropriate; those he chooses to court are practicing later courtship behavior while he is still working out the early stages of the process.

If courtship was a rational process, the problem would be less complex, but clearly it is not. Young people marry to escape from home, to rescue one another, because they simply fall in love, because of a desire to have children, and for many other reasons. The first encounter between two young people can lead to unpredictable outcomes. A particular problem for the human adolescent is his simultaneous involvement with his family and his peers. The ways he must behave to adapt to his family can prevent his normal development with people his own age. Essentially it is a weaning problem, and the weaning process is not complete until the child is out of the home and has established intimate bonds outside his family. The long nurturing period required for human development can induce the youngster never to leave home rather than prepare him for a separate life. The mother bear will send her cubs up the tree and abandon them. Human parents can turn their children loose, but they can also entangle them perpetually in the family organization.

Many adolescents who become peripheral people never became sufficiently detached from their families or origin to go through the necessary stages of selecting a mate and building their own nest. In some cultures mate selection is explicitly defined as the right of the parents, but even in cultures with more romantic ideas about marriage the child is not entirely free to select his companions of the opposite sex. As soon as a young man ventures out from his own family and associates seriously with a young woman, two sets of parents become part of the decision-making process. Even when young people select mates out of spite because their parents oppose the choice, they are still caught up in the parental involvement, because the choice is not an indepedent one. What was once thought of as a "neurotic choice of partners" evidently involves a family decision process.

For many adolescents, help from a professional therapist becomes an initiation ceremony, in that it provides a relationship with an outsider whose goal is to help him achieve independence and maturity. It is one way the culture helps ease the young person out of his tight family organization and into a marriage and family of his own.

Therapy, when it is successful, shifts the young person into a life where he can make the most of his potential abilities. When it is not successful, the person becomes a peripheral creature, and the therapy can contribute to that failure. The more drastic the intervention of a therapist—for example, by imposing hospitalization or by insisting upon years of treatment—the more permanent the stigma of being a "special" person that adheres to the adolescent. The therapeutic relationship in itself can prevent, rather than improve, his chances. Long-term treatment can introduce an abnormal bias into a young person's life in many ways: it continues the financial involvement of the parents, produces a reliance upon a paid relationship as a substitute for more natural relationships, and creates a species of adolescent peculiarly focused upon being conscious of why he does whatever he does and with a restricted ideology of explanation.

As therapists improve in skill, the goals of treatment become more precisely formulated and therapeutic techniques more efficient. Major change came with the realization that all adolescents with problems cannot be fitted into a single method of therapy; each individual is in a unique context, and the therapy must be flexible enough to adapt to the needs of the particular situation. The treatment of most adolescents comes about when these young people feel they cannot participate as they wish in love or work, and so they set the goals the therapist should help them achieve. Often both the therapist and the patient have formulated a goal, but in the process of treatment a third kind of goal appears that was not anticipated by either participant. When a professional helper intervenes in a person's life, the outcome is by no means predictable.

One of the problems for a clinician dealing with young people is that he must have sufficient wisdom to be a guide and yet not have so stereotyped a view that he must "adjust" young people to his idea of how they ought to live. It is usual, for example, for young people to marry and rear children, yet many people who do not choose that way can lead quite satisfactory lives. If a young person seeks therapy because he wishes to marry or succeed in a career and cannot, a clinician should know how to help him toward his goal; if, however, a young person does not choose that way of life, to impose it upon him because it is "accepted" behavior is unrealistic and might hamper therapeutic efforts. Fortunately, our American culture is still sufficiently diverse to allow people to live in ways that do not conform to the middle-class norm of the nuclear family in the suburb.

If a clinician believes that a goal of therapy is to introduce complexity and richness into a person's life, he is more occupied with encouraging alternative ways of living than conformity to a socially accepted pattern. The problem for the clinician is to recognize that the narrow lives many young people lead result from their lack of success in disentagling themselves from their families. For example, some young people live socially deviant lives because they are part of a youth culture seeking alternative life styles. Others live in deviant ways because it is their function in the family to be a failure. They are not responding to their peers but to what would happen at home if they chose a more conventional path, and although they appear to have made a choice, they are really responding helplessly to a family entanglement. To talk to them about a different way of life is like talking to a prisoner about how he might use his freedom. The difficulty for the clinician is to determine the restrictions that prevent the young person from achieving a more complex and interesting life, which is often impossible without meeting with the entire family.

Just as young people may avoid marriage for reasons within the family, they can also rush into marriage prematurely in an attempt to disengage themselves from an unfortunate family network. Often a clinician's task is to restrain the young person from entering the next stage of family life too quickly, before he or she has recognized the possible diversity of ways of life.

Dr. Erickson's approach to resolving problems in the courtship stage is presented in Chapter III.

MARRIAGE AND ITS CONSEQUENCES

The importance of a marriage ceremony not only to the young couple but to the entire family is beginning to become more apparent as more young people give it up. Rituals that may seem superfluous to young people can be important demarcations of stages, which help everyone involved to make the shift to new ways of relating with one another. In most cultures the ceremonies surrounding birth, puberty, marriage, and death are protected as crucial to stable living.

Whatever the relationship between a courting couple before marriage, the ceremony shifts the nature of that relationship in unpredictable ways. For many couples the honeymoon period and the time together before they have children is delightful. For others it is not; bewildering stress can occur, rupturing the marital bond or producing symptoms in the individuals before the marriage has well begun.

Some marriages are troubled from the beginning because of the purpose of the marriage. For example, young people who marry largely to escape from their families may find, once they are married, that the reason for their marriage has disappeared. They have escaped, but into a marriage that has no other purpose, and if it is to continue, some other basis for it must be found. The illusion of what marriage will achieve is often far removed from what it is actually like.

Although the symbolic act of marriage has a different meaning for everyone, it is primarily an agreement that the young people are committed to each other for life. In this age of easy divorce, marriage can be entered into with reservations, as a trial. Yet insofar as it is a commitment, the young people will find themselves responding to one another in new ways. Sometimes they feel trapped and begin to act rebellious, quarreling over authority problems; or they feel free to "be themselves" and behave in ways their spouses find unexpected. By the act of marriage, the couple are absolved from holding back from one another; this move toward unreserved intimacy may be welcome but it can also be frightening. Many conservative young people still postpone sexual relations until they are married, and different ideas about that adventure, as well as previous exaggerated expectations, can cause disappointment and confusion.

As the married couple begin to live together, they must work out a number of agreements necessary to any pair living in intimate association. They must agree about ways of dealing with their families of origin, their peers, the practical aspects of life together, and the subtle as well as gross differences between them as individuals. Either implicitly or explicitly, they must resolve an extraordinary number of questions, some of which could not be anticipated before marriage, including who will decide where they are to live, how much influence the wife is to have on her husband's career, whether either should judge the other's friends, whether the wife should work or remain at home, and hundreds of others —even so apparently trivial a matter as who will pick up whose clothes. Their information about marriage and their actual experience of it are two different orders of knowledge.

As they work out a new relationship with each other, the young couple must also devise ways for dealing with disagreements. Often in this early period they avoid open controversy or critical statements because of the benevolent aura of the new marriage and because they do not wish to hurt each other's feelings. In time, the controversial areas they avoid become larger, and they find themselves continually on the edge of a quarrel and mysteriously irritable with each other. Sometimes the issues that cannot be discussed become built into the marriage. More usually, one person brings up a minor issue, the other retaliates in kind, and they have an open fight, which makes explicit matters which up to then have been communicated only indirectly. Often such a fight is frightening because of the unexpected emotions aroused, and the couple make up and vow never to quarrel again. But gradually issues they can't discuss again build up until there is another flare-up and another fight. In the process, they work out ways of resolving disagreements and settling issues. Sometimes the solutions are themselves unsatisfactory, leading to increasing discontentment, which emerges later in the marriage. For example, a couple may find that controversy can be resolved only if one partner gives in to the other more than he or she feels is appropriate. In this early period, husbands and wives learn the manipulative power of weakness and illness, as well as the power of force.

Most of the decisions made by a newly married couple are influenced not only by what they learned in their separate families but by the current entangling alliances with the parents, which are an inevitable aspect of the marriage. Individually, the young people must make the shift from being dependent on their parents to relating to them as independent adults, and behave differently toward them.

The decisions the newly married pair make cannot be easily separated from parental influence. For example, whether or not the wife is to work or where the young couple will live is influenced by parental views. The young people must establish a territory with some independence from parental influence, and the parents in turn must change their ways of dealing with their children after marriage. Too much benevolent help can be as damaging to the young couple as unconstructive censure. When parents continue to provide financial support, there is an implicit or explicit bargain about their right to dictate a way of life in return for their support. Giving money can be either helpful or detrimental, and questions about it arise: should it be given in cash, in gifts, to one or the other, or to the two as a couple? Is it given freely or with the implied criticism that is should not be necessary? A schism can be created in a new marriage because of the nature of parents' involvement in it, often without any awareness of what is causing the bad feeling. When the marriage is caught up in conflicts with extended kin, symptoms can develop. A wife whose husband cannot prevent the intrusion of his mother into the marriage, for example, may develop symptoms as one way of dealing with the situation.

Some couples attempt to make their own territory totally independent by cutting themselves off from their extended families. Usually this is not successful and tends to erode the marriage, because the art of marriage includes achieving independence while simultaneously remaining emotionally involved with one's relatives. (Cases illustrating ways of resolving problems of early marriage are presented in Chapter IV.)

CHILDBIRTH AND DEALING WITH THE YOUNG

Part of the adventure of marriage is that just as the problems of one stage are beginning to be resolved, the next stage has begun to provide new opportunities. A young couple who have worked out an amiable way of living together during the period of early marriage find that childbirth raises new issues and unsettles old ones. For many couples this is a delightful period of mutual anticipation and welcoming of a child, but for others it is a period of distress that takes different forms. The wife may become extremely upset during pregnancy, she may have mysterious physical problems that prevent carrying a child to term, or she may begin to behave in disturbed and bizarre ways immediately after the birth of the child. Alternatively, the husband or some member of the extended family may develop distress that coincides with the event of childbirth.

When a problem arises during this period, the "cause" is not easily determined because so many different established arrangements in the family system are revised by the arrival of a child.

Young couples who consider their marriage a trial find separation is less possible. Other couples who thought they were committed to each other discover themselves feeling trapped with the arrival of a child and learn for the first time the fragility of their original marriage contract.

The kind of game a couple has worked out before childbirth is an intimate game of two. They have learned to deal with each other and find ways of resolving many issues. With the birth of a child, they are automatically in a triangle. It is not a triangle with an outsider or a member of the extended kin; jealousy of a new kind can develop when one spouse feels the other is more attached to the child than to him or her. Many of the issues the couple face begin to be dealt with through the child as he becomes scapegoat and excuse for new problems and old ones not previously resolved. Husbands and wives on the edge of separation can now agree they must stay together for the child's sake, when they might not have separated at any rate. Wives who are discontented can decide it is because of the child rather than face older issues with the husband. For example, a mother of an eighteen-year-old psychotic daughter once protested that her daughter always came between her and her husband. She cited as evidence a letter she had written when the daughter was a few months old, which pointed out to her husband that he and the daughter were always siding together against her. If an infant becomes a part of a triangle in this way, when she is old enough to leave home a crisis arises because the couple face each other without the child as a device between them; issues that were not resolved many years previously, before the child's birth, are reactivated.

In many instances, a marriage is precipitated because of a pregnancy, and the young couple never experience life together as a partnership of two. The marriage begins and continues as a triangle until the children leave home. Often a marriage that is forced in this way does not become a problem. In other cases, the child is the excuse for the marriage and can be blamed for all marital and extended-family difficulties.

The imminent birth of a child represents the coming together of two families and creates grandparents, aunts, and uncles on both sides. Such simple arrangements as visiting agreements become revised when a grandchild appears. The two families may quarrel over such matters as what the child is to be named, how he is to be raised and educated, which family will influence his development, and so on. Often the extended kin have considered the marriage a temporary one until the arrival of a child forces the issue. The possibility, or actuality, of a defective child can raise potential doubts about all branches of the family and be used as ammunition in a family struggle.

Set farther apart from their families by the arrival of a child, the young couple is also further entangled within the family system. As parents, they are now more individuated as adults and less children themselves, but the child brings them further into the total network of relatives as old bonds change their nature and new ones are formed.

When distress arises during this period, it often takes the form of symptoms or disturbance in one of the participants. However, the person exhibiting distress is not necessarily the appropriate focus of treatment. A disturbed wife can be responding to a husband who now feels trapped because a child is on the way, or she may be responding to a crisis in the extended family.

As a young married couple survive the birth of children, they become excessively occupied for a period of years in taking care of little ones. Each arrival changes the nature of the situation and raises new as well as old issues. The pleasures of child rearing are often balanced by the stress on the parents of continual involvements in complex problems they must learn to deal with largely on their own, because they are reluctant to use the child-rearing methods of their parents in this time of change.

It is at the stage of caring for young children that a special problem arises for women. Having babies is something they looked forward to as a form of self-fulfillment. Yet caring for small children can be a source of personal frustration. Having been educated in preparation for the day when they would be adults and able to make use of their special abilities, they find themselves cut off from adult life and living in a world of children again. In contrast, the husband is usually able to participate with adults in his working world and enjoy the children as an added dimension to his life. The wife who finds herself confined largely to conversation with children can also feel herself denigrated with the label of "only" housewife and mother. A longing for more participation in the adult world for which she was prepared can lead her to feeling discontented and envious of her husband's activities. The marriage can begin to erode as the wife demands more child-rearing help from her husband and more adult activities, while he feels that he is being burdened by wife and children and hampered in his work. Sometimes a mother will attempt to exaggerate the importance of child rearing by encouraging a child to have an emotional problem, which she can then devote her attention to. The task of the therapist is to solve the problem of the child by helping the mother to disengage herself from him and find a more fulfilling life of her own.

Despite the difficulties that arise with small children, the most common period of crisis is when children start school. In the past, when a child began to misbehave or was reluctant to go to school, the usual procedure was to allow him to remain at home while he entered individual therapy, in the hope that he would recover and ultimately be willing to go to school. In the meantime, he was falling more and more behind his peers. With the family orientation, it has become more common to get the child to school and treat his total situation, recognizing that the problem might be either in the home, the school, or both. At this age the child often malfunctions, partly because of what happens within the complex organization of the family, but also because he is becoming more involved outside the family. Conflicts between the parents about child rearing become most manifest when their product is put upon display. Going to school also represents for them their first experience of the fact that their children will ultimately leave home and they will face only each other.

It is at this stage that the structure of the family becomes most visible to a therapist consulted because of a child problem. The communication patterns in the family have become habitual, and certain structures are not adaptable to the child's becoming involved outside the family. Several types of unfortunate structures are commonly found, all of them concerned with the breaching of generation lines within the family. The most usual problem is for one parent, usually the mother, to side consistently with a child against the other parent, usually the father, protesting that he is too hard on the child, while he protests that she is too soft. In this triangle the parents are trying to save the child from each other, offering the child the opportunity to play one parent off against the other. This triangle can be described in many ways, and a useful way is to see one parent as "overinvolved" with the child. Often the mother is both helpful and exasperated with the child, frustrated in her attempts to deal with him. Father is more peripheral, and if he intervenes to help mother, she attacks him and he withdraws, leaving her unable to deal effectively with the child. This pattern repeats itself endlessly, preventing the child from maturing and the mother from becoming disengaged from child rearing for a more productive life of her own. As the pattern continues, the child becomes the means by which the parents communicate with each other about those issues they cannot deal with directly. For example, if there is an issue about father's masculinity that cannot be faced within the marriage, mother can question whether the son is not too effeminate while father can insist that the boy is sufficiently masculine. The child cooperates by behaving feminine enough to provide mother with an argument and masculine enough to support father. The child has the appearance of not quite knowing which sex he is as he performs like a metaphor within this triangle. As the child moves outside the home, the established pattern is threatened, and symptoms in the child can signal the family's difficulty in getting past this stage.

This triangle can occur even if the parents are divorced, since legal divorce does not necessarily change this type of problem. If a mother who is raising a child alone presents him as a problem, an alert therapist looks for a separated husband who is still involved, and his goal is to help the family through the process of actually disengaging a member.

In one-parent families, a typical structural problem at this stage is a grandmother who consistently sides with a child against the mother. If mother is young, grandmother often treats her and her child as if they were siblings, and the child is caught in a struggle between mother and grandmother across generation lines. This is especially typical of families who live in poverty.* In the middle class, a mother often separates from her husband after a struggle with him over the child, and grandmother substitutes to continue the struggle.

These cross-generation struggles within a family often become evident only when the child reaches the age when he should become involved in the community outside the family. At that point, family patterns that have functioned with tolerable success break down and a therapist is asked to intervene to help the family into

* Salvador Minuchin et al., *Families of the Slums* . . . (New York: Basic Books, 1967).

the next stage. (Erickson's approaches to such problems are presented in Chapters V and VII.)

MIDDLE MARRIAGE DIFFICULTIES

Among most species of animals, a family unit composed of parents and children is of brief duration. Typically, the parents annually produce offspring and the young go off into the world to reproduce their kind, while the parents begin a new brood. Human parents must continue to be responsible for their children for a period of many years, and they must continue to associate with them while making the shift from treating them as children to treating them more as peers. Ultimately, as the parents age, the children begin to take care of their parents. This arrangement is unique and requires that family members adapt to extraordinary changes in relationship to one another over the years. As relationships change within the family, the marital relationship undergoes constant revision.

To talk of a marital problem is to create an entity of "marriage" that overlooks all the forces outside the marriage that have an influence on it. The boundary we draw around a married couple, around a nuclear family, or around a kinship system is an arbitrary one for discussion purposes. When we examine the influence of welfare on the poor family, or the intrusion of a corporation into the private lives of middle-class executives, it becomes obvious that the problems of a married couple are only partially described by focusing upon the couple. If a man is out of work and his wife is receiving welfare funds, the "marital problem" includes the way the government has intervened in their marriage. Similarly, a marriage can have as a major source of difficulty the intrusion of a mother-in-law, the behavior of children, or any number of other factors. It is important to keep always in mind that a family is an ongoing group subject to changing external influences, with a history and a future together and with stages of development as well as habitual patterns among the members.

In the family as we know it today, the couple who have been married for ten or fifteen years face problems that can be described in terms of the individual, the marital pair, or the whole family. At this time the husband and wife are reaching the middle years of their life cycles. Often this is one of the better periods of life.

The husband can be enjoying success in his work and his wife can share in the success they have both worked toward. The wife, too, is more free as the children make fewer demands, and she can develop her talents and further her own career. Earlier difficulties the couple may have experienced have become resolved with time, and their approach to life has mellowed. It is a period when the marital relationship is deepening and broadening, and when stable relationships with the extended family and a circle of friends have been established. The difficulties of rearing small children are over, and are replaced with a joint pleasure in watching the children grow and develop in surprising ways.

The clinician sees families at this stage not when life is going well but only when it is going badly. For many families it is a difficult time. Often the husband has reached a point in his career where he realizes he is not going to fulfill the ambitions of his youth. His disappointment can affect the whole family and particularly his status with his wife. Or, conversely, the husband may be more successful than he had anticipated, and while he enjoys great respect outside the home, his wife continues to relate to him as she did when he was less important, with consequent resentments and conflicts. One of the inevitable human dilemmas is the fact that when a man reaches his middle years and has gained in status and position, he becomes more attractive to young females, while his wife, who is more dependent upon physical appearance, is feeling less attractive to males.

When the children have all entered school, the wife feels she must make changes in her life. The increased leisure forces her to consider her earlier ambitions for a career, for example, and she can be uncertain about her abilities. The cultural premise that being a housewife and mother is not enough becomes more of a problem as the children need her less. At times she may feel that her life is being wasted in the home and that her status is declining, just as her husband is feeling more important.

By these middle years, the married couple have been through many conflicts and have worked out quite rigid and repetitive ways of dealing with one another. They have maintained stability in the family by means of complicated patterns of interchange for resolving problems and for avoiding resolutions of them. As the children develop and the family undergoes change, the previous patterns can prove inadequate and crises can arise. Sometimes there is an accumulation of problem behavior, such as drinking or violence, which passes the toleration point. One or both of the spouses can feel that if life is ever going to be less miserable, they must make the break now before they grow older.

The middle years can force a couple to a decision about whether to stay together or to go their separate ways. This period when the children are less often at home also forces the parents to realize that ultimately the children will be gone altogether, and they will be faced only with each other. In many cases, they have agreed to stay together for the children's sake, and as they see the time approaching for the children to leave, they enter marital turmoil.

Severe marital strain and divorce can occur in these middle years, even though the couple have survived many previous crises. Most other periods of family stress occur when someone is entering or leaving the family. In the middle years the cast is not changing; yet in a sense it is, because this is the time when the children are making the shift from childhood to young adulthood. What is known as adolescent turmoil can be seen as a struggle within the family system to maintain the previous hierarchical arrangement. For example, a mother may have evolved ways of dealing with her daughter as a child and ways of dealing with competing females, yet when the daughter matures into a competing female, the mother cannot relate to her in any consistent way. The father, who is caught between them, can find the experience bewildering. A similar shift occurs as sons grow up into young men and the father must deal with a son as his child and yet also as an adult male. Symptoms may appear in a child or a parent as a way of stabilizing the system, but perhaps more often than at other periods the presenting problem is acknowledged marital distress.

Resolving a marital problem at the middle stage of marriage is often more difficult than in the early years when the young couple are still in a state of instability and working out new patterns. By the middle stage, the patterns are set and habitual. Often the couple have tried various ways of reconciling differences and have returned to old patterns despite the distress. As one typical pattern for stabilizing the marriage is for the couple to communicate with each other through the children, a crisis arises when the children leave home and the couple again come face to face with each other.

WEANING PARENTS FROM CHILDREN

It appears that every family enters a period of crisis when the children begin to move out, and the consequences are various. Often the marriage is thrown into a turmoil, which progressively subsides as the children leave and the parents work out a new relationship as a pair. They succeed in resolving their conflicts and manage to allow the children their own mates and careers, making the transition to becoming grandparents. In families where there is only a single parent, the loss of a child can be felt as the beginning of an old age of loneliness, but the loss must be survived and new interests found. Whether parents get past this period as part of the normal process depends to some extent upon how severe it is for them and to some extent upon how a helper intervenes at the crucial time.

In many cultures, the weaning of children and parents from each other is assisted by a ceremony that defines the child as a newly created adult. These initiation rites give the child a new status and require the parents to deal with him differently from that point onward. In middle-class America, there is no such clear demarcation; the culture has no way of announcing that the adolescent is now an individuated adult. School graduation partially serves this purpose, but graduation from high school is often only a step on the way to college, with continued parental support. Even marriage, in cases where parents continue to support the couple, does not clearly define the separation or offer a ceremonial completion of weaning.

Sometimes the turmoil between parents comes when the oldest child leaves home, while in other families the disturbance seems to become progressively worse as each child leaves, and in others as the youngest is about to go. In many cases, parents who have watched their children leave one by one without difficulty suddenly have difficulty when one particular child reaches that age. In such cases, the child has usually been of special importance in the marriage. He may have been the one through whom the parents carried on most of their communication with each other, or the one they felt most burdened by and were held together by in their common concern and care for him.

A marital difficulty that may emerge at this time is that the parents find they have nothing to say to each other and nothing to share. They have not talked to each other about anything except the children for years. Sometimes the couple begin to quarrel about the same issues they quarreled about before the children came. Since these issues were not resolved but merely put aside by the arrival of children, they now arise again. Often the conflict leads to separation or divorce—an event that to the observer can seem tragic after so long a marriage. Often, too, if the conflict is severe, there are murder threats and suicide attempts.

It does not seem accidental that people most frequently go crazy—become schizophrenic—in the late teens and early twenties, the age when children are expected to leave home and the family is in turmoil. Adolescent schizophrenia and other severe disturbances can be seen as an extreme way of attempting to solve what happens to a family at this stage of life. When child and parents cannot tolerate becoming separated, the threatened separation can be aborted if something goes wrong with the child. By developing a problem that incapacitates him socially, the child remains within the family system. The parents can continue to share the child as a source of concern and disagreement, and they find it unnecessary to deal with each other without him. The child can continue to participate in a triangular struggle with his parents, while offering himself and them his "mental illness" as an excuse for all difficulties.

When parents bring an adolescent to a therapist as a problem, the therapist can focus upon him and place him in individual treatment or hospitalize him. If this is done, the parents appear more normal and concerned and the child manifests more extreme behavior. What the expert has done is to crystallize the family at this stage of development by labeling and treating the child as the "patient." The parents do not have to resolve their conflict with each other and move on to the next marital stage, and the child does not have to move toward intimate relationships outside the family. Once this arrangement has been made, the situation is stable until there is improvement in the child. If he becomes more normal and seriously threatens to marry or succeed in supporting himself, the family once again enters the stage of the child's leaving home, and so conflict and dissension arise again. The parents' response to this new crisis is to take the child out of treatment, or to rehospitalize him as a relapsed case, and once again the family stabilizes. As this process repeats itself, the child becomes "chronic." Often a therapist will see the problem as child versus parents and side with the victimized child, bringing about more difficulty for the family. With a similar view, the hospital doctor will sometimes advise the young person to leave his family and never see them again. Consistently this approach fails; the child collapses and continues his chronic career.

Although we don't know much about how a child disengages himself from his parents and leaves home, it looks as if he would lose if he went to either of two extremes. If he leaves his family and vows never to see them again, his life usually goes badly. If, in this culture, he stays with his parents and lets them run his life, that too goes badly. He must become separated from his family and yet remain involved with them. This balance is what most families manage and what contemporary family therapists seek.

The family therapist who is offered an adolescent as a case does not see the child as the problem but rather the whole family situation. His goal is not to bring about understanding and togetherness between child and family but to function as an initiation ceremony, dealing with the family in such a way that the child shifts to join the adult world and the parents learn to treat him and each other differently. If the therapist eases the child out of the family and resolves the conflicts that have arisen around the separation, the child abandons his symptoms and is free to develop in his own way.

As the young person leaves home and begins to establish a family of his own, his parents must go through the major change of life called becoming grandparents. Sometimes they have little or no preparation for taking this step if the proper marriage rituals have not been gone through by the children. They must learn how to become good grandparents, work out the rules for participating in their children's lives, and manage to function with only each other in the household. Often in this period they must also deal with the loss of their own parents and the consequent grief.

One aspect of the family we are learning about is the natural process by which difficulties are remedied as they arise. An example is the arrival of a grandchild. A mother once said as a joke that she kept on having more children so that she would not spoil the youngest one. Often mothers are overinvolved with the youngest child and have difficulty disengaging from him as he moves toward a more independent life. If at that point an older child produces a grandchild, the arrival of the new child can free the mother from her youngest child and involve her in the new stage of becoming a grandparent. If one thinks of the natural process in this way, one realizes the importance of maintaining the involvement of the generations with each other. If young people cut themselves off from their parents they deprive their child of grandparents and also make it more difficult for their parents to get past stages in their own lives. Each generation is dependent upon every other generation in complex ways that we are beginning to understand as we watch the disruption of families in these changing times. (Erickson's conception of the importance of continuity in family life is most apparent in the ways he resolves problems of disengaging and re-engaging young people with their parents, described in Chapter VIII.)

RETIREMENT AND OLD AGE

When a couple have succeeded in turning loose their children so they are less involved with them, they often seem to come to a period of relative harmony that can continue through the husband's retirement. Sometimes, however, retirement can complicate their problem as they are faced with each other twenty-four hours a day. It is not unusual for a wife to develop some incapacitating symptom at the time of her husband's retirement, and the focus of a therapist should be upon easing the couple into a more amiable relationship rather than treating the problem as one involving only the wife.

Although the individual emotional problems of older people can have diverse causes, a first possibility is the protection of someone else. For example, when a wife developed an inability to open her eyes, the problem was diagnosed as hysterical. The emphasis was upon her and her stage of life. From a family point of view, her disability could be seen as a way of supporting her husband through a crisis. The problem arose at the time of her husband's retirement, when he was deposed from an active, helpful life to what in his view was being put on the shelf with no useful function. When his wife developed her problem, he had something important to do—help his wife recover. He took her from doctor to doctor, arranged their living situation so that she could function even though unable to see, and became extremely protective. His involvement in the problem became evident when his wife improved and he began to be depressed, cheering up only when she relapsed again. The helpful function of problems, apparent throughout family life, is equally important when a couple have only each other through their declining years.

In time, of course, one of the partners dies, leaving the other to live alone and find a way to be involved with their families. Sometimes an older person can find a useful function; sometimes he is merely superfluous as times change and old people are seen as irrelevant to the action in the younger generation. At this stage the family has to face the difficult problem of caring for the older person or extruding him into a home where others will care for him. This, too, is a crisis point, which is often not easily managed. Yet how the young take care of the old becomes the model for how they will be taken care of as they too grow old, as the family cycle continues without end.

III

THE COURTSHIP PERIOD: CHANGING THE YOUNG ADULT

When young people graduate from the juvenile to the adult status, they enter a complex social network that requires a variety of kinds of behavior. A primary task at this time is to engage successfully in courtship behavior. Success in this adventure involves many factors: the young people must overcome personal inadequacies, they must be able to associate with people their own age, they must achieve adequate status in their social network, they must have become disengaged from their family of origin, and they require a society stable enough to allow the steps of courtship to go to their completion. Many problems that handicap a young person at this time of life can arise, and therapy can resolve some of them.

The difficulties take many forms—an overconcern with physical inadequacies, unfortunate social behavior, failures in mental processes, fears that handicap the person's mobility, fears of the opposite sex, and so on—and they can have different functions. If a young person is needed within his or her family of origin, problems that force him to fail in work and courtship and collapse back within his family may arise. This aspect of the problem will be discussed in Chapter VIII. Sometimes the difficulties are not in relation to the family of origin but in relation to peers. Whatever the function of the problem, the goal of therapy can be seen as helping the young person past the courtship stage into marriage. This does not mean that everyone should marry or that it is abnormal not to, but many young people who seek therapy at this time have that end in mind.

A series of Milton Erickson's cases will be offered here to illustrate ways of resolving some of the problems of the young at this stage. Generally, there are two types of problem young people: those who are beginning to drop out of the normal stream of living and those who have already become peripheral and are clearly social deviants. With both types, Erickson puts a primary emphasis upon shifting them toward success in work and love. He does not usually review their past with them, nor does he help them to understand why they have problems. His general approach is to accept the young person's way of behaving while simultaneously introducing ideas and acts that lead to change. What he does with a particular patient will vary, and therefore he approaches each new young person with an open mind as to possible interventions. In one case he might work with hypnosis to provide an elaborate shifting of ideas, in another he might focus on reducing a problem to absurdity, and in another he might require quite specific acts. For example, a young man came to him who was suffering from asthma and was completely dependent upon his mother. "He was Mama's little asthmatic boy," said Erickson, "and she was a sweet mother who would bring him a glass of water, a sandwich, a napkin. I persuaded the young man to take a job in a bank—he was totally uninterested in banking. Then I saw him once a week, once in two weeks, once in three weeks. Each time I asked a question about some little detail about banking that he could answer. He took great pleasure in telling me about them. Every time he made a mistake in his work, I showed an interest in the procedure by which it was corrected, never the details of how he made the mistake. How was it corrected, and what was the attitude of so-and-so who helped correct the error? Later he became quite enthusiastic and looked upon banking as a delightful temporary job to earn money for college. Previously he hadn't planned to go to college. Now his view of his asthma attacks is that they are a nuisance, and his enthusiasm is in his college plans."

It is typical of Erickson in his work with young people not to point out, or interpret, that they have a fear of this or that. His focus is upon bringing about change and expanding the person's world, not upon educating him about his inadequacies. His approach involves action to bring about change.

One essential requirement for a young person to succeed in courtship or in work is the ability to be geographically mobile. If someone cannot travel from place to place or enter certain buildings, he or she is socially incapacitated in this age of mobility. It appears unique to the human species that an individual can define public space as off limits. Sometimes a fear of certain areas is called a phobia, but Erickson is reluctant to describe a problem in this way. For example, in talking about a young man who worked at a minor job beneath his ability and who traveled by back streets and alleys and was unable to enter many public buildings, Erickson said, "Why treat this as a fear of streets and buildings? In this particular case the young man was elaborately avoiding women, and with a mother like his, he had a reason to be fed up with them. I didn't talk to him about his fear of women. I showed an interest in his physique and worked with him on what sort of apartment a man with his musculature and strength and brains should have. He moved into an apartment of his own away from his mother. We discussed his biceps and his quadriceps, and it wasn't possible for him to take pride in those without being proud of what was in between. As his body image improved, he changed his ways. Why should I ever tell him he was afraid of women? He isn't any more. He's married."

An example of a mobility problem, and Erickson's way of intervening to make a change, is the case of a young man who could not cross certain streets or enter certain buildings without falling down in a faint. There was one restaurant in particular—

we will call it the Loud Rooster—he was unable to enter. He also had a variety of other forms of avoidance, including an avoidance of women. As Dr. Erickson reports:

I decided that I could get this young man over his problem of entering this particular restaurant, and in that way I could help him over other fears, particularly his fears of women. I asked him how he felt about going to dinner at the Loud Rooster, and he said he would inevitably faint. Then I described various types of women to him; there is the young naïve woman, the divorcée, the widow, and the old lady. They could be attractive or unattractive. I asked him which was the most undesirable of those four. He said there was no question about it—he was quite afraid of girls, and the idea of associating with an attractive divorcée was the most undesirable thing he could think of.

I told him that he was going to take my wife and me out to dinner at the Loud Rooster and there would be someone else going along with us. It might be a young girl, a divorcée, a widow, or an old lady. He should arrive at seven o'clock on Tuesday. I said I would drive because I didn't wish to be in his car when he was likely to faint. He arrived at seven, and I had him wait nervously in the living room until the other person who would accompany us arrived. Of course I had arranged with an extremely attractive divorcée to arrive at seven-twenty. She was one of those charming, easily met people, and when she walked in I asked him to introduce himself. He managed to, and then I told the divorcée our plans. The young man was taking us all out to dinner at the Loud Rooster.

We went to my car, and I drove up to the restaurant and parked the car in the parking lot. As we got out, I said to the young man, "This is a graveled parking lot. That's a nice level spot there where you can fall down and faint. Do you want that place, or is there a better one that you can find?" He said, "I'm afraid it will happen when I get to the door." So we walked over to the door, and I said, "That's a nice-looking sidewalk. You'll probably bang your head hard if you crash. Or how about over here?" *By keeping him busy rejecting my places to faint, I kept him from finding a place of his own choosing.* He didn't faint. He said, "Can we get a table just inside by the door?" I said, "We'll take the table I picked out." We went clear across to an elevated section in the far corner of the restaurant. The divorcée sat beside me, and while we were waiting to give our order, the divorcée and my wife and I talked about matters that were over the young man's head. We told abstruse and private jokes and laughed heartily at them. The divorcée had a master's degree, and we talked about subjects he didn't know anything about and told mythological riddles.

The three of us had a good time and he was out of the swim and feeling increasingly miserable. Then the waitress came to the table. I picked a fight with her. It was a disagreeable, noisy fight, and I demanded to see the manager and then had a fight with him. While the young man sat there intensely embarrassed, the fight culminated with my demand to see the kitchen. When we got there, I told the manager and the waitress that I was ribbing my friend, and they fell in line with it. The waitress began to slam dishes angrily down on the table. As the young man ate his dinner, I kept urging him to clean up his plate. So did the divorcée, adding such helpful comments as "The fat's good for you."

He lived through it and took us home. I had tipped off the divorcée, and she said, "You know, I feel in the mood to go dancing tonight." He could only dance a little bit, having hardly learned it in high school. She took him dancing.

The next night the young man picked up a friend of his and said, "Let's go out to dinner." He took his friend to the Loud Rooster. After what he had been through there, nothing else was to be feared; the worst had happened, and anything else would be a welcome relief. He could also enter other buildings from then on, and this laid the groundwork for getting him over his fear of certain streets.

This case illustrates Erickson's way of arranging that a fearful person enter the place he fears while blocking off the kind of behavior usually associated with the fear. In this instance Erickson was personally involved and managed the situation, taking his therapy out of the office into the area where the fear occurred. He forced the young man to survive a situation he thought he could not.

In a quite different approach, Erickson resolved a fear of traveling for a young man who insisted that he wanted only that one problem solved. The young man could only drive a car on certain streets, and he could not drive outside the city limits. If he drove to the edge of town, he became nauseated, and after vomiting he would faint. Driving with friends did not help. If he kept going, he would only recover and then faint again. Erickson required him to drive to the edge of town at three o'clock the next morning, wearing his best clothes. It was an untraveled highway with wide shoulders and a sandy ditch running alongside. When the young man reached the city limits, he was to pull over to the edge of the road, leap out of the car, and rush to the shallow ditch beside the road. He was to lie down there at least fifteen minutes. Then he was to get back into the car, drive one or two car lengths, and repeat the lying down for another fifteen minutes. Repeating this again and again, he was to continue until he could drive from one telephone pole to the next, stopping at the first evidence of any symptoms and spending fiften minutes on his back in the ditch. Under protest, the young man followed the procedure. He later reported, "I thought it was a damn-fool thing you made me promise to do, and the more I did it the madder I got. So I just quit and began to enjoy driving." Thirteen years later, he still had no problem in driving his car.

Whether Erickson uses hypnosis or not, he typically directs people to behave in particular ways. Although many therapists are reluctant to tell people what to do, partly because they fear the person will not do it, Erickson has developed a variety of ways to persuade people to do what he says. Commenting on this once in a conversation, he said, "Patients usually do what I tell them, often largely because I expect them to. A patient said to me, 'You never make an issue of my doing what you say, you just expect it in such a way that I have to do it. When I balked and tried to avoid it, I always wanted you to try to force me, and you'd always stop short. Then I'd try a little harder to make you force me to do it.' In that way she would come closer to me in the performance of what I wanted.

"But, you see, that's the way human beings are. Whenever you start depriving anyone of anything, they are going to insist that you give it to them. When I instruct a patient to do something, that patient feels I'm ordering him. They want me to be in the unfortunate position of failing at that. Therefore they've got to keep me in the active task of ordering them. When I stop ordering them at the right moment, then they substitute for me and do things for themselves. But they don't recognize that they are substituting for me."

Viewing the giving of directives in this way, Erickson takes into account, and is not overconcerned with, the idea that giving directives will make a person dependent upon the therapist. When the focus is upon moving a person into involvements with other people, they become independent of the therapist. A case example illustrates his use of directives to resolve an extremely difficult problem in a short space of time.

A twenty-one-year-old girl came to Erickson and said she wanted help. She would like to get a husband and have a home and children, but she had never had a boy friend and felt she was hopeless and destined to be an old maid. She said, "I think I'm too inferior to live. I've got no friends, I stay by myself, and I'm too homely to get married. I thought I'd see a psychiatrist before I committed suicide. I'm going to try you for three months' time, and then if things aren't straightened out that's the end."

The young lady worked as a secretary in a construction firm and had no social life. She had never dated. A young man at her office showed up at the drinking fountain each time she did, but even though she found him attractive and he made overtures, she ignored him and never spoke to him. She lived alone and her parents were dead.

The girl was pretty, but she managed to make herself unattractive because her hair was straggly and uneven, her blouse and skirt didn't match, there was a rip in her skirt, and her shoes were scuffed and unpolished. Her main physical defect, according to her, was a gap between her front teeth, which she covered with her hand as she talked. The gap was actually about one-eighth of an inch wide and not unsightly. Generally, this was a girl going downhill, heading for suicide, feeling helpless about herself, and resisting any acts that would help her achieve her goal of getting married and having children.

Erickson approached this problem with two major interventions. He proposed to the girl that since she was going downhill anyhow, she might as well have one last fling. This last fling would include taking the money she had in the bank and spending it on herself. She was to go to a particular store where a woman would help her select a tasteful outfit, and to a particular beauty shop where she would have her hair properly done. The girl was willing to accept the idea, since it was *not* a way of improving herself but part of going downhill and merely having a last fling.

Then Erickson gave her a task. She was to go home and in the privacy of her bathroom practice squirting water through the gap between her front teeth until she could achieve a distance of six feet with accuracy. She thought this was silly, but it was partly the absurdity of it that made her go home and practice squirting water conscientiously.

When the girl was dressed properly, looking attractive, and skillful at squirting water through the gap in her teeth, Erickson made a suggestion to her. He proposed that when she went to work the following Monday she play a practical joke. When that young man appeared at the water fountain at the same time she did, she was to take a mouthful of water and squirt it at him. Then she was to turn and run, but not merely run; she was to start to run toward the young man and then turn and "run like hell down the corridor."

The girl rejected this idea as impossible. Then she thought of it as a somewhat amusing but crude fantasy. Finally she decided to do it. She was in a mood for a last fling anyhow.

On Monday she went to work dressed in her new outfit and with her hair done. She went to the water fountain, and when the young man approached, she filled her mouth with water and squirted it on him. The young man said something like "You damn little bitch." This made her laugh as she ran, and the young man took after her and caught her. To her consternation, he grabbed her and kissed her.

The next day the young lady approached the water fountain with some trepidation, and the young man sprang out from behind a telephone booth and sprayed her with a water pistol. The next day they went out to dinner together.

She returned to Erickson and reported what had happened. She said she was revising her opinion about herself and wanted him to do a critical review of her. He did, pointing out, among other things, that she had cooperated well with him, that she had dressed badly before but now dressed well, and that she had previously thought she had a dental defect instead of an asset. Within a few months she sent Erickson a newspaper clipping reporting her marriage to the young man, and a year later a picture of her new baby.

This case demonstrates an approach that appears to be outside the stream of traditional therapy. It is not typical of any therapeutic school, including hypnotherapy. Yet it is typical of Erickson's work, and I think it developed out of his hypnotic orientation. Just as a hypnotist typically accepts the resistance of a subject and even encourages it, Erickson accepted the way this girl dealt with him and encouraged it—but in such a way that change could take place. This girl defined herself as going downhill and heading for the end of the road. Erickson accepted this and encouraged it, only adding that she should have one last fling. The girl was also hostile to men and would not make an effort to be nice to them. Erickson accepted this behavior, and essentially arranged that she spit on a man. Yet the consequence was, to her, quite unexpected. His way of motivating her to do what he asked, and his way of handling her resistance, was an approach characteristic of hypnosis. However, he brought the social setting into play. Instead of having her follow directions deliberately and then have a spontaneous happening by herself, he had her follow directions and then have a spontaneous happening because of the response of someone else.

There are, of course, other aspects of this case uniquely Ericksonian. His way of turning a symptom into an asset is typical, and so is his willingness to intervene, bring about a change, and disengage himself so the patient can develop independent of him, while he checks to be sure the improvement continues. There is also his use of whatever is available in the social context of the person. Not only did he have a fashion consultant and a hairdresser he could make use of, but the one man on this girl's horizon was immediately included in her future.

Another case example illustrates Erickson's use of directives to help a young woman achieve independence from her family and from him by guiding her past the courtship stage into marriage.

A physician in a nearby city sent a girl to me with the suggestion that I would probably have to put her into a mental hospital. She had a variety of fears and was terribly inhibited. The fears had become extreme in the last four years when she became engaged to a boy in the Air Force. Each year she postponed the marriage. She agreed to marry him in June, and then put it off until December. In December she put it off until the next June. During these years she developed almost incapacitating fears. She couldn't ride in a bus or a train or an airplane. In fact, she couldn't go past a railroad station because there were trains there, and she couldn't go near an airport. She hated to get into a car, and only with aid from her mother and her aunt could she get in a car to drive here to see me.

The girl was from a very proper Spanish family. She told me she loved this boy, who was now discharged from the Air Force and living in North Dakota. She wanted to marry him. She showed me his letter. But she was afraid, afraid, afraid. I had the boy write me a letter to find out his views on the marriage, and he wanted to marry her.

I thought the girl would turn out all right if her horrible fears were corrected, but I knew that would take some time. The first thing I did was move her out of her maternal home into her own apartment. She could go home on weekends. Her grandmother laid down the law to her about not moving, but I had laid down the law first. Somehow I was more effective than grandmother.

Then I focused upon solving the problem of her traveling. I told her to take a bus trip, and she was to shut her eyes and back into the bus. She did that. I don't know what the other passengers thought of that. This pretty Spanish girl with her eyes shut backing into a bus. She was so distressed about having to back into the bus that she didn't seem to realize the bus was a means of transportation to visit me in Phoenix.

Later I had her board a train backwards. The conductor didn't like it, but his comments didn't bother her because getting on a train was so horrible. I had her practice riding on buses and trains sitting in the back seat looking out the window.

When the question of sex came up, this shy and inhibited girl developed deafness. She just turned blank and apparently couldn't see or hear. Yet she wanted to get married.

I told her the next time she came in for an interview, I wanted her to bring, in her handbag, the shortest pair of short-shorts imaginable. I said she was going to take them out of the bag and show them to me. She did that. Then I gave her a choice. At her next interview with me she would either walk in wearing those short-shorts or she would put them on in my office. She made her preference and chose to walk in wearing them. I wanted to talk about sex with her as part of her preparation for marriage, so I said, "Now you're going to listen to me when I discuss sex, or I'll have you take those shorts off and put them on in my presence." She listened to me on the subject of sex and wasn't deaf.

When she was able to travel, was able to wear shorts, and could talk about sex, I said that since she wanted to get married, she was not to postpone that any more. I said, "This is the first of July. You have until the seventeenth of this month to marry the guy. You have to take a train up to North Dakota to see him and visit his family, and you don't have much time if the marriage is going to take place before the seventeenth."

She made the trip to North Dakota, and after that he came down and married her. She has two children now.

At times Erickson will be quite direct about a person's fears and how he or she should deal with them, and at other times he is extremely protective and subtle in his moves for change. An example of the more subtle approach is a case he dealt with many years ago when a young woman developed a fear that made courtship impossible.

As he reports it, a capable twenty-three-year-old woman began to be distressed and ineffectual in her work. She gradually withdrew from all social relationships and remained secluded in her room. If her roommate pleaded with her, she would eat, but most of the time she sobbed and expressed a wish to die. When asked what was wrong, she became blocked and inhibited. She was seen by several psychiatrists and had had some therapy but showed no improvement. She was still unable to discuss her problem, and her family considered hospitalization. Erickson decided to use hypnosis with her, but without her knowledge since she had proved so resistant with other psychiatrists.

From family and friends he learned that her family had been rigid and moralistic and that her mother had died when she was thirteen years old. She had a close girl friend, and they both fell in love with the same man. The girl friend married the man, and later died of pneumonia. The man moved away, but a year later he returned and they met by chance and began to see each other. She was "so much in love she walked on air," according to her roommate. One evening she returned from a date with the young man sick, nauseated, and with her dress stained with vomit. She said she was not fit to live, and when asked if the man did anything to her she began to vomit and cry. When the young man tried to call on her, she had another spell of vomiting and refused to see him.

The young man reported to a psychiatrist that on the evening of the date they had stopped the car to watch the sunset. Their conversation had become serious, and he told her of his love for her and his wish to marry her. He had hesitated to say this before because of the girl's friendship with his dead wife. She seemed to reciprocate his feelings, but as he leaned to kiss her she fended him off, vomited, and became hysterical. She sobbed words like "nasty," "filthy," and "degrading." Refusing to let him take her home, she told him he must never see him again and rushed away.

Erickson approached the case by having the woman's roommate confide to her that she was receiving hypnotic psychotherapy and wanted her to accompany her to a session as a chaperone. The patient consented, but without interest and in a listless fashion. Erickson sat the two girls in adjacent chairs and offered a prolonged, tedious, and laborious series of suggestions to the roommate, who soon developed an excellent trance, thereby setting an effective example for the intended patient. He reports:

> During the course of this trance, I gave suggestions to the roommate in such a way that by imperceptible degrees they were accepted by the patient as applying to herself. It was possible to give a suggestion to the roommate that she inhale and exhale more deeply, so timing the suggestion as to coincide with the patient's respiratory movements. By repeating this carefully many times, I could finally see that any suggestion given to the roommate with regard to her respiration was automatically performed by the patient as well. Similarly, the patient having been observed placing her hand on her thigh, I suggested to the roommate that she place her hand upon her thigh and that she should feel it resting there. Such maneuvers gradually and cumulatively brought the patient into a close identification with her roommate so that my suggestions applied to the patient as well. Gradually, it became possible for me to make suggestions to the roommate *while looking directly at the patient*, thus creating in the patient an impulse to respond, such as anyone feels when someone looks at him while addressing a question or a comment to another person.
>
> At the expiration of an hour and a half, the patient fell into a deep trance. Several things were done to ensure her cooperation and to make sure that there would be opportunities to use hypnotic treatment in the future. She was told gently that she was in a hypnotic trance and reassured that I would do nothing that she was unwilling to have me do. Therefore there was no need for a chaperone. I told her that she could disrupt the trance if I should offend her. Then I told her to continue to sleep deeply for an indefinite time, listening to and obeying only every legitimate command given her. *Thus she was given the reassuring but illusory feeling that she had a free choice*. I took care that she had a friendly feeling toward me, and for future purposes I secured a promise from her to develop a deep trance at any time for any legitimate purpose. These preliminaries were time-consuming but vitally necessary for safeguarding and facilitating the work to be done.
>
> Accordingly, I gave emphatic instructions "to forget absolutely

and completely many things," carefully omitting to specify just what was to be forgotten. The exploratory process that lay ahead would be helped by this permission to repress the more painful things, since it would automatically be applied to those that were most troublesome.

Next, I progressively disoriented her as to time and place, and then gradually reoriented her to a vaguely defined period in childhood lying somewhere between the ages of ten and thirteen.

The years from ten to thirteen were chosen because they just preceded her mother's death and must also have included the onset of her menstruation and therefore have been the critical turning point in her general emotional life and psychosexual development.

She was at no time asked to name and identify specifically the age to which she became reoriented in the trance. By being allowed to avoid this specific detail, she was compelled to do something more important; namely, to speak in general terms of the total experience those years had meant.

Presently the patient showed by the childishness of her posture, manner, and replies to casual remarks that she had regressed to a juvenile level of behavior. Then I told her emphatically, "You know many things now, things you never can forget no matter how old you grow, and you are going to tell me those things now just as soon as I tell you what I'm talking about." These instructions were repeated over and over with admonitions to obey them, understand them fully, and be prepared to carry through all of these suggestions. This was continued until her general behavior seemed to say, "Well, what are we waiting for? I'm ready."

I asked her to relate everything she knew about sex, especially in connection with menstruation, during the general period of this hypnotically reestablished but purposely undefined period of her childhood. The patient reacted with some fright, and then in a tense and childlike fashion she proceeded obediently to talk in brief disconnected sentences, phrases, and words. Her remarks related to sexual activity, although in the instructions given her the emphasis had been not upon intercourse but upon menstruation.

"My mother told me all about that. It's nasty. Girls mustn't let boys do anything to them. Not ever. Not nice. Nice girls never do. Only bad girls. It would make mother sick. Bad girls are disgusting. I wouldn't do it. You mustn't let them touch you. You will get nasty feelings. You mustn't touch yourself. Nasty. Mother told me never, never, and I won't. Must be careful. Must be good. Awful things happen if you aren't careful. Then you can't do anything. It's too late. I'm going to do like mother says. She wouldn't love me if I didn't."

No attempt was made to introduce any questions while she was talking, but when she had ceased, I asked her, "Why does your mother tell you these many things?"

"So I'll always be a good girl" was the simple, earnest, childlike reply.

My stratagem was to adopt a point of view as nearly identical with that of the mother as I could. First I had to identify entirely with this mother. Only at the end did I dare to introduce a hint of any qualifying reservations. Therefore I began by giving the patient immediate and emphatic assurance: "Of course you will always be a good girl." Then, in a manner in harmony with the mother's stern, rigid, moralistic, and forbidding attitudes (as judged from the patient's manner and words), I carefully reviewed each idea attributed to the mother in the same terms, and earnestly *approved* them. I admonished her to be glad that her mother had already told her so many of those important things that every mother should tell her little girl. Finally I instructed her to "remember telling me about all of these things, because I'm going to have you tell me about them again some other time."

Gradually and systematically I reoriented her to her current age and situation in life, thereby reestablishing the original hypnotic trance. However, the earlier instructions to "forget many things" were still in effect, and an amnesia was induced and maintained for all of the events of the hypnotically induced state of regression.

Upon awakening, she showed no awareness of having been in a trance, but complained of feeling tired and remarked spontaneously that perhaps hypnosis might help her since it seemed to be helping her roommate. Purposely, I made no reply to this. Instead, I asked abruptly, "Will you please tell me everything you can about any special instructions concerning sexual matters that your mother may have given you when you were a little girl?"

After a show of hesitation and reluctance, the patient began in a low voice and with a manner of rigid primness to repeat essentially the same story that she had told in the earlier regressive trance state, except that this time she employed a stilted, adult vocabulary and sentence structure, and made much mention of her mother. She said, "My mother gave me very careful instructions on many occasions about the time I began to menstruate. Mother impressed upon me many times the importance of every nice girl protecting herself from undesirable associations and experiences. Mother made me realize how nauseating, filthy, and disgusting sex can be. Mother made me realize the degraded character of anybody who indulges in sex. I appreciate my mother's careful instruction of me when I was just a little girl."

She made no effort to elaborate on any of these remarks and was obviously eager to dismiss the topic. When she had concluded her account of her mother's teachings, I systematically restated them to her without any comment or criticism. Instead, I gave full and earnest approval. I told her that she should be most grateful that her mother had taken advantage of every opportunity to tell her little daughter those things every little child should know and should begin to understand in childhood. After making an appointment for another interview the next week, I hastily dismissed her.

At the second appointment, the patient readily developed a deep trance, and I drew her attention again to the fact that her mother had lectured her repeatedly. I asked, "How old were you when your mother died?" She replied, "I was thirteen." Immediately, with quiet emphasis, I said, "Had your mother lived longer, she would have talked to you many more times to give you advice. But because she died when you were only thirteen, she could not complete that task and you had to complete it without her help."

Without giving her any opportunity to accept or reject this comment or to react to it in any way, I quickly diverted her by asking her to describe the events that had occurred immediately after she had awakened from her first trance. As she completed the account, I drew her attention to the repetitive character of her mother's lectures, and made the same careful comment on the unfinished nature of her mother's work. Then I reoriented her to the same period of early childhood. I emphasized sharply the fact that these lectures had all been given to her *in childhood. And as she grew older, her mother would have had more to teach her.* I suggested that she might well begin the task of continuing for herself the course of sexual instruction her mother had begun but had been unable to finish because of her death. She might best begin by speculating seriously about what advice her mother would have given her during the years intervening between childhood and adolescence and between adolescence and adult womanhood. As she accepted this suggestion, I added instructions to take into consideration all intellectual and emotional aspects. Immediately after this instruction, I said that upon awakening she should repeat all of the various accounts she had given in this hypnotic session.

The patient's waking account was decidely brief. She slowly combined everything she had said into a single, concise story. Significantly, she spoke in the past tense: "My mother attempted to give me an understanding of sex. She tried to give it to me in a way that a child such as I was could understand. She impressed upon me the seriousness of sex; also, the importance of having nothing to do with it. She made it very clear to me as a child."

She made this statement with long pauses between each sentence, as though thinking profoundly. She interrupted herself several times to comment on her mother's death and the incompleteness of her instruction, and to remark that had her mother lived, more things would have been told her. Repeatedly she said, as if to herself, "I wonder how Mother would have told me the things I should know now." I seized upon this last remark as a point for terminating the session and dismissed her.

Promptly upon arrival for the third session, she was hypnotized and instructed to review rapidly and silently all the events of the two previous sessions and to recall the instructions and suggestions she had been given and the responses she had made. Her final statement summarized her performance most adequately. She said, "You might say that Mother tried to tell me the things I needed to know, that she would have told me how to take care of myself happily and how to look forward confidently to the time when I could do those things appropriate to my age—have a husband and a home and be a woman who has grown up."

I told her that when she awoke she was to completely forget all three sessions, including even the fact that she had been hypnotized, except that she would be able to recall her first stilted, prim waking account. This amnesia was to include any new and satisfying understanding she had come to possess. She was told further that upon awakening she would be given a systematic review of her sex instruction as I had learned about these matters from her. But because of the all-inclusive amnesia this review would seem to her to be a hypothetical construction of probabilities built by me upon the first waking account. She was to listen with intense interest and ever growing understanding. She would find truths and meanings and applications understandable only to her in whatever was said. As those continued and developed, she would acquire a capacity to interpret, apply, and recognize them as actually belonging to her, and do so far beyond any capacity that I might have to understand.

At first glance, it would seem strange to suggest repression of insight as one of the culminating steps in a therapeutic procedure. However, this measure was employed for three reasons. In the first place, it implies that much of the affective insight may either remain or again become unconscious without thereby lessening its therapeutic value. Secondly, it protects the subject from the disturbing feeling that anyone else knows the things about her that she now knows, but wishes to keep to herself; hence the importance of the suggestion that she would understand far more than I would. Thirdly, by looking upon the material as a purely hypothetical construction of probabilities by me, the patient could recover insight gradually in a slowly progressive fashion as she tested this hypothetical structure.

I awakened her and offered to speculate upon the probable nature and development of the sex instruction she had been given and reviewed all the material she had furnished in general terms that permitted her to apply them freely to her own experiences.

In this way I could give the patient a general review of the development of all the primary and secondary sexual characteristics: the phenomenon of menstruation, the appearance of pubic and axillary hair, the development of her breasts, the probable interest in the growth of her nipples, the first wearing of a brassière, the possibility that boys had noticed her developing figure and that some of them had slapped her freshly, and the like. I named each in succession without placing emphasis on any individual item and followed this with a discussion of modesty, the first stirrings of sexual awareness, autoerotic feelings, the ideas of love in puberty and adolescence, and the possible ideas of where babies came from. In this way, without any specific data, a wide variety of ideas and typical experiences were covered by name. After this, I made general statements about the speculations that might have passed through her mind at one time or another. This again was done slowly and always in vague general terms, so that she could make a comprehensive and extensive personal application of these remarks.

Shortly after this procedure was begun, the patient responded by a show of interest and with every outward manifestation of insight and understanding. At the conclusion, she declared simply, "You know, I can understand what has been wrong with me, but I'm in a hurry now and I will tell you tomorrow." This was her first acknowledgment that she had a problem.

Instead of permitting her to rush away, I promptly rehypnotized her and emphatically instructed her to recover *any and all* memories of her trance experiences that would be valuable and useful; she was led to view *all of them* as possibly useful. This diverted her attention from any conflicting feelings about those memories and assisted in their free and full recovery. I told her she should feel free to ask advice, suggestions, and any instruction she wished, and to do so freely and comfortably. As soon as this instruction had been firmly impressed, I awakened her.

Immediately, but with less urgency, she said that she wanted to leave but added that she would first like to ask a few questions.

I said she could, and she asked me to state my personal opinion about "kissing, petting, and necking." Very cautiously and using her own words, I expressed approval of all three, with the reservation that each should be done in a manner that conformed with one's own ideas and that only such amorous behavior should be indulged in as would conform to the essential ideals of the individual personality. The patient received this statement thoughtfully, and then she asked for a personal opinion as to whether it was right to feel sexual desire. I replied cautiously that sexual desire was a normal and essential feeling for every living creature and that its absence from appropriate situations was wrong. I added that she would undoubtedly agree that her own mother, were she living, would say the same thing. After thinking this over, she left hastily.

The next day the patient returned to declare that she had spent the previous evening in the company of her suitor. With many blushes she added, "Kissing is great sport," and she departed quickly.

A few days later I saw her by appointment, and she held out her left hand to display an engagement ring. She explained that as a result of her talk with me during the last therapeutic session she had gained an entirely new understanding of many things. This had made it possible for her to accept the emotion of love and to experience sexual desires and feelings so that she was now entirely grown up and ready for the experiences of womanhood. She seemed unwilling to discuss matters further, except to ask whether she might have another interview with me in the near future. She explained that at that time she would like to receive instruction about coitus, since she expected to be married shortly. She added with some slight embarrassment, "Doctor, that time I wanted to rush away— By not letting me rush away, you saved my virginity. I wanted to go right to him and offer myself to him at once."

Some time later I saw her at her request and gave her a minimum of information. I found that she had no particular worries or concern about the entire matter and was straightforward and earnest about her desire to be instructed. Shortly afterward she came in to report that she was to be married within a few days and that she looked forward happily to her honeymoon. About a year later she returned to report that her married life was all she could hope for, and that she was anticipating motherhood with much pleasure. Two years later I saw her again and found her to be happy with her husband and baby daughter.

It seems evident that in a variety of ways Erickson offers a young person the permission of an adult, and so the adult world, to engage in behavior that was forbidden when the person was younger and the behavior was not appropriate. This initiation into mature views can be done actively and directly or indirectly with a variety of subtle suggestions. Erickson manages to do it in terms the young person can comprehend most easily.

This case illustrates a number of aspects of Erickson's approach. Most important is his elaborate protection of the young lady. She is gracefully eased into the treatment situation, gently induced into a trance, and carefully protected from any ideas that might be upsetting to her. She is also protected from an impulsive action when he restrains her from rushing off to her boy friend. Not only does Erickson demonstrate vast experience with the control of ideas coming into awareness; he also shows acute awareness of the actual social situation of young people.

Just as young women must be able to establish intimate relationships, so must a young man succeed in that endeavor. When a young man seeks a mate, many factors are involved, and a primary necessity is an ability to achieve a normal sexual response.

By late adolescence, the male is learning to become emotionally aroused by a female and is learning to establish bonds with females in preparation for a more permanent union. In this period, which is usually one of sexual trial and error, the young man who consistently experiences defeat by being unable to participate adequately in sexual relations is handicapped in the mate-selection process. The most common problems, besides an inability to associate comfortably with females at all, are premature ejaculation and impotence. In either case, the sexual contract is not fulfilled and frustration, rather than increasing experience in the more subtle intimacies of a relationship, develops.

A young man requested that Dr. Erickson treat him for premature ejaculation by using hypnoisis. Dr. Erickson reports:

> This young man was thirty years old and unmarried when he came to me. He had suffered from premature ejaculation during his first attempt at sexual relations when he was twenty years old. He had had a most unhappy reaction to that experience and thought it was punishment for his immorality. He felt damaged and incompetent. From then on, he became obsessional about the subject and read everything he could find on sex. He sought new and different women from every stratum of society, racial group, and physical type, all to no avail. He had really proved to himself that he suffered from premature ejaculation.

When I asked him for a complete description of his behavior in the sexual act, he declared that it was invariably the same whether his partner was an aging, drunken prostitute or an attractive, charming, well-educated girl. He never had any difficulty in securing and maintaining an erection, even after ejaculation. However, upon an attempt at insertion, ejaculation occurred first. Many times he had disregarded the premature ejaculation and engaged in active coitus, but this gave him neither pleasure nor satisfaction. He regarded it as an unpleasant effort in a desperate desire to achieve sexual competence. Usually he would persist in this intravaginal masturbation until ready for the second ejaculation, whereupon he would unwillingly but compulsively withdraw. He would then be unable to gain insertion until he had completed the second ejaculation externally. He sought me out as a last resort.

A half dozen sessions were taken up with letting him bemoan his difficulties. But he did go into a trance, with a considerable amount of posthypnotic amnesia. He was questioned extensively in a trance about his current liaisons, and I learned that he was assiduously courting a prostitute who lived in an apartment house in a second-floor suite, located above the entrance to a court. Inside the court, it was necessary to go up a stairway and along a balcony before reaching her apartment. I offered the suggestion that when he visited her he would develop an erection immediately upon entering the court and maintain it until he left the court either alone or in her company. He never did have any trouble getting an erection, so let him get it as he entered the court. Then I spent about two hours in a long, rambling conversation. However, systematically and unobtrusively I interwove into the monologue a whole series of posthypnotic suggestions. I made confusing elaborations until the entire list had been presented. I suggested that neurotic ideas serve a purpose for the personality. That was one of the posthypnotic suggestions. Neurotic manifestations are often seemingly constant but are fundamentally inconstant, since the purpose they serve changes as time passes and circumstances change and the personality alters. Many varieties of neurotic symptoms can actually reverse, and do reverse. Correction of a neurotic problem can occur effectively and quite accidentally because of coincidental measures as well as by deliberate effort. No neurotic can really know what will happen with his problems at a *given* time. Repression of a neurotic problem can occur by the development of another, which in itself is beneficial. A specific neurotic symptom, such as premature ejaculation, can without warning be reversed into a frightening delay in ejaculation, a delay of half an hour or more. He would really have something to worry about if that ever happened to *him*. He really would know how to worry both consciously and unconsciously. Such a development would undoubtedly result in a totally unexpected internal ejaculation. Then he would be confronted by the tremendous problem of accomplished sexuality, which would require constructive utilization.

For the next week or ten days there would be a growing unrest in him presaging an impending change in his life. Here he was forbidden discussion and was told to do nothing for a while, not even to think, but just to rest comfortably. I gave him an appointment for the next day, which was Tuesday, and for Wednesday, and for Friday. On Tuesday I saw him briefly but did not allow him to talk. I told him he would be given, in return for the briefness of the interview, a very special appointment on Sunday. I knew that Saturday night was his regular meeting with this prostitute. The Wednesday appointment was similarly handled, and there was further emphasis on the Sunday appointment, to the effect that he would really have to give out for that interview. Friday's interview was also briefly handled, with emphasis upon the special character of what he would have to relate on Sunday. Three brief interviews, full fee charged, and a promise of making up for that shortness of time by a special interview on Sunday. However, when he came in on Sunday morning he explained to me that he had something more urgent than whatever I had in mind for that appointment. Because of certain developments he had experienced, what I was interested in would have to be postponed.

His story was that the three previous brief interviews, or brush-offs, as he termed them, had made him restless, unhappy, uncertain. He had been so ill at ease after the Friday interview that he sought out a girl he had been seeing frequently but with whom he had not yet had sex relations. He suggested dinner and the theater. However, during the evening he had been inattentive to his companion and preoccupied. Recurrently the question popped into his mind of whether or not he actually could ejaculate intravaginally. A doubt about whether he could—previously he had known that he couldn't! But he was doubting whether he could. Almost at once the idea would elude his mind when he tried to remember what he'd been thinking. Shortly the idea would again pop into his mind only to elude him again. Over and over this occurred.

As he was returning his companion to her apartment, he developed an erection upon entering the courtyard of her apartment house. This persisted, although he was still so preoccupied with his elusive thought that he did not contemplate sex relations. Nevertheless, upon entering the apartment his partner manifested such aggressive, amorous behavior that he promptly went to bed with her. Because he was still preoccupied, he allowed her to take the aggressive role, and his reaction to the insertion was one of sudden fear that he would *not* be able to have an ejaculation. So absorbing was this fear that "I forgot completely all of my past popping off. All I could think of was that I wanted to pop into her and I was afraid I couldn't." He responded to this fear by active coitus, and for some unknown reason "watching the minute hand on my wrist watch, which I never wear to bed." As the end of half an hour approached, he became increasingly excited and at the same time more anxious and fearful. Then suddenly, but without knowing the time until some twenty minutes later, he experienced a satisfying intra-vaginal ejaculation. His erection continued, and after a short rest after withdrawal he engaged in active coitus and had a completely satisfying intravaginal ejaculation, and he waited for detumescence before withdrawal. He slept comfortably, and the next day he went for an automobile trip. On the following evening, Saturday, there occurred further normal sexual activity. Upon completing his description, the patient asked, "Is there any explanation why I've become normal?" I replied that neither he nor I need explain the normal, that it was infinitely more pleasurable to accept the normal as something to which everybody is entitled.

His relationship with the woman continued for about three months before they drifted apart. Several other relationships were formed before he became seriously interested in marriage. He then became engaged.

Sometimes some type of sexual difficulty will prevent a young person from engaging in ordinary social relations, and at other times a symptom will prevent him from working or going to school. During the Second World War, when entering the Army was more popular than it is today, Erickson was a consultant on a draft board and helped many young men enter the Army when they wished to and could not. Often these young men had relatively minor problems, but of the kind that would prevent them from functioning in the Army like their peers. A common problem was bedwetting, which is a particularly embarrassing problem for a young adult. A case example illustrates how Erickson resolved a lifelong bedwetting problem in a single session for a young man who wished to be drafted.

During the psychiatric examination a selectee disclosed a history of bedwetting since the age of puberty. He had never dared to be away from home overnight, although he had often wished to visit his grandparents and other relatives who lived at a considerable distance. He particularly wished to visit them because of his impending military service. He was distressed to learn that enuresis would exclude him from the service, and he asked if something could be done to cure him. He explained that he had taken barrels of medicine, had been cystoscoped, and had had numerous other procedures employed upon him, all to no avail.

I told him that he could probably get some effective aid if he were willing to be hypnotized. He agreed readily and quickly developed a profound trance. In this trance state I assured him most emphatically that his bedwetting was psychological in origin and that he would have no real difficulty in overcoming it if he obeyed instructions completely.

In the form of posthypnotic suggestions I told him that, after returning home, he was to go to a neighboring city and engage a hotel room. He was to have his meals sent up to him and was to remain continuously in his room until three nights had elapsed. Upon entering the room he was to make himself comfortable and to begin to think about how frightened and distressed he would be when the maid, as his mother always did, discovered a wet bed the next morning. He was to go over and over these thoughts, speculating unhappily upon his inevitable humiliated, anxious, and fearful reactions. Suddenly the idea would cross his mind about what an amazing but bitter joke it would be on him if, after all this agonized thinking, the maid were surprised by a *dry* bed.

This idea would make no sense to him and he would become so confused and bewildered by it that he would be unable to straighten out his mind. Instead, the idea would run through his mind constantly and soon he would find himself miserably, helplessly, and confusedly speculating about his shame, anxiety, and embarrassment when the maid discovered the *dry* bed instead of the wet bed he had planned. The rationale of the three nights was this: if the plan were effective, the first night would be one of doubt and uncertainty, the second one of certainty, and the third would bridge a transition from bedwetting anxiety to another anxiety situation. This thinking would so trouble him that finally, in desperation, he would become so sleepy that he would welcome going to bed because, try as he might, he would not be able to think clearly.

On the first morning his first reaction would be one of abject fear of remaining in the room while the maid discovered the *dry* bed. He would search his mind frantically for some excuse to leave, he would fail, and he would have to stare wretchedly out of the window so that she would not see his distress.

The next day, beginning in the afternoon, the same bewildered, confused thinking would recur with the same results, and the third day would be another repetition of the same.

I instructed him that when he checked out of the hotel after the third night, he would find himself greatly torn by a conflict about visiting his grandparents. The problem of whether he should visit the maternal or the paternal set of grandparents first would be an agonizing, obsessional thought. This he would finally resolve by making the visit to the first set one day shorter than that to the second. Once arrived at his destination, he would be most comfortable and would look forward happily to visiting all of his relatives. Nevertheless, he would be obsessed with doubts about which to visit next, but always he would enjoy a stay of several days.

All of these suggestions were repetitiously reiterated in an effort to ensure the implantation of these pseudo-problems in order to redirect his enuretic fears and anxieties and transform them into anxieties about visits with relatives instead of anxiety about a wet bed for his closest relative, his mother.

He was dismissed after approximately two hours' work with a posthypnotic suggestion for a comprehensive amnesia. When he awakened, I told him briefly that he would be recalled in about three months and that he would undoubtedly be accepted for military service then.

Ten weeks later he was sent to me again as the consultant for the local draft board. He reported in detail his "amazing experience" at the hotel, with no apparent awareness of what had occasioned it. He explained that he "almost went crazy in that hotel trying to wet that bed but couldn't do it. I even drank water to be sure, but it didn't work. Then I got so scared I pulled out and started to visit all my relatives. That made me feel all right, except for being scared to death about which one to see first, and now I'm here."

I reminded him of his original complaints. With startled surprise, he replied, "I haven't done that since I went crazy in the hotel. What happened?" I replied that what had happened was that he had stopped wetting the bed and now could enjoy a dry bed. Two weeks later he was seen again at the induction center, at which time he was readily accepted for service. His only apparent anxiety was concern about his mother's adjustment to his military service.

Erickson doesn't necessarily use hypnosis with problems, particularly bedwetting difficulties. He has many alternative procedures, and he also likes to point out that getting a young adult over this kind of difficulty frees him to shift into normal behavior in many other areas.

Young people can set themselves apart by some form of deviant behavior, and they can also be deviant in some physical way that handicaps them in courtship. Sometimes there is a physical problem, such as obesity, that makes the person unattractive. At other times they avoid making themselves attractive to the opposite sex. Sometimes Dr. Erickson works directly on helping young people reshape themselves. In other cases he might focus on their conception of themselves, particularly their body image.

When working with young women, Erickson makes maximum use of his own masculinity. He assumes that if he persuades a woman that she is attractive to *him*, she will generalize that idea to an acceptance of herself as attractive to men. Within the safe relationship of therapy, the woman can feel herself admired by a man, and then she is diverted to appropriate males in her social network and responds to them differently than she has in the past. Erickson uses the relationship with himself as a ritual that induces in the young woman a courtship frame of mind that makes success with men possible.

As an example, a young lady came to see Erickson for help because she felt she was horribly fat. She was overweight, but actually not as unattractive as she insisted. She was a churchgoing girl who was extremely prim and proper. Her prudishness, as well as her conception of herself as horribly fat, was causing her to avoid normal courtship activity. Erickson reports:

> When I saw the girl waiting to see me, it was immediately apparent that she was quite a proper and prudish girl. I had her come into the office and sit down, and although I was courteous, I only glanced briefly at her. Then I asked her to tell me her story, and as she talked I picked up a paperweight from my desk and examined it. While she told me her problem, I only glanced at her occasionally and directed most of my attention to the paperweight.
>
> When she finished, she said she wondered if I would be willing to accept her as a patient, since she was so hideously unattractive. Even if she did reduce, she would still be the homeliest girl in creation.
>
> I responded by saying, "I hope you'll forgive me for what I've done. I haven't faced you as you talked, and I know that is rude. I've played with this paperweight instead of looking at you. I found it rather difficult to look at you, and I'd rather not discuss why. But since this is a therapy situation, I really must tell you. Perhaps you can find the explanation. Well, let me put it this way. I have the

very strong feeling that when you reduce—at least everything I see about you; that's why I keep avoiding looking at you—indicates that you will be even *more* sexually attractive. I know that's something that should not be discussed between you and me. But you are, of course, extremely attractive sexually. You'll be much more so after you've reduced. But we ought not to discuss that matter."

As I spoke, the young lady flushed and blushed and squirmed. What I said wasn't too traumatic, but according to her code it was horribly unpleasant. Yet here was a man she respected immensely who said she was attractive sexually, and who noticed it immediately.

Later she reduced, and in the most polite way reported to me that she had fallen in love with an older man who was not interested in her. I told her that it was a great compliment to the man for her to fall in love with him. Since she had now learned to compliment a man, she would undoubtedly turn her affections to some man closer to her age. But she ought to keep on complimenting the older man for a while. Later she lost interest in me and became engaged to a man her own age.

When Erickson uses his maleness in this way, he is particularly concerned that the relationship with him does not become a substitute for a natural relationship with a male in the patient's social situation. Therefore, once courtship behavior is aroused, it is directed toward the appropriate social setting of the girl's life. Unlike therapists who think in terms of long-term therapy and deep, continuing emotional involvement with a therapist, Erickson works as rapidly as possible to disengage himself and focus the female patient on other men. Sometimes he does this after a period of time and sometimes quite rapidly.

Although one thinks of the courtship period as one involving young people, a problem at this stage can continue for a period of years. As a woman or man grows older, the difficulties of getting past this stage can increase. Less willing to take the risk of attempting to mate, a woman can arrange her appearance and behavior to prevent that possibility. The more set she is in her trajectory toward being a peripheral woman, the more dramatic the means necessary to produce a basic change in her way of life. Sometimes Erickson does this quickly by setting up an intensely personal, but safe, relationship with a man that provides the impetus to allow her to risk normal intimate relationships.

A woman came to Erickson because her only friends in the

world, a professional couple, were also friends of his and had referred her. She was thirty-five years old and was a bit more than pleasingly plump. Although she had a plain but decidedly attractive face, anyone seeing her for the first time would think, "Good God, why doesn't she wash her face and comb her hair and put on a dress instead of a gunny sack."

She entered the office hesitantly and explained in a prim and impersonal manner that she felt wretched and frustrated. She had always wanted to get married and have children, but she could never even get a date. She had worked her way through college while supporting and taking care of her invalid mother and had no social life. She knew she was slightly overweight, but she felt that some men like plump girls and there was no reason for her isolation. She was intelligent, cultured, interesting, and desperate because she was thirty-five years old, and she wanted something done quickly. She said her therapy would have to be rapid, since she had accepted a position in a distant city, where she was determined that she would either be different or give up. Therefore something drastic was called for. Furthermore, her funds were limited.

This woman was a conscientious worker and was retained by her employer only because of the excellence of her work. She was cold, impersonal, seclusive, and withdrawn in her habits. Her only friends were the professional couple, and with them she was a charming conversationalist and showed intelligence and a wide range of interests. Except for monthly visits with them, she remained in her apartment by herself. She wore steel-rimmed glasses and no makeup, and her clothes did not fit and were of clashing colors. Her personal habits were untidy, her hair was never well combed, her ears were always dirty, and so was her neck. Frequently her fingernails were obnoxiously dirty. If anyone mentioned these matters to her, she would freeze them with her cold and impersonal behavior. She had never had a date. Erickson reports:

I said to the woman, "You want therapy, you want it fast, you're getting desperate. Do you want me to give it to you in my way? Do you think you can take it? Because I can give it to you rapidly, thoroughly, effectively, but it will be a rather shocking experience." She said she felt desperate enough to accept anything. I told her to think the matter over for three days, and during this time she was to decide whether she really wanted therapy and wanted it sufficiently drastic to benefit her. I assured her she could be benefited greatly, but that it would require great personal strength to withstand the therapeutic assault that would be necessary under the short-term conditions she proposed. I used the word "assault" deliberately for its multiple possibilities. I said she would have to promise absolutely not to discontinue therapy and to execute fully every task I assigned her, no matter what it was. Before making such a promise, she should think over all the possible implications—especially unpleasant ones—of what I had said. She returned in three days and promised absolutely to meet all the demands placed upon her.

I had a long session with her, starting with the question "How much money do you have?" She said she had saved one thousand dollars and was prepared to pay that amount over at once. I instructed her to place seven hundred dollars in a checking account with full expectation of spending all of that amount on herself in an unexpected fashion. Then I presented her with a mirror, a tape measure, scales, and a weight chart.

For over three hours I did a comprehensive, completely straightforward critique of her weight and appearance, with all possible proof to back it up. Each fingernail was examined and the amount of dirt described in detail—her fingernails were in mourning, this one and this one and this. Holding a mirror, I had her describe for me the dirt on her face and neck and the lines of perspiration. With two mirrors, she described her dirty ears. I commented critically about her uncombed hair, her ill-fitting dress, the clashing colors. All of this was done as one might do a physical examination. These things were discussed as matters she could correct without any help from a therapist and for which she herself was totally at fault. These were expressive of willful self-neglect.

Then I handed her a washcloth and instructed her to wash one side of her neck and view the contrast with the unwashed side. This was exceedingly embarrassing to her. I concluded the interview with a summary statement that she was a sorry-looking mess. However, she was to make no purchases until she was so instructed. She was merely to continue working, but to think over the truth of everything that had been said to her. I told her our next appointment would be in two days, and it would be equally long and quite possibly even more devastating.

She appeared promptly for the next interview, embarrassed and hesitant about what might happen next. She wore no makeup, but otherwise she was remakably well groomed except for the poor fit of her dress and the loud colors of the cloth. Of course, she had gone home and bathed thoroughly after the previous session. I had approved of the washed side of her neck, and therefore I approved of her bathed body. Her hesitancy indicated some uncertainty about what might be examined this time.

Systematically I reviewed the previous interview and the changes she had succeeded in making; this was discussed in a cold, impersonal manner. Then I told her to prepare herself for a new, highly important, but hitherto neglected, unrealized, and disregarded matter of the greatest importance to her as a living creature. The matter was something she could no longer neglect or disregard— she would never be able to put out of her mind that "something" which was apparent and recognized by everyone with whom she came in contact. It would be continuously in her consciousness and compel her to behave normally and rightfully with a pleasing and satisfying self-awareness. I told her this would be revealed to her as she took her departure. Then, as she went to the door to leave the office at the end of the interview, I said there was something I wanted her to do. She stood there prim and rigid, waiting to hear what it was. I said, "You are never going to be able to forget again that you have a pretty patch of fur between your legs. Now go home, undress, get in the nude, stand in front of a mirror, and you will see the three beautiful badges of womanhood. They are with you always wherever you go, and you cannot forget them ever again."

She appeared for the next appointment promptly, exceedingly embarrassed in manner. Without any preliminaries, I told her, "You have money set aside for some special purpose. Go to the department store. They have a beauty counselor there, and in a straightforward fashion tell her that you are a sorry mess, that you know nothing about self-grooming, that you want her to teach you all you need to know. You'll find her a charming, warmhearted, sympathetic, understanding woman. Have her outfit you completely. You'll enjoy knowing her and find it thrilling to have her teach you what you need to know. In three weeks there is a dance for all of the employees where you work, and you will be routinely invited. You are to go. In preparation, go to a dance studio and learn rapidly how to dance well. Have the beauty counselor select the material for a formal dress to wear at that dance. Take the material to Mrs. —— who is a seamstress and explain that you wish her to supervise you in making the dress. The sewing will be done entirely by you. Your next appointment will be on the way to the dance."

On the evening of the dance, she walked in really well dressed. She was embarrassed, blushing, and tastefully gowned. She had lost excess weight and was animated and vivacious and charmingly self-conscious. Three months later, after taking her new position, she became acquainted with a college professor. A year later they were married. She has four children now.

Often Erickson's approach involves the use of sensible, ordinary procedures, such as learning to groom oneself or to dance, combined with an intimate encounter that forces the person to accept these sensible procedures when he has not done so before. He makes maximum use of both himself and community facilities. In this case, he used himself to provide a prudish woman an intimate relationship with a male, which included discussing unmentionable things. He also made use of an available beauty consultant and a seamstress.

A conversation about brief-therapy techniques that took place a number of years ago will offer a more detailed portrait of the dilemmas of young women, as well as the ways in which Erickson deals with them. A young man who was attempting to understand and use Dr. Erickson's method presented him with a series of cases and asked him how he would approach these problems.

INTERVIEWER: A girl was referred to me for relief of pain from severe premenstrual cramps. She was incapacitated about eight hours a day once a month; forced to go to bed. She has had this pain since she was fourteen years old. I have seen her for two sessions and I'm not at all sure I can help her. Yet I feel that her problem isn't very complicated. She started to menstruate at twelve —perfectly normal. At thirteen she was in a city during a bombing raid. She lived up on the hillside and saw the raid but she wasn't injured in any way. For a year after that she didn't menstruate. She returned to the States with her mother, and at the age of fourteen she began to menstruate again. This was very painful. She had menstruated painfully ever since.

ERICKSON: Is she a pretty girl?

INTERVIEWER: Yes.

ERICKSON: Does she think so?

INTERVIEWER: Yes, she does. She is not by any means fully confident that she is pretty. She works a little too hard at it.

ERICKSON: What do you think about that?

INTERVIEWER: What do I think about it? Well, I think she is twenty-eight years old and isn't married for reasons she doesn't understand.

ERICKSON: And yet she is a pretty girl? And she works too hard at it. You see, in brief psychotherapy one of the important considerations is the body image. By body image I mean how does the person look upon herself? What sort of image do they have of themselves? She's a pretty girl, she works too hard at it. She is telling you that she has a defective body image. And it is so tremendously important that she have a good body image. A good body image implies not only the physical self, as such, but the functional self, and the personality *within* the body. Does she know that it is *all right* to know that she has very pretty eyes? Does she know that it is *all right* for her to be aware of the fact that her chin is too heavy? Is it *all right* for her to have a pretty mouth, but to have her ears set unevenly? Does she know that the individuality of her face is the thing that gives her individual appeal?

INTERVIEWER: Is that the way you would put it to her?

ERICKSON: That's the way it should be put to her. You'll see these pretty girls that absolutely depreciate themselves. They are unaware that they are trying to classify their looks in terms of other people's looks. And they usually think about a symptom of some sort that proves to them conclusively that they are not adequate people. The girl with the painful menstruation—exactly what does she think about her body? Are her hips too large, or her ankles too large? Is her pubic hair too scarce—too straight—too curly? Or what about it? It may be too painful a thing for her ever to recognize consciously. Are her breasts too large? Too small? The nipples not the right color? In brief psychotherapy, one of the first things you do, whether it's a man or a woman, is to try to find out what their body image is.

INTERVIEWER: And how do you find this out?

ERICKSON: Sometimes, after a few minutes with a patient, with a girl in particular, I ask her what her best features are. And why. I make it a straightforward inquiry. In the same way that one would do a physical examination. You start to examine the scalp and you work down to the soles of the feet. It's purely an objective examination. You really want to know what the body image is, so you do a physical examination of the body image.

INTERVIEWER: I see. What this girl does is work a little too hard at looking feminine. Her curls are placed just so, her makeup is just so, her earrings just so.

ERICKSON: In other words, what does she lack in her body image that is feminine, so that she has to overdo or overemphasize the external evidence of femininity? What deficiency does she think she has in her genitals? In her breasts, in her hips, in her figure, in her face?

INTERVIEWER: Well, how do the patients accept such an objective consideration of their genitals? Do they take your discussion so objectively?

ERICKSON: They do for me. You see a girl come in with a very crooked part in her hair. The next time she comes in, her hair is combed slightly differently, but with a crooked mid-line part. And you ought to wonder about her attitude toward her genitals.

INTERVIEWER: If the part is crooked, you should wonder that?

ERICKSON: Yes. Because bear in mind that our own familiarity with ourselves, our physical selves, is so great that we never really appreciate that familiarity—consciously. How do you recognize that a woman is wearing falsies?

INTERVIEWER: I don't know how I would recognize it, except in terms of the proportion with the rest of her body.

ERICKSON: I'll demonstrate to you. I ask a woman to sit up straight and pretend that she has a mosquito on her right shoulder; then I ask her to please swat it. First I'll show you how I swat it. (Demonstrates swatting with arm not touching chest.) Now I'll exaggerate as I show you how she swats it—you see, she detours her elbow in accord with the actual size of her breast.

INTERVIEWER: Oh, I see. With falsies she brushes her breast.

ERICKSON: Yes. If she's got very small breasts, practically no breasts, she tends to swat her shoulder in much the same way I would. And if she has got large breasts she makes a large detour.

INTERVIEWER: That's a simple test.

ERICKSON: A very simple test. When I see a patient with a defective body image, I usually say, "There are a number of things that you *don't* want me to know about, that you *don't* want to tell me. There are a lot of things about yourself that you don't want to discuss, therefore let's discuss those that you are willing to discuss." She has blanket permission to withhold anything and everything. But she did come to discuss things. And therefore she starts discussing this, discussing that. And it's always "Well, *this* is all right to talk about." And before she's finished, she has mentioned everything. And each new item—"Well, this really isn't so important that I have to withhold it. I can use the withholding permission for more important matters." Simply a hypnotic technique. To make them respond to the idea of withholding, and to respond to the idea of communicating.

INTERVIEWER: I see.

ERICKSON: Their withholding is essentially a mere matter of shuffling the order in which they present, and that's sufficient withholding.

INTERVIEWER: It also forces them to think of what they

would normally withhold, which they probably hadn't thought much about before.

ERICKSON: There is the girl who has had a series of affairs and is too distressed to tell you about it. You have given her permission to withhold. She knows you don't know about the affairs. She starts thinking—well, number one is all right to tell about. Number five is all right to tell about. Not number two. And she tells about number four, number six, number three, number seven, number two. *She has withheld* number two. In fact, she has withheld all of them except number one. Because she didn't give them in order— one, two, three four, five, six, seven.

INTERVIEWER: It's a play on the word "withheld."

ERICKSON: The unconscious *does* that. And you've got to be aware of it. Therefore you suggest that they withhold—*and they do.* And you also suggest that they tell—*and they do.* But they withhold and they tell responsively. And as long as they are going to withhold, *you ought* to *encourage them* to withhold. In discussing your body image—the way you view yourself, the way you appear in your mind's eye, the way you think about your body. Certainly you don't want to tell me about certain parts of your body—and yet there are parts of your body you do want to discuss. For example, your chin and your mouth. You may even think about your ankles. You may think about your abdomen, the hair on your head. And by saying "the hair on your head," how many girls are aware of the maidenhead? The part in your hair, and how do you feel about it?

INTERVIEWER: And that's a play on the word "part"?

ERICKSON: No, it's a play on the fact that there is a genital groove. And there *is* a part in the hair.

INTERVIEWER: Apparently you do this not just to get an idea of their body image, but to make them very conscious of their body.

ERICKSON: Make them conscious of their body. And *"as you sit there,"* you can think about what you ought to discuss about yourself." "As you sit there" seems to be a transitional phrase. But what do you sit on? And what kind of a body do you want? The kind of body that would please a woman with another type of personality? Or the kind of body that would please you with *your* personality? And how much do you know about it?

INTERVIEWER: And you assume that a menstrual pain is related to this kind of difficulty?

ERICKSON: Yes, I do.

INTERVIEWER: Naturally, with my background, I get curious about the history. It interests me that this girl lost her menstrual functions for a year, from age thirteen to fourteen.

ERICKSON: Yes, and one of the first things I would want to know about would be what she thought about the impermanence of life, and the impermanence of the body, and how a body can come to a sudden and violent end. And the threat of death. This body of hers is doomed to go only to dust, and every menstrual period brings her closer to death, and it's a painful thing.

INTERVIEWER: This is a different way to look at menstruation.

ERICKSON: But it does, you know.

INTERVIEWER: Oh, yes, it does, I know. But it also tells her that she is a woman, but she is not pregnant. That's the sort of thing I think about.

ERICKSON: But you think of menses in terms of male thinking, in terms of biological thinking.

INTERVIEWER: And how does a woman think about it differently? In terms of aging?

ERICKSON: What does every woman think about? When she gets old enough, she won't menstruate. When she gets old enough, she will cease to menstruate. And therefore it is a totally different thing to her as a person. Within the privacy, in the separateness of her own living, menstruation is a living thing. Just consider how a woman thinks about her twenty-fifth birthday. It isn't a twenty-fifth birthday—it's a quarter of a century. And how does she *feel* about her thirtieth birthday? She is forever leaving her twenties. And then the horrible dread of leaving—*leaving*—the thirties. And that twenty-fifth birthday is a quarter of a century. And the tremendous emphasis that you find from Arizona to Massachusetts on the quarter of a century. Now, when did she stop menstruating?

INTERVIEWER: Age thirteen. She had lost her father when she was three years old. Then during a bombing raid she lost her stepfather in the sense that he left at once to go to war. The mother divorced him while he was gone. The girl not only stopped menstruating at that time but she developed a morning sickness where she was dizzy and nauseated for a period of months. Almost as if she was trying to substitute a family of her own for the family she was losing. At least, it looked to me like a pregnancy idea.

ERICKSON: She lost her father when she was three, and her stepfather at the time of the bombing. If she were three years old, she could look forward to the return of a father. And how could she resume her three-year-old status?

INTERVIEWER: You would look upon it as a regression?

ERICKSON: Yes, because at age three, with her current memories and understanding, she could really look forward to having a stepfather come into the home. Now—with the bombing, the city didn't function, everything in the home was thrown out of function. *Her* function was thrown out, too. She was part of a totality.

INTERVIEWER: Yes, she describes it as if everything stopped functioning—if not quite in those terms, very close to it. She was taken out of school, she was taken away from her friends, she was taken away from her stepfather, and so on.

ERICKSON: She wasn't big enough to go to school. She was taken out of school. Not big enough to go to school, not big enough to menstruate.

INTERVIEWER: Why would it begin again painfully?

ERICKSON: Why not assume a legitimate painfulness?

INTERVIEWER: What do you mean?

ERICKSON: The first beginning of menstruation could occur easily, naturally—without any particular associations. So it could be painless. Then you interrupt a function—for which you have learned all the sensations—and then it occurs suddenly and unexpectedly. The loss of it has been a painful thing. And here all of a sudden you are reminded by the reappearance of all the painfulness of her loss of affection, plus the normal congestion of the tissues. And so it's a legitimate painfulness. You break your arm, it's put in a cast. Gradually you become accustomed to the cast. The cast is taken off and you try to bend your arm—it's painful.

INTERVIEWER: Yes.

ERICKSON: It's a legitimate pain, too. The pain of disuse. Yet you want it to be a movable arm. But it's not painful because of conflicts. Why shouldn't interrupted menstruation recur with pain? And that in itself could frighten her and raise the question in her mind "Is it always going to be painful?" And then she could look forward to painful menstruation. She will have a month's time in which to anticipate painful menstruation—and verify it.

INTERVIEWER: I am sure that's exactly what she does in that way—spends a month expecting it.

ERICKSON: Yes, she has had added proof. And I would raise with her the question "What is your cycle?" "How many pads a day do you use?" "Does it always come regularly?" "Is it in the morning?" "In the afternoon, or at night?" "Or just at random?"

INTERVIEWER: Apparently regular and in the morning.

ERICKSON: And I would throw in the question "How many pads a day?" Because that really makes it an embarrassingly intimate question. "Do you soak the pads through?" "Or do you change them as *soon* as they begin to get moist?" She has already said that it's regular, it's in the morning. "And how would you feel if it happened a day before you expected it? And not in the morning, but at night. And how would you feel about that?" The first thing I would want to do is displace the time of the hurt.

INTERVIEWER: You mean displace the time, then you can do something about the pain?

ERICKSON: If I displace the time, then it's not the *expected period*, and the expected period is a painful period. The unexpected period is not painful, because it happened unexpectedly. And then you have that implanted in her mind. She is too intent on questions about "How many pads?" "Do you let them soak through?" She isn't paying too much attention consciously to the suggestions for displacement.

INTERVIEWER: And they are more effective if she gives less conscious attention to them?

ERICKSON: She is within hearing distance of you—she hears everything you say—she came in to talk to you—she is going to listen with both her conscious mind and her unconscious mind. And you just remain aware of that fact. "And how would you feel if it occurred unexpectedly—during the night?" But you see I use the word "feel." But it has a different connotation from—pain.

INTERVIEWER: Oh, I see.

ERICKSON: So I have actually changed a feeling of menstruation from pain into another kind of feeling. Now another thing is to emphasize the handling of painful menstruation. So many therapists, medical men, overlook the patient's rights. And they try to relieve a girl of painful menstruation by a blanket removal. When any girl comes to me to be relieved of the pain of menstruation, I make it very clear to her that she wants to be relieved of the pain of menstruation—as far as she knows. But there certainly is likely to occur, in her lifetime, an occasion in which she *might want* a painful period. She *might* like to escape some social engagments, by virtue of complaining about her painful menstruation. She might like to skip the university examination. She might like to get an extra day off from the office. So be realistic about it. She wants to be relieved of painful menstruation when it's convenient for her. The unconscious is a lot more intelligent than the conscious. The girl comes to you for relief of painful menstruation, and you blandly, blithely, give her suggestions to be free, and her unconscious knows that you don't understand the problem. You are telling her now, as a menstruating creature, to be free of pain, and she knows very well that she's going to get married, and she is going to have a baby, and she is going to have interruption of menstruation, and that not one of the suggestions you have given her is so worded that it applies until after she begins a new history of menstruation. She rejects your offering of relief because you haven't taken into consideration the natural course of events. And she is acutely aware of that in her unconscious and really scorns you because you just assume that she's never really going to have an interruption. But she is. She may get sick. Maybe in her past she did get sick, and had to interrupt menses. And her unconscious, seeking help from you, *wants* you to consider her as an individual who is going to encounter such and such things. When you give her the privilege of having painful menstruation as a way of talking her husband into buying her a new fur coat, you have given her the privilege of keeping pain and not keeping it. Then it's her choice; you are not forcibly taking something away from her that she feels belongs to herself. You are just offering her the opportunity of dropping it when it's convenient, and keeping it when it's convenient. Just as you let them withhold.

INTERVIEWER: Well, that's true of most symptoms, isn't it? It's the proper attitude.

ERICKSON: It's the proper attitude. A woman in her thirties sucked her thumb, scratched her nipples until they were always scabbed, and scratched her belly button until it was scabbed. She had done it ever since childhood. She sought therapy for that, and I told her no, I wouldn't give her therapy for it, that I would just simply cure it—in less than thirty seconds' time. She knew that was impossible. And she wanted to know how I could cure it in thirty seconds' time. And I told her—all she had to do was say yes. And she knew *that* did not alter anything. "To say yes and mean yes." "The next time you want to scratch your nipple, I want you to do it. You can come into this office, expose your breasts and your nipple, and do it. Will you do it?" She said "Yes," and then said "You know I'll never do it. I never will." And she meant "*I never will do it.*" She was talking about not coming into the office.

INTERVIEWER: Yes.

ERICKSON: "That's right, you never will do it." Her unconscious knew, and her unconscious took all of *her* intensity and transferred it to her.

INTERVIEWER: To get back to the body image and thinking about this girl again, when you get an idea of the defects of the body image, what do you then do in the way of revising this?

ERICKSON: What do you do? A girl came in to see me because she was nervous. She was fearful, tremulous, uncertain. She didn't like people and they didn't like her. And she was so shaky it was hard for her to walk. She was afraid of people, and when she ate in a restaurant she brought a newspaper to hide behind. She went home by way of alleys to avoid being seen. She always went to the cheapest restaurants—so people could look at her and despise her. And besides, she wasn't fit to look at. I had her draw her portrait.

And she tested out her sketching ability. And there is her portrait —you see it?

INTERVIEWER: It's obscure. Merely unrelated parts.

ERICKSON: Finally she drew this calendar picture of herself in the nude. First a head with no body, and then her final picture of herself.

INTERVIEWER: Now, what did you do with her from the first drawing to the last drawing? In the way of overcoming this defective body image?

ERICKSON: First I asked her if she really wanted therapy. Would she really cooperate with therapy. She said she had no choice, and I agreed with her. And she really had no choice, except in the matter of therapist, and since she had come to me and had made that first difficult step, it would even be worse to have to find another—because she'd have to make the first step all over. That ensured her staying with me.

INTERVIEWER: I see.

ERICKSON: She didn't recognize that I was putting a barrier into her seeking someone else. But it *was* there, and I told her that therapy would be in relationship to all of her functions as a person, which included not only the way she worked, and walked in the streets, but the matter of eating and sleeping, and recreation. Eating implies what? Urination, defecation, too. Try to eat without including those—you have to. And every little child learns that you eat and sooner or later you move your bowels. That's one of the fundamental learnings, and you always retain that. And I mentioned it to her through eating. All of her functions as a person. Not as a personality, but as a person. A person who ate, slept, and worked, engaged in recreation—so that was inclusive of everything. And I would have to know all the things that she *could* tell me. And all the things that I could think about.

INTERVIEWER: That's kind of a tricky phrase right there, isn't it? You would have to know *all* the things—that she *could* tell you. That's an endangering statement with the danger suddenly taken away.

ERICKSON: And all the things that I could think about—and I dared to think about a lot of things. Which actually signified to her that nothing, absolutely nothing, wouldn't be included. Everything would be included—all that she could tell about, all that I could think about. And I am a doctor and I can really think—and I really know. And yet it is said so gently. But every bit of knowledge that she could ascribe to her physician was put out in front right there. And one of the first things I wanted to know about her was how did she think of herself as a person—or perhaps the best way to tell me would be to tell me what she felt she looked like. "Well," she said, "I am a blonde." "And you have two eyes, and two ears, and one mouth, and one nose, and two nostrils, and two lips, and one chin. What do you think about those? And you are blonde, you stated. What kind of a blonde?" "A dirty-dishwater blonde." What more do you need? "And my teeth are crooked, my ears are too large, my nose is too small. All I can say is that I am just a very ordinary girl." And very ordinary implies what? When she went from her face to "very ordinary girl" she was describing herself. All the rest of her body was implied by "very ordinary girl." Then I wanted to know if she would tell me whether she took a tub bath or a shower. I asked her to describe to me in detail how she got into the shower, to describe in detail what she did in the shower, and after she turned off the shower. She would have to visualize herself —I am keeping her in the nude right in front of me, am I not? But she was in the nude, and once having been in the nude for me, then "Now, if you were to see your body in the nude, without your head being visible, would you recognize your body?" You know it is awfully hard to recognize your voice on a tape. She started to think about recognizing her body in the nude—but there she was again nude. "Now I can tell you something about your body that you don't know, and I never have seen it. You undoubtedly are pretty sure that you know the color of your pubic hair. I've never seen it, I never expect to see it. I don't think that you know the color of it." Now that's one thing she's certain about.

INTERVIEWER: That not only makes her think about it, but it makes her go home and check it, too.

ERICKSON: Her first answer was "Naturally the same color as the hair on my head, a dishwater blonde," and with the natural normal pigmentation of the body your pubic hair is going to be darker than the hair on the head—that I know. Therefore I can tell her, "You say your pubic hair is the same color as the hair on your head, and I say it isn't." She checks it, and finds that I *am* right. I've *really* demonstrated—I've given her a chance to take issue with me. Disputing her *knowledge* of her body. But what about my impolite mentioning of her pubic hair? That isn't the issue. The issue is that I've challenged her knowledge. And she's going to prove to herself that I am ignorant—not that I am intrusive. So she's fighting—a false battle. She can't tell me I am right or wrong without bringing up the subject of pubic hair. "And what color are your nipples? I wonder if you really know." They can't miss the issue of intellectual awareness—I wonder if you really know. "Naturally the color of my skin." "I don't think they are. That's something you'll find out, that they *aren't* the color of your skin." So she's got an issue there to fight on, a purely intellectual one. She's going to fight, but she's fighting on my territory.

INTERVIEWER: Yes, she is. And the fact that you were right about the color of the pubic hair must make it all the more clear that she has been in the nude with you.

ERICKSON: Oh, yes. And the fact that I am right about her nipples. And when she tells me that her hips are *too large*, I can flippantly tell her, "The only use they have for you is to sit upon." How can you dispute that without getting into an awful mess of arguments. They are made up of muscles and fat and that's an unmentionable topic. But that they are useful in climbing stairs—

INTERVIEWER: And useful in attracting men?

ERICKSON: *That* I mention later. Then I can point out later that people view things differently. Who is it? Which woman is it in Africa that has the duck-bills? I can't remember the name. You know, the duck-billed women with their lips sticking way out with platters in their lips. "And do you know that the men in that tribe think those are beautiful, and they're astonished that the American men would consider the kind of lips that you have as beautiful." What have I said?

INTERVIEWER: You slipped in a very nice compliment there.

ERICKSON: I'm presenting the male point of view. It's nothing personal.

INTERVIEWER: Yes, and you've made it so general that it can't be just you.

ERICKSON: And that is the sort of thing one does in brief psychotherapy.

INTERVIEWER: Well, one of the problems in brief psychotherapy, it seems to me, is getting the patient to feel that this isn't just your personal opinion, but that everybody else would have the same opinion, or at least other men would.

ERICKSON: Not that every man will have the same opinion, but that men have a masculine point of view. That women have a feminine point of view. A man doesn't want to kiss a mustache, and very often women do.

INTERVIEWER: But that's a nice twist there; if you pay her a compliment on her attractive lips, she can either deny it, thinking you are wrong, or accept it, thinking this was your opinion but not the opinion of men in general.

ERICKSON: That's right. And I teach the functions of the body. "You eat—what kind of stomach trouble do you have?" "What kind of constipation do you have?" "How well do you eat?" "What respect have you got for your stomach—do you eat good food or do you insult it with anything that's handy?" With that sort of frontal attack, which cannot be objected to, it was possible to inquire what is the attitude she should have toward her breasts, her genitals, her hips, her thighs, her ankles, her knees, her abdomen. And were her teeth too crooked? Were they really? How *would* a man looking at her smile react to it? Would his eyesight be so deficient that he could see only those two crooked teeth, or would he see her lips? Would he see her chin, would he like her smile? Did he have the *right* to see what *he* wanted to see? What he liked to see? Did she have the right to say, "I'm now smiling, and look at my crooked teeth?" He might prefer to notice the shape and thickness of her lips.

INTERVIEWER: You try to get her interested in the possibility of feeling attractive, is that it?

ERICKSON: No. To recognize that any man that chooses can look upon her and behold something beautiful. And men vary in their taste.

INTERVIEWER: I have often wondered how you set it up so that patients do what you tell them to do. How you commit them to it.

ERICKSON: Often by giving them a contest. For example, a patient was not getting along in her job—all the usual complaints. The first time that she came in I noticed that her hair was very, very poorly combed. She noticed me looking at her hair and said, "Don't do what my boss does; he keeps telling me to comb my hair and I do my level best." And I said, "You want to get along better in your job, and you do do your level best with your hair, but I wonder how afraid you are of looking your best?" So I told her she could find that out by going home, taking a shower, and washing her hair. "And you are going to find out a number of things about yourself."

INTERVIEWER: Leaving it that open?

ERICKSON: That open.

INTERVIEWER: And what did she find out?

ERICKSON: She told me later she took a shower, dried herself very carefully, stood in front of a mirror, got her hand mirror out so she could get a back view, and spent an awful lot of time examining her body. Examining it against the background of her boss finding fault with the way she combed her hair. And she resented her boss criticizing her. The more she scrutinized herself, with that background of her resentment toward her boss, the more she approved of her body.

INTERVIEWER: It's extraordinary the way you manage to turn opposition in a contest to something productive for the person rather than something destructive to the person.

ERICKSON: But all you are doing is using the narcissism with which you are born.

INTERVIEWER: You could have a contest with a patient in which the patient proves you are wrong by staying sick, but you ask them to turn it around so they prove you are wrong by doing something beneficial to them. What's most interesting to me about it is how you dismiss the whole etiology of it.

ERICKSON: Etiology is a complex matter and not always relevant to getting over a problem. A man can go through the marriage ceremony, and now that he and his wife are pronounced man and wife, he finds he can't enjoy sexual relations. It doesn't mean that there is any one specific etiological factor. If you think of a boy growing up, and sometimes I describe this process to male and particularly to female patients, there is so much he must learn along the way. He has to learn the sensations in his penis; the sensations in the glans penis, the shaft, the skin, the foreskin, the feeling of the urethra. A boy learns this as he grows up, and when he reaches puberty he has to learn to have an ejaculation and have it in a satisfying way. But even then he has a lot to learn, since he must learn the very difficult thing of giving and receiving sexual pleasure. From whom can he first learn that? From someone who talks his language. Not the language of dresses and dolls, but of home runs and touchdowns. Can you wrassle, and how far can you jump is what concerns him, not what shade of color goes with this, and how you do your hair. That's alien language, offensive language. So he seeks out other boys. He's got to learn how to give and how to receive sexual pleasure from someone else. And so at a very elementary level he exchanges views on whether or not their penises are identical, shaped the same, because you've got to identify with someone else. Boys size up each other's muscles. They size up each other's ability to jump, to play ball, and they size up the ability of the other chap to have an ejaculation. And how far can you shoot when you come? And they handle each other. Now how do they handle each other? Sometimes manually. Sometimes by observing it. Sometimes by hearing about it. Is that the homosexual stage, or is it a fundamental, elementary level of learning how to give and to receive sexual pleasure in relationship to another person? And you'd better start with somebody that uses your language than some alien creature who talks another kind of language entirely. Who's got an alien body, can't play ball, can't wrassle, can't do anything interesting. Hasn't even got muscles. Now, all these learnings don't develop separately. The boy has to learn how to produce an ejaculation in himself by manual stimulation, friction, and so on. He's got to be aware of the fact that other boys do. But to be mature and a man, he's got to make provision for emotional values. And so he develops wet dreams. At first these dreams are pretty vague. But he sleeps quietly, doesn't touch himself, but in relationship to ideas and thoughts and feelings he gets an erection and he has a wet dream, he has an ejaculation. And he has to have enough ejaculations, enough wet dreams, so that in his response to feelings, thoughts, dream images, he can have a correct ejaculation. And often his mother says he's abusing himself, and his learning is impeded. He's not having those wet dreams to spite his mother; he's having those wet dreams because physiologically he's learning something. Organizing actual physical experience with concepts of feelings and experiences and memories and ideas. Vague, it's true, but nevertheless very vital to him. But sexual development doesn't occur in orderly units. There must be a mixture of responding to boys and then beginning to respond to girls. Learning to roller skate at the rink, where they learn to engage in pleasurable, rhythmical, physical activity with one another. The beginning of dancing with girls, and then the discovery that girls are fun to go hiking with. Along with this is a discovery that girls have other qualities than the purely physical— some can be a whiz at math. And so the boy has to learn all of those things at the elementary level, and as they learn that, and as they observe their elders, they learn what a girl is. And all that crude, coarse talk that is so condemned. They crudely wonder about the girls, their hips, their breasts—and their willingness to pinch a girl on the buttocks, and to accidentally bump her breast with their hand or their elbow. Until they have really located the breasts so that they can help a girl put on a sweater and then draw a hand over it. But first they poked it with their elbow, or bumped it. The crude searching is for the location. The crude bumping of buttocks with a girl, the crude slapping, and their crude talk. Because they lack the language of refinement, and the language of emotional regard. They have to confirm their own observations of others, and so you have those bull sessions in which sex is mentioned, and their instinctual drives keep forcing them to make further and further extensions. And the first love affair. The girl is put upon a pedestal, and kept there, and worshiped from afar, because they're not sufficiently familiar with the opposite sex to dare to let her be too close. She is a strange creature. And they keep the girl on the pedestal until she shows clay feet. And they erect another pedestal for another girl, but this time it's not so high, until that girl shows clay feet. Until finally the girl and the boy meet on a level where they can actually look each other straight in the eye. Without the boy craning his neck. But of course the girls put the boys on pedestals until they show clay feet. And everything the boy does the girl does in her own way. The boy has to speculate on what kissing is. My son knew what kissing was when he was eleven years old. It was disgusting. He wondered when he'd ever degenerate to that. But while he is speculating on when he is going to degenerate to that, he's also recognizing the fact that he will achieve that. And how do boys and girls actually learn about sex itself? By that time they have enough general understanding, they can seek out information from books, from elders, from trusted people, and they can correlate it, without necessarily experimenting. A certain number of boys just cannot correlate and synthesize their information, and they go in for experimentation. Necking from the neck up, from the waist up, from the waist down, depending upon their general—if you want to call it that—moral background. So do some girls have to learn by actual experimentation.

Then another consideration that is so often overlooked is the biological development of an individual. A man can have sexual relations with a woman, and it is a biologically local performance. The sperm cells are secreted, and once that process has been completed—the manufacture of the sperm cells—the man's body has no longer any use for them. They serve no purpose to him. They are useful only when the man gets rid of them by depositiing them in the vagina. And so a man's sexual performance biologically is a purely local phenomenon and can be accomplished very quickly, in the space of seconds. It's just local, and once he has deposited the sperm cells he's all through with the sexual act. Biologically speaking, when a woman has intercourse, to complete that single act of intercourse biologically, she becomes pregnant. That lasts for nine months. She lactates; that lasts another six months. And then she has the problem of caring for the child, teaching it, feeding it, looking after it, and enabling it to grow up. And for a woman the single act of intercourse, in our culture, takes about eighteen years to complete. A man—eighteen seconds is all that is necessary. How is a woman's body built? Very few people stop to realize it—how completely a woman's body enters into the sexual relationship. When a woman starts having an active, thoroughly well-adjusted sexual life, the calcium of her skeleton changes. The calcium count increases. Her foot gets about a fourth of a size larger, her eyebrow ridges increase a little bit. The angle of jaw shifts, the chin is a little bit heavier, the nose a trifle longer, there's likely to be a change in her hair, her breasts change in either size or consistency or both. The hips, mons Veneris, change in either size or consistency or both. The shape of the spine alters a bit. And so physiologically and physically the girl becomes different in as short a time as two weeks of ardent love-making. Because biologically her body has to be prepared to take care of another creature for nine long months inside, and then for months and years afterward with all her body behavior centering on her offspring. And with each child there's a tendency for a woman's feet to get larger, the angle of her jaw to change. Every pregnancy brings about these tremendous physical and physiological changes. A man doesn't grow more whiskers because he's having intercourse, his calcium count doesn't alter any, his feet don't enlarge. He doesn't change his center of gravity one bit. It is a local affair with him. But intercourse and pregnancy are a tremendous biological, physiological alteration for a woman. She has to enter it as a complete physical being. Now, where in all this is the etiology of a particular sexual problem. So often it is assumed that some simple trauma in the past is the whole cause of a difficulty. Or some self-discovery about an idea in therapy will transform the person. I see the problem more as one of arranging a situation where a person can make use of what he has learned and have the opportunity to learn more of what he must know to enjoy himself sexually.

INTERVIEWER: You don't feel that exploring the past is particularly relevant? I'm always trying to get clear in my mind how much of the past I need to consider when doing brief therapy.

ERICKSON: You know, I had one patient this last July who had four or five years of psychoanalysis and got nowhere with it. And someone who knows her said, "How much attention did you give to the past?" I said, "You know, I completely forgot about that." That patient is, I think, a reasonably cured person. It was a severe washing compulsion, as much as twenty hours a day. I didn't go into the cause or the etiology; the only searching question I asked was "When you get in the shower to scrub yourself for hours, tell me, do you start at the top of your head, or the soles of your feet, or in the middle? Do you wash from the neck down, or do you start with your feet and wash up? Or do you start with your head and wash down?"

INTERVIEWER: Why did you ask that?

ERICKSON: So that she knew I was really interested.

INTERVIEWER: So that you could join her in this?

ERICKSON: No, so that she knew I was *really interested*.

IV

CHARACTER REVISION OF THE YOUNG ADULT

When a young person's problem is so severe that he has essentially put himself outside of human involvements, Erickson will attempt major revision of his nature. His approach is much the same as when he does brief therapy, but the intervention is more comprehensive. Often when Erickson has a person in therapy for months or years, he does not have daily or weekly interviews with him. He might see him for a period of time, recess, and then see him again for a period of time. He likes to start changes that can continue without his constant involvement. In such cases the duration of treatment might be for several years, but the number of therapy sessions are relatively few in contrast with other types of long-term therapy.

When a young person withdraws from all social involvements,

it can be for a variety of reasons. In the first case to be reported here, a young woman withdrew from the world for what she considered a major physical defect. A concern with physical appearance is typical in adolescence, although rarely is it so severe as in this case. Usually at this time young people compare themselves with a cultural ideal and find themselves lacking. Typically, they overcome these concerns as part of normal courtship activity. Girls feel themselves attractive when boys find them attractive. However, at times a girl can develop such a preoccupation with what she considers a physical abnormality that she avoids those social situations that might help her resolve the difficulty. Sometimes it is a real physical defect, at other times it is what other people would consider a minor flaw but is extremely important to her. A vicious circle can begin in which the girl withdraws more and more from other people, and as she withdraws she becomes more and more preoccupied with her physical defect because she has fewer other interests, and so she becomes even more withdrawn. Often in such cases any reassurance from a parent is dismissed by the girl as benevolently motivated and so biased. Sometimes a girl will develop this kind of concern because of a family problem; for example, she can negate her physical attractiveness as a way of dealing with a mother who is jealous. Sometimes, too, a blossoming girl sets off a conflict between mother and father as the mother responds to her as a competing female or the father uses her against his wife. At other times such a preoccupation with a real or imagined physical defect can seem to just happen, and no amount of logical argument can dissuade the girl that she is too unattractive for human intercourse.

Milton Erickson has not only had many years of professional experience in dealing with young people in his practice but he has had the personal experience of rearing eight children of his own. His wife once estimated that they would have had an adolescent in the home for thirty years. Erickson thinks about the problems of young people within a framework of knowledge about their sensitivities.

A seventeen-year-old girl began to refuse to leave the house at a time when she should have entered college. She was withdrawing from the world because her breasts had failed to develop, although otherwise she was physically normal. She had received extensive medical treatment for this problem, including experimental endocrinological therapy, with no result. Now, because of her increasingly disturbed emotional state, the possibility of a mental hospital was being considered. Erickson went to her home to treat her and found her hiding behind the sofa. When she was discovered there, she rushed behind the piano. Only when she learned that she was not going to receive any more medical help, and so "no more medicines or needles," would she even talk to Erickson. He began to work with her and found her a good hypnotic subject. He reports:

> During the first interview, which lasted several hours, I talked to her about her personality assets, both in and out of the trance state. I found she had a puckish sense of humor, with an interest in being dramatic, and so I made use of this in my opening gambit. I reminded her of the old song about the toe bone being connected to the foot bone, and so forth. When she was interested, I offered her a paraphrase about the endocrine system, saying that just as the foot bone is connected to the ankle bone, so is the "adrenal bone" connected to the "thyroid bone," with each "supporting and helping" the other.
>
> Next I gave her suggestions to feel hot, to feel cold, to have her face feel uncomfortably hot, to feel tired, and to feel rested and comfortable. She responded well to these suggestions, and so I suggested that she feel an intolerable itch upon her feet. I told her to send this intolerable itch away, but not to the nethermost depths. She was to send the itch to the "barren nothingness" of her breasts, a fitting destination for so intolerable an itch. However, in further punishment of the itch, it would become a constantly present, neither pleasant nor unpleasant, noticeable but undefined feeling, making her continuously aware of the breast area of her body. This series of suggestions had the multiple purpose of meeting her ambivalence, puzzling and intriguing her, stimulating her sense of humor, meeting her need for self-aggression and self-derogation, and yet doing all this without adding to her distress. It was done so indirectly that there was little for her to do but accept and respond to the suggestions.
>
> I suggested to her that, at each therapeutic interview, she visualize herself mentally in the most embarrassing situation that she could possibly imagine. This situation, not necessarily the same each time, would always involve her breasts, and she would feel and sense the embarrassment with great intensity, at first in her face, and then, with a feeling of relief, she would feel that weight of embarrassment move slowly downward and come to rest in her breasts. I gave her

the additional posthypnotic suggestion that, whenever she was alone, she would regularly take the opportunity to think of her therapeutic sessions, and she would then immediately develop intense feelings of embarrassment, all of which would promptly "settle" in her breasts in a most bewildering but entirely pleasing way.

The rationale of these suggestions was rather simple and direct. It was merely an effort to shift to her breasts, but in a pleasant and constructive manner, such unfortunate destructive psychosomatic reactions as "terrible, painful knots in my stomach over just the slightest worries."

The final set of hypnotic instructions was that she have a thoroughly good time in college. Making the suggestions in this way effectively bypassed all discussion of her withdrawn behavior and college attendance.

I explained that she could, in addition to handling her academic work adequately, entertain herself and mystify her college mates delightfully by the judicious wearing of tight sweaters and the use of different sets of falsies of varying sizes, sometimes not in matched pairs. She was also instructed to carry assorted sizes in her handbag in case she decided to make an unexpected change in her appearance, or, should any of her escorts become too venturesome, so that she could offer them a choice with which to play. Thus her puckish activities would not lead to difficulties.

I first saw her in mid-August and gave her weekly appointments thereafter. The first few of these she kept in person, and they were used to reiterate and reinforce the instructions previously given her and to ensure her adequate understanding and cooperation. After that, she kept, by permission, three out of four appointments "in absentia." That is, she would seclude herself for at least an hour and develop, in response to posthypnotic suggestions, a medium-to-deep trance state. In this state, she would review systematically and extensively all previous instructions and discussions and whatever "other things" might come to her mind. I made no effort to determine the nature of those "other things," nor did she seem to be willing to volunteer information, except to say that she had thought of a number of other topics. The other appointments she kept in person, sometimes asking for information, sometimes for trance induction, almost always for instructions to "keep going." Occasionally she would describe with much merriment the reactions of her friends to her falsies.

She entered college in September, adjusted well, received freshman honors, and became prominent in extracurricular activities. During the last two months of her therapy, her visits were at the level of social office calls. In May, however, she came in wearing a sweater and stated with extreme embarrassment, "I'm not wearing falsies. I've grown my own. They are large medium size. Now tell them to stop growing. I'm completely satisfied."

At my request, she underwent a complete physical examination, with special reference to her breasts. A report of this was sent to me and she was physically normal in every regard. Her college career was successful, and subsequent events are entirely satisfactory.

Whether or not the hypnotherapy had anything to do with her breast development I do not know. Quite possibly the development was merely the result of a delayed growth process. It might have been as a result of all the medication she had received. Or it might have been a combined result of these, favorably influenced by her altered emotional state. But at all events, she entered college and began to enjoy life instead of continuing her previous pattern of withdrawal.

One of Erickson's characteristics is his willingness to be flexible in every aspect of his therapy. Not only is he willing to see patients in the office, in the home, or in their place of business, but he is also willing to have short sessions or interviews lasting several hours. He might use hypnosis, or he might not. He will involve all family members at times and not at other times. As in this case, he is also willing to have a session in the form of a social call.

A more severe problem was once presented to Erickson when a twenty-one-year-old woman telephoned him and asked for help, saying she was certain he would not want to see her. When she arrived in the office, she said, "I told you so, I will go now. My father is dead, my mother is dead, my sister is dead, and that is all that's left for me." Erickson approached the problem in the following way:

I urged the girl to take a seat, and after some rapid thinking I realized that the only possible way of communicating with this girl had to be through unkindness and brutality. I would have to use brutality to convince her of my sincerity. She would misinterpret any kindness and could not possibly believe courteous language. I would have to convince her beyond a doubt that I understood her and recognized her problem, and that I was not afraid to speak openly, freely, unemotionally, and truthfully.

I took her history briefly and then asked the two important questions: "How tall are you and how much do you weigh?" With a look of extreme distress, she answered, "I am four feet ten inches.

I weigh between two hundred and fifty and two hundred and sixty pounds. I am just a plain, fat slob. Nobody would ever look at me except with disgust."

This comment offered me a suitable opening, and so I told her, "You haven't really told the truth. I'm going to say this simply so that you will know about yourself and understand that I know about you. Then you will believe, really believe, what I have to say to you. You are *not* a plain, fat, disgusting slob. You are the fattest, homeliest, most disgustingly horrible bucket of lard I have ever seen, and it is appalling to have to look at you. You have gone through high school. You know some of the facts of life. Yet here you are, four feet ten inches tall, weighing between two hundred and fifty and two hundred and sixty pounds. You have got the homeliest face I have ever seen. Your nose was just mashed onto your face. Your teeth are crooked. Your lower jaw doesn't fit your upper jaw. Your face is too damned spread out. Your forehead is too hideously low. Your hair is not even decently combed. And that dress you are wearing—polka dots, millions and billions of them. You have no taste, even in clothes. Your feet slop over the edges of your shoes. To put it simply—you are a hideous mess. But you do need help. I'm willing to give you this help. I think you know now that I won't hesitate to tell you the truth. You need to know the truth about yourself before you can ever learn the things necessary to help yourself. But I don't think you can take it. Why did you come to see me?"

She answered, "I thought maybe you could hypnotize me so I could lose some weight." I answered her, "Maybe you can learn to go into a hypnotic trance. You're bright enough to graduate from high school, and maybe you're bright enough to learn how to go into hypnosis. I'd like to have you go into hypnosis. It's an opportunity to say a few more uncomplimentary things to you: Things I don't think you could possibly stand to hear when you are wide awake. But in the trance state you can listen to me. You can understand. You can do something. Not too dam much, because you are horribly handicapped. But I want you to go into a trance. I want you to do everything I tell you to do because the way you have gobbled up food to make yourself look like an overstuffed garbage pail shows you need to learn something so you won't be so offensive to the human eye. Now that you know I can tell you the truth, just close your eyes and go deeply into a trance. Don't fool around about it, just as you don't fool around in making yourself a disgusting eyesore. Go into a completely deep hypnotic trance. You will think nothing, see nothing, feel nothing, do nothing, hear nothing except my voice. You will understand what I say—and be glad that I am willing to talk to you. There is a lot of truth I want to tell you. You couldn't face it in the waking state. So sleep deeply in a deep hypnotic trance. Hear nothing except my voice, see nothing, think nothing except what I tell you to think. Do nothing except what I tell you to do. Just be a helpless automaton. Now, are you doing that? Nod your head and do exactly as I tell you because you know I'll tell you the truth. The first thing I am going to do is to get you—rather order you—to tell me certain facts about yourself. You can talk even though you are in a deep trance. Answer each question simply but informatively. What is important about your father?"

Her answer was, "He hated me. He was a drunk. We lived on welfare. He used to kick me around. That's all I ever remember about my father. Drunk, slapping me, kicking me, hating me." "And your mother?" "She was the same, but she died first. She hated me worse than my father did. She treated me worse than he did. They only sent me to high school because they knew I hated high school. All I could do at high school was study. They made me live in the garage with my sister. She was born defective. She was short and fat. She had her bladder on the outside of her body. She was always sick. She had kidney disease. We loved each other. We only had each other to love. When she died of kidney disease they said, 'Good.' They wouldn't let me go to the funeral. They just buried the only thing I loved. I was a freshman in high school. The next year my mother drank herself to death. Then my father married a woman worse than my mother. She didn't let me go in the house. She would bring slop out to the garage and make me eat it. Said I could eat myself to death. It would be good riddance. She was a drunk like my mother. The social worker didn't like me, either, but she did send me for some medical examinations. The doctors didn't like to touch me. Now my stepmother and my sister are all dead. Welfare told me to get a job. I got a job scrubbing floors. The men there make fun of me. They offer each other money to have sex relations with me, but nobody will. I'm just not good for anything. But I would like to live. I've got a place where I live. It's an old shack. I don't earn much—eat corn-meal mush and potatoes and things like that. I thought maybe you could hypnotize me and do something for me. But I guess it isn't any use."

In a most unsympathetic, peremptory fashion I asked, "Do you know what a library is? I want you to go to the library and take out books on anthropology. I want you to look at all the hideous kinds of women men will marry. There are pictures of them in books in the library. Primitive savages will marry things that look worse than you. Look through book after book and be curious. Then read books that tell about how women and men disfigure themselves, tattoo themselves, mutilate themselves to look even more horrible. Spend every hour you can at the library. Do it well and come back in two weeks."

I awakened her from trance with this posthypnotic suggestion and she left the office in the same cringing fashion as she had entered it. Two weeks later she returned. I told her to waste no time —to go into a trance, a deep one, immediately. I asked if she had found some pictures unpleasant to her. She spoke of finding pictures of the steatopygous women of the Hottentots, and of duck-billed women, and giraffe-necked women, of keloid scarification in some African tribes, of strange rituals of disfigurement.

I instructed her to go to the busiest section of the city (in a waking state) and watch the peculiar shapes and faces of the things that men marry. She was to do this for one whole week. The next week she was to look at the peculiar faces and peculiar shapes of the things that women will marry, and to do this wonderingly.

She obediently returned for the next appointment, went into a trance, and stated with simple wonderment that she had actually seen women almost as homely as she was who wore wedding rings. She had seen men and women who seemed to be man and wife, both of whom were hideously fat and clumsy. I told her that she was beginning to learn something.

Her next assignment was to go to the library and read all the books she could on the history of cosmetology—to discover what constituted desirable beauty to the human eye. She made a thorough search, and the next week she entered the office without cringing, but she was still clad in her polka-dot dress. Then I told her to return to the library and look through books dealing with human customs, dress, and appearance—to find something depicted that was at least five hundred years old and still looked pretty. Ann returned, developed a trance immediately upon entering the office, sat down, and spoke eagerly about what she had seen in books.

I told her that her next assignment would be very hard. For two weeks she was to go first to one women's-apparel store and then another, wearing her frightful polka-dot dress. She was to ask the clerks what she really ought to wear—to ask so earnestly and so honestly that the clerks would answer her. She reported after this assignment that a number of elderly women had called her "dearie" and explained to her why she should not wear millions and millions of polka dots. They told her why she should not wear dresses that were unbecoming and served to exaggerate her fatness. The next assignment was to spend two weeks in obsessive thinking: Why should she, who must have been born weighing less than twenty pounds, have added such enormous poundage? Why had she wrapped herself up in blubber? From that assignment, she reported, she couldn't reach any conclusions.

Again in the trance state, she was given another assignment. This time to discover if there was really any reason why she had to weigh what she did—to be curious about what she might look like if she weighed only 150 pounds and was dressed appropriately. She was to awaken in the middle of the night with that question in mind, only to fall asleep again restfully. After a few more trances in which she reviewed all her assignments, she was asked to recall, one by one, each of her assignments and to see whether they especially applied to her.

Ann was seen at two-week intervals. Within six months she came in, with great interest, to explain that she could not find any reason why she should weigh so much—or why she should dress so atrociously. She had read enough on cosmetology, hairdressing, and makeup. She had read books on plastic surgery, on orthodontia. She asked piteously if she could be permitted to see what she could do about herself.

Within another year's time, Ann weighed 150 pounds. Her taste in clothes was excellent, and she had a much better job. She was enrolling in the university. By the time she graduated from the university, even though she still weighed 140 pounds, she was engaged to be married. She had had two teeth that had developed outside of the dental alignment removed and replaced. Her smile was actually attractive. She had a job as a fashion artist for catalogues and newspapers.

Ann brought her fiancé to meet me. She came into the office first and said, "The darn fool is so stupid. He thinks I'm pretty. But I am never going to disillusion him. He's got stars in his eyes when he looks at me. But both you and I know the truth. I have difficulty keeping below a hundred and fifty—and I am afraid I am going to start gaining again. But I actually know that he loves me this way."

They have been married for fifteen years, and they have three handsome children. Ann talks freely of her therapy, since she remembers everything that was said to her. She has said more than once, "When you said those awful things about me, you were so truthful. I knew that you were telling me the truth. But if you hadn't put me in a trance, I wouldn't have done any of the things you made me do."

One of the more interesting aspects of this case is the way Erickson arranged that after six months of treatment the girl *requested* that she be able to do something about making herself more attractive. She was not then resisting change but piteously seeking it. By then she was sufficiently knowledgeable and motivated enough to make a change possible. As he often does, Erickson made use of community facilities, such as the public library. Rather than help her understand why she was overweight—the traditional approach—he required her to spend two weeks of obsessive thinking about the reasons why she was overweight. When she could not find any reasons for why she should weigh so much, it was reasonable to allow her to lose weight.

A more extreme example of Erickson's long-term therapy was his work with a young man who was a migratory laborer with homosexual leanings. Over a period of a few years he was transformed into a college graduate with a preference for females. This case is presented in detail, since it illustrates many aspects of Erickson's therapeutic procedures that have been touched on more briefly in preceding cases. Erickson reports:

> When Harold called me, he did not actually ask for an appointment, but in a weak and hesitant voice managed to express the question whether a few minutes of valuable time could be wasted upon him. When he arrived in the office, his appearance was incredible. He was unshaven and unwashed. His hair, which he cut himself, was too long, with a ragged and chopped look. His clothes were filthy, and his workmen's shoes were cracked and broken in the uppers and laced with packing-box cord. He stood there pigeon-toed, wringing his hands while his facial muscles contorted. Suddenly he jammed his hand into his pocket and pulled out a bunch of crumpled dollar bills.. He dropped them on my desk, saying, "Mister, that's all I got. I didn't give my sister all she wanted last night. I'll pay you more just as quick as I get it."
>
> I stared at him in silence, and he said, "Mister, I ain't very smart or much good. I don't never expect to be much good, but I ain't bad. I ain't nothing but a damn dumb no-good moron, but I ain't never done nothing wrong. I work hard—see—them hands prove it. I got to work hard, because if I stop I got to sit down and cry and be miserable and want to kill myself, and that ain't right. So I just keep on working fast and I don't think nothing and I can't sleep and I don't want to eat and I just hurt all over and, Mister, I can't stand it no more." Then he began to cry.
>
> When he paused for breath, I asked him, "And what is it you wish me to do for you?"
>
> With sobs he said, "Mister, I'm just a moron, a dumb moron. I can work. I don't want nothing but to be happy instead of scared

to death and crying and wanting to kill myself. You're the kind of doctor they had in the Army to straighten out guys that went off their rockers, and I want you to straighten me out. Mister, help me, please. I'll work hard to pay you, Mister, I got to have help."

He turned away and walked toward the office door, his shoulders slumped and his feet dragging. Waiting until he reached for the doorknob, I said, "Listen you, listen to me. You're nothing but a miserable moron. You know how to work, you want help. You don't know nothing about doctoring. I do. You sit down in that there chair and you let me go to work."

I phrased that statement deliberately in keeping with his mood and in a fashion calculated to arrest and fixate his attention. When he sat down, bewildered, he was virtually in a light trance. I continued, "As you sit there in that chair, I want you to listen. I will ask questions. You will answer and you will tell not a damn bit more and not a damn bit less than I got to know. That's all you do —no more."

In response to questions, Harold managed to give a history of himself. In summary, he was twenty-three years old, the eighth child in a family of seven sisters and five brothers. His parents were illiterate immigrants, and the entire family grew up in poverty. Because of lack of clothing, Harold missed much schooling. He dropped out of high school to help support his younger siblings after completing two years with failing grades. At the age of seventeen he joined the Army, where, after basic training, he spent his two years' service as a "yard bird." After his service, he joined his twenty-year-old sister and her husband in Arizona and found they had both become seriously alcoholic. He shared his earnings as a manual laborer with them and had no other family contacts. He had tried some night-school education and failed at it. He was living at a minimal-subsistence level, renting a wretched one-room shack, and his diet was discarded vegetables from the produce market and cheap meat stewed together over a hot plate secretly connected to an outdoor outlet of a neighboring shack. He bathed infrequently in irrigation canals, and in cold weather he slept in his clothes because of insufficient bedding. With encouragement, he managed to say that he abhorred women, and no woman in her right mind would want a feeble-minded man like him. He was a queer, and there should be no effort made to change him on that score. His occasional sexual involvements were with "young punks."

The way Erickson approached this case is typical of his methods, and various aspects of the therapy will be summarized. However, it should be kept in mind that this is a brief outline of an extraordinarily complex approach to treatment; each therapeutic maneuver is inextricably connected with every other maneuver, and a selection of points to highlight necessarily oversimplifies the case.

When Harold entered the office, Erickson decided to accept him as a patient almost immediately. He felt "there existed a wealth of strong personality forces which quite conceivably would justify therapy. His unkempt appearance, his desperation, the inconsistency of his language and ideas, and the tremendous callousing of his hands from manual labor gave an impression of a therapeutic potential."

However, when the man made his desperate plea, Erickson did not respond immediately with helpfulness. He allowed him to go even further toward the end of his rope by allowing him to turn to leave the office feeling rejected. Only when he reached for the doorknob to leave did Erickson respond. As he puts it, "When the patient turned to leave the office, he was emotionally at the lowest possible ebb. He had come for help, and he was leaving without it. Psychologically he was empty. At that moment I thrust a series of suggestions upon him which by their very nature required him to respond positively. From a depth of despair he was suddenly thrust into a position of actual hopefulness, which was a tremendous contrast."

Harold defined himself as a moron, a dumb moron, and Erickson accepted this view as he typically accepts a patient's view. As he puts it, "The fact that from the beginning there was a difference of opinion between us about his being a moron was irrelevant and not germane to the situation. To the very limit of his ability to understand in that situation, he was a stupid moron totally uninterested in, and actually intolerant of, any contrary opinion." How extreme is Erickson's ability to "accept" is indicated by the fact that it was not until Harold was in college that this agreement between them that the man was a moron was dropped.

Erickson's opening statement confirmed the man's language as appropriate, identified the two participants and defined their tasks—he was to do the doctoring and the patient was to follow instructions—and provided the patient with a secure framework. Harold was to tell him "not a damn bit more and not a damn bit less" than he needed to know. Furthermore, his saying "That's all you do——no more" afforded Harold a sense of certaintly and security. As Erickson puts it, "However illusory such security might be, it was valid to him." He adds, "By replying to questions under these conditions, he was absolved from any need to pass judgment upon his answers. Only *I* could do so, and even then it would apparently be only judgment of quantity of information, not of emotional quality or value." Later in the interview, which continued into a second hour during this session, Erickson assured him there was another matter or two or three concerning therapy that had not yet been mentioned. Since therapy was a sharing of responsibility, Harold would have to add other items he considered unimportant or not significant. As it was put, "Special things about which they ain't nothing been said yet, all gotta be told anyhow. But these is gonna be special things only." In response to this, Harold declared that since he was sharing responsibility, he would have to inform Erickson that he was "queer." He could not tolerate women and preferred fellatio with men. He wanted no effort made to change him to heterosexuality and asked for a promise about that. Erickson responded in a typical manner; he offered a compromise that left him free to achieve his own ends by promising that every effort would be made to abide by Harold's needs "as he progressively understood them." Neither he nor the patient was to define prematurely a goal that was yet undetermined, and neither one could give orders to the other. Each person had to do his own job with complete respect for the other person's honest efforts.

Erickson, more than many therapists, seeks goals as specific as possible from his patients in the initial sessions. He will inquire, and then inquire again, as he did later in this session. On the second inquiry about what he wanted, Harold explained that he was feeble-minded, a moron, that he "didn't have no brains or no education," and he was qualified only for manual labor. He was "all twisted up and mixed up in the head" and he wished to be "straightened out" so he "could live happy like other feeble-minded morons." When he asked if he was expecting too much for himself, Erickson assured him emphatically that "under no circumstances would he be given more than his rightful share of happiness" and also that he would have to accept "all the happiness that was rightfully his, no matter how small or large a portion it was." Approaching him in this way, Erickson committed him to accepting all therapeutic benefits to which he was entitled while also defining the situation as one in which he could accept or reject in actual accord with his needs. As Erickson puts it, in this way "nothing alien to the personality results, the person is prepared for both positive and negative reactions, and he has an inner sense of obligation of tremendous motivational force."

Later, when Erickson defined the task of therapy as "to tell ideas and to get them straight no matter what they were, so that nobody nohow would be mixed up in the head not even to please somebody," Harold responded with a hope that not too much would be expected of him. He was assured that he should only do as much as he could—in fact, he "damn well better not do no more than what he could because it would just waste time."

By the end of the interview, the relationship was defined by Erickson as "You let me stick to the doctoring—that's my business —and you stick to getting no weller than you can—that's your business." As Erickson puts it, "This negative formulation implied most effectively and acceptably a positive goal of actually getting well. Thus both positive and negative desires are united to achieve a common goal, wellness—a goal he could feel was limited but which was not."

To summarize Erickson's initial encounter with this patient, the therapeutic stance taken is one that assumes the patient is going in two contradictory directions at once. The patient is defining the relationship as one in which he is a person desperately seeking assistance, and at the same time one in which he will resist any change. Erickson responds at two levels, which satisfy both definitions of the patient. He accepts the request for help by defining himself as the preson who will take charge and do the doctoring and the patient is to follow instructions. Within that framework, he simultaneously defines a relationship appropriate for someone resisting change and unwilling to follow direct instructions by (a) motivating the patient toward change when he increased his desperation with a delay of offer of help, (b) communicating in the patient's language and agreeing with the man's definition of himself as a moron, (c) defining tolerable limits of what the man is to do and not do, (d) making more self-revelation easier, (e) limiting what is expected of him in terms of goals in an ambiguous way and reassuring him that he is not to do more that he can and to get no more well that he can, and (f) defining the situation as one in which "neither one can give orders to the other."

What appears complex and contradictory in these therapeutic maneuvers is the simultaneous defining of relationships in contradictory and ambiguous ways, as is true of any psychotherapy. By definition, psychiatric patients are suppliants seeking help, but, also by definition, there is nothing wrong with them in the usual sense—their problem is the unfortunate way they deal with other people, particularly people who offer them assistance. Therefore there must be a framework of helpful assistance, but within that framework there must be an avoidance of a direct demand for more "normal" behavior; that is, behavior appropriate to a helping relationship. In other words, there must be a framework defining the relationship as one designed to induce change, and within that framework no *direct* request for a change but an acceptance of the person as he is. Throughout the case, when Erickson requests a change it is defined to the patient as an extension, really quite a minor one, of the way he already is. This is why Erickson defines the therapy in agreement with the patient as one in which there will be no attempt at a *real* change; it is merely that a feeble-minded moron is being helped to continue as he is but to be happier and a better worker.

WORK AND THE ACHIEVEMENT OF APPROPRIATE STATUS

In the treatment of Harold there were two main emphases; an increase in his career position in society, and an increase in his ability to be social, especially to behave in appropriate ways with females. There two goals are in many ways inextricable, since a certain competence in socializing is essential to a career, but they will be presented here as separate.

Harold was usually seen in one-hour sessions, although occasionally the interviews were two hours long. "At first a light trance was almost always employed, but as therapy progressed, a medium and then from time to time a profound trance state was utilized." The hypnosis was used to ensure that instructions would be followed, to provide amnesia at times and so bypass resistance, and in the later stages to provide experience in distorting the patient's subjective sense of time so that more could be accomplished in shorter time periods.

Special training was given him, in both waking and trance states, to talk freely and to discuss his ideas easily. This was accomplished by having him give at tedious length a comprehensive account of his day's work and other activities. Questions, suggestions, and discussion were interjected by Erickson into this account, so that Harold was being trained both to be communicative and to be receptive to ideas.

In the first therapeutic session, Harold was told authoritatively, "I don't want no arguments with you. I'm going to show you some ideas and explain them. I want you to listen and understand and find out if they belong to you and how you can use them your way, just your way, not mine, not the way of anybody else, just your way. You put everything you got into it, but not a bit more. You gotta be you, the way you really are."

Harold had said his sisters and his mother were intensely religious but he himself was not. However, the Bible was "the most important thing in the world," even though he "was uninterested in it." With this as background, Erickson began to confirm Harold's feeling of the importance of work as well as his feeble-mindedness. He said, "You believe in the Bible, it's the most important thing in the world. That's right and it's O.K. Right here I want you to know something and understand it. Somewhere in the Bible it says that you always got the poor with you. And the poor are the hewers of wood and the drawers of water. That's day labor and you can't run the world without it. It's awful important. I just want you to understand that."

This led to a discussion, in the first and future sessions, of the importance to all society of the labor performed by the "feeble-minded." Woven into this account was Harold's work history and its significance for him as a producer and legitimate member of society. With these ideas there was a systematic, but deliberately scattered, emphasis upon the value and importance of physical attributes. Muscle size, strength, coordination, and skill as well as the importance of the physical senses were brought into the discussion.

For example, working in irrigation ditches "ain't just muscle power. You gotta have that, but you gotta get just the right size shovel full of dirt or you get tired before you get a day's work done. Same way working with cotton. You can't chop it or pick it, even if you got the muscles, if you ain't got the know-how to see and feel the job just right." With this kind of discussion, unnoticeably, unobtrusively, there was an increasing emphasis on recognizing the coordination of the muscles with the senses and a respect and admiration for the reality around him as well as his part in that reality. Since he derogated himself, there was a discussion of assembly-line workmen and athletes as merely muscle men lacking in intelligence. Similarly, I pointed out that there were cooks who only possessed a skilled sense of taste and not much intelligence. This was done to lay a broad foundation for the idea that even the most feeble-minded person can and does learn a great variety of things. When he seemed to grasp this, I offered him a long and interesting dissertation on the *idiot-savant*, with case histories and careful emphases upon their capabilities and deficiencies. In particular, Railroad Jack proved to be someone who aroused Harold's intense interest and admiration. I closed this discussion, with Harold deeply hypnotized, with the statement that he was "*neither an idiot nor a savant, just somewhere in between.*" Before he could realize the significance of that remark, I awakened him with amnesia and dismissed him. Part of the value of the use of hypnosis is the use of amnesia whenever a crucial or highly significant suggestion is offered that might be disputed or questioned. A rejection of a valuable idea is prevented and the patient can continue to develop it later.

Often therapeutic suggestions can be platitudinous in character; as such they are generalizations whose personal applications are not realized immediately and later become indisputable. Examples are "It ain't just what you say, or how you say it; it's what it really means to you that counts," or "They ain't nobody who can't learn something good, something interesting, something awful nice and good from every baby, every kid, every man, *every woman*," or "Nobody can tell what a baby is going to grow up to be, and nobody knows what he's gonna be like five years from now or even a year."

With an emphasis upon the range of possibilities of the feeble-minded, and questions about the potential capability of anyone, Erickson introduced uncertainty into the question of Harold's potentialities. Yet this was done in such a way that the uncertainty could not be easily disputed or rejected.

Concurrently with an emphasis upon the usefulness of the feeble-minded, Erickson began to focus upon what is required of a good worker. Usually he finds some positive aspect of a person's life and makes use of it like a lever to shift the patient's behavior. In this case Harold was proud of being a good worker, and so Erickson organized his suggestions around that. First he began with the need of a worker for a feeling of physical well-being, and later he emphasized the importance of a good diet and had Harold learn good cooking. To learn to cook well, Harold had to obtain cookbooks at the library, and so he learned to use the library. Erickson also persuaded him to provide good meals, rather than money, for his alcoholic sister and her alcoholic husband, and in the process Harold learned to look upon that couple as examples of self-neglect and self-destruction. The motivation for these activities was defined in terms of Harold's expressed wish to be a good worker. At this beginning stage, Harold accepted the idea that a good worker generally should take care of his physical self, including having proper shoes to provide him with an ability to work better. However, he began to show resistance when the idea was applied to himself. Therefore Erickson shifted to talking about work in the cotton fields.

Out of this developed a discussion of the tractor as a piece of farm machinery unsuited for anything except manual labor. Then I pointed out that a tractor needed the right kind of care. It needed to be kept oiled, greased, cleaned, and protected from the elements. It should be properly fueled with the right kind of oil and gas, certainly not aviation gas, and the valves should be ground, the spark plugs cleaned, the radiator flushed out, if the tractor was to be a useful manual laborer. I drew other comparable analogies and said, "You know, you gotta do some things right, even though you don't want to," but what those "things" were I left carefully undefined for Harold.

He responded by appearing at the next interview in clean clothes. He seemed hostile and belligerent as he waited for my comments on his appearance. I said, "Well, it's about time you took care of your clothes instead of wasting money on your carcass buying new ones because they wear out so fast." With this phrasing, Harold's insistence upon his inferiority and his acceptance of the idea of self-care were both confirmed, thereby committing him to continue to take care of himself. He sighed with relief and spontaneously developed a trance state to avoid any further discussion of his clothes. At once I told him, with a labored but self-defeating effort to be amusing, the story of the parsimonious farmer who knew that a mule is rightly a "work horse," but instead of feeding it grass he put green glasses on it and fed it excelsior. Then he complained that after he had trained it to live on excelsior, it died before he could get any work out of it. Before Harold could react to this, I read and discussed "The Deacon's Masterpiece, or The

Wonderful One-Hoss Shay." Then I dismissed him in a rather confused and uncertain frame of mind.

He appeared for the next interview with his hair neatly barbered for the first time, with new clothes, and obviously freshly bathed. Embarrassed, he explained that his sister and her husband had sobered up to celebrate their wedding anniversary and he felt he should go. I replied that some things just have to be done, and when the habit is formed it's not too difficult to continue. Harold also added that as a present to his sister he had taken her to *his* dentist and *his* physician for a checkup and examination. Except for a subsequent mention of a change of address "a while ago," nothing further was said about his improved physical care or his improved standard of living.

With Harold dressing well and living more comfortably, Erickson began to encourage him to investigate his potentialities by arranging a failure.

I encouraged him to enroll in an evening class in algebra. Both he and I knew he could not handle the work, but I felt it was desirable to emphasize, and thus dispose of, negative considerations before attempting the positive. A patient has a continuing need to feel himself in the right, even when he is wrong, and a therapist needs to join the patient on this. Then, when the time comes for the patient to correct his mistake, he and the therapist can do this jointly and so the therapy is a more cooperative endeavor. Harold soon announced with pleasure that he was unable to master the algebra, and with similar pleasure I announced my satisfaction with the failure. It proved that Harold had been wrong in enrolling in the course with the idea of discovering *if he could pass* the course, instead of enrolling to discover *that he could not.* This statement bewildered Harold, but the reason for phrasing it in this way was to lay the groundwork for later attempts in school.

With the failure safely accomplished, Harold was receptive to other instructions.

At this point Erickson began to instruct him to socialize more, which will be discussed under that heading, but one social visit was important to his increasing ability to work.

I assigned Harold the task of making another new acquaintance by giving him an address and telling him to go there and learn well and thoroughly, overlooking nothing, and to visit frequently.

During the next few weeks, while he was executing this assignment, I forbade him discussing it with me so that whatever he did would be entirely his own action and responsibility. Such an instruction also compelled him to put forth more effort for the eventual discussion of what he had done.

The person I sent him to was a man named Joe, aged thirty-eight, with whom he developed almost immediately a warm friendship. Joe suffered from asthma and arthritis. Confined to a wheel chair, he attended to his own wants and supported himself. In anticipation of being unable to walk, he had built into his cabin a wealth of mechanical contrivances of all sorts to meet his needs. He earned his living by repairing radios and electrical appliances, doing the neighborhood mending and odd jobs of reweaving, and, above all, professional baby sitting. His knowledge of story, song, and verse and his powers of mimicry enthralled both children and adults. Joe also did his own cooking, and he exchanged recipes with others and counseled neighborhood brides in cooking.

Joe had not completed the sixth grade, and his intelligence quotient was 90 or less, but he had a retentive mind, listened well, and possessed a rather remarkable fund of facts and philosophical ideas. He enjoyed people and was cheerful and inspiring despite his physical handicaps.

Out of this friendship, which continued for two years before Joe's sudden death from a coronary attack, Harold derived immeasurable benefit. Little was said about Joe to me, and the friendship remained Harold's own, unshared, and so his own accomplishment.

Harold was also given instructions to visit the local library and become thoroughly acquainted with children's books, which he did partly because of Joe's influence. He spontaneously began to explore the rest of the library and began to share conversations with Erickson about books and ideas, some contributed by Joe and some from his reading.

Two areas that caused Harold emotional distress at the mention of them were the art of cooking and the art of writing. However, Erickson began to discuss cooking as an attainment of the highest skill, and at the same time he derogated it as something that even the feeble-minded can do, even a woman. Writing was discussed as a great accomplishment, but derogated as something little children can learn to do, the feeble-minded can do it, and even women. Writing was reduced still further by equating it with the crooked marks and lines a woman makes when she writes shorthand.

Since Harold had sought therapy to secure a modicum of pleasure in living Erickson reviewed with him possible sources of recreational pleasure.

Harold liked music and in fact owned a radio, although he felt guilty about this since he did not feel he deserved to possess it. I impressed upon him the fact that, for the time being only, he needed the radio and had to use it by medical command. I said "for the time being only" to enable him to accept a command as one limited and restricted in character. Any future rejection by him of the command could then be regarded as cooperation, since it had been for a short time only.

I further offered the rationalization that just as a good workman should exercise his body, he should also exercise his eyes and ears and total physical self. With the establishment of the radio as a legitimate part of his life and his genuine interest in music, the development of recreational interests became relatively easy, because other therapeutic suggestions could be fitted into his interest in music. For example, as a posthypnotic suggestion he was told that a tune he would like would run through his mind. He would want to learn that tune well, but it would be best remembered only when he ate a hamburger. In this way, unobtrusively, an alteration of his diet was effected.

At each session Harold was encouraged to give an account of what music and songs he had enjoyed lately, and every effort was made to fit their titles, or quotations from them, into therapeutic suggestions. For example, suggestions were drawn from "Doing What Comes Naturally," "Accentuate the Positive; Eliminate the Negative," and "Dry Bones" ("The toe bone connected to the foot bone," etc.). However, all songs by female singers or those extolling women tended to be rejected by him until later in therapy.

I encouraged him to beat time to music in a variety of ways and to hum an accompaniment. Then, over some resistance, I persuaded him to accompany the singer vocally. Finally I induced him to invest in a tape recorder so that he could record the music and record his own singing, alone or in conjunction with the singer on the radio. Harold derived so much pleasure from these activities that it became possible to confront him with a more threatening constellation of ideas. I suggested that he learn to play some instrument, preferably a banjo or a guitar, to accompany himself. However, I then rejected this idea, since Harold was only qualified for manual labor requiring strong muscles, not *delicate* muscular skills. I debated this problem pro and con, with repeated expressions of regret that were actually indirect hypnotic suggestions. Finally, we found a solution; Harold could acquire rapidly all the fine muscular skills and coordination he had never had a chance to develop by learning shorthand and typing. These skills were no more than any feeble-minded moron or dumb cluck of a woman could do, since shorthand was only purposely making little fine crooked marks with a pencil, and typing was just hitting keys, like one does on a piano, but in typing you can see at once any mistakes and correct them. Perhaps such an argument to a patient in the ordinary waking state might have been ridiculous and futile; in the trance state a patient is attentive and responsive to ideas and oriented to the question of benefit and help rather than concerned with logical relationships and coherencies.

Harold became both distressed and determined. He followed the suggestions and developed a tremendous motivation to learn both shorthand and typing, practicing them faithfully and intensively. He learned rapidly and was encouraged to do so by his admiration for his friend Joe's manual dexterity and skill in fine movements.

The next step was to urge him to take weekly piano lessons "to speed up learning typing and playing the guitar." He was referred to an elderly woman piano teacher whose husband was ill, and he was able to obtain lessons in return for yard work. Harold accepted this arrangement, and did not recognize that he was placed in special contact with a woman, a contact that placed him both in a learning role in relation to a woman and also in a position where he could enact the role of a competent male. (This circumstance occurred without previous planning and was seized upon to achieve these ends.)

With the increased expenses of his tape recorder, his guitar, his typewriter, and his improved living conditions, Harold began to seek better employment. A fellow workman taught him how to drive an automobile, and this led to a truck-loading job and then to a well-paying truck-driving job.

A session was devoted to summarizing his past work history, his improvements and progressive achievements, but I also discounted these as being a process of "living from day to day at the same old job without anything new coming up." Finally, I encouraged him to begin to explore Help Wanted advertisements. By chance, an ad appeared inquiring for an amanuensis who was unattached and willing to work at any hour of the day or night and to live in an isolated mountain cabin. He must be able to type and take shorthand. Harold sought an interview and was hired at a salary of $410 per month. His employer was a wealthy, rather eccentric, aged recluse whose hobby was having copies made of old manuscripts and books, which he would then discuss and annotate. Harold did the secretarial duties, and when the cook was off for a day or two he would do the cooking. He was well qualified for this, since his therapy included the study of cookbooks and the cooking of meals at his sister's home.

Harold's performance pleased his employer, and in addition to salary and maintenance he was furnished with a complete wardrobe for his visits to town for supplies. A business suit was provided for his frequent visits to the library for reference books.

Harold worked at this job for eighteen months, seeing me from time to time for two-hour sessions. He matured greatly in his thinking, his academic orientation broadened tremendously, and the range of his interests and awareness increased as a result of long discussions with his scholarly employer. Finally his employer closed up his Arizona home, giving Harold three months' severance pay.

Within a few days Harold secured another well-paying job as a combination secretary and office manager. He was hesitant about accepting it because of his mental limitations, but finally he took it, expecting to be discharged shortly for incompetence. He explained that he had applied for the position because "he didn't really know any better."

At this point Harold was hypnotized and required to review comprehensively his entire work experience. Particularly, he was to contrast "mercilessly" the early period of his life with the eighteen-month period of employment as secretary. He did this review with an appearance of emotional distress. He was dismissed with the posthypnotic suggestion that he would return with a most important question in the form of a tentative idea.

At the next session Harold said, "I've been feeling pretty damn punk, all tore up inside, just like I got to do something but don't really know what. Maybe I've got part of the answer figured out. It's silly to say it, but I got a feeling I got to go to college even though I know I'll flunk out." He added that there were lots of things he wanted to get straight, like adventures in life, like enjoying a sunrise, and he added, "Oh, there's hundreds of things, and, man, *I'm rarin' to go.*"

I informed him, in an authoritative manner, "All right, you will go to college. But this time you won't make the mistake you did when you took the algebra course—to see if you could pass instead of to discover you couldn't. Next September you will enroll for a full regular college course, and by midsemester you will have discovered how much of it you will fail." I added that between now and then he would explore the simple, nice little things that constitute the greater part of life.

During the next three months Harold was seen once a week, and the character of the interviews was markedly changed. Usually he spent the time asking me about my own views on various subjects. He behaved in the manner of a curious man seeking how another man, whom he respected and liked, viewed and did things, sought recreation, felt and thought about an endless variety of topics.

In September Harold registered for a full regular course of sixteen hours. He did not ask me for any opinion or advice about actual courses or procedures of enrolling without a high-school diploma, and I gave him none. Harold's conviction that he was feeble-minded had not yet been dissipated, so again I assured him he would have to wait until midsemester to learn what he was failing. Since he could be certain of failing, he could enroll with every feeling of confidence. Nothing beyond his abilities or that would even tax his capacities was being expected. However, *in order to achieve that failure*, he had to enroll successfully.

As the weeks passed, Harold did not attempt to discuss his studies. After the midsemester examinations, he reported with astonishment that he had been *given* good grades in everything. I replied that midsemester was really a bit too early to expect instructors to be able to judge new students adequately. He would have to wait until the end of the semester for a correct determination of his abilities. In this way, the non-discovery of his failures was defined as the fault of his instructors. Yet Harold was being committed to accepting his future semester grades as "a correct determination of his abilities."

It might be difficult to conceive that a patient undergoing therapy should be so blandly oblivious of how well he was actually doing in school. However, one must remember that hypnosis was employed, that amnesias were used, and distractions and redirection of attention undoubtedly aided his ability to conceal from himself what was occurring.

Harold received all A's at the end of his semester, and without calling for an appointment he appeared at the office. He was upset, and felt he had been wrong. I assured him he had not been wrong, merely mistaken in many things. He developed a profound trance, and I gave him the posthypnotic suggestion, "As you arouse, you will know your grades. You will know that topic is a settled issue. Any discussion can be held at any convenient time, since it is no longer an urgent issue but a decided matter of fact."

Harold continued in college successfully while facing a new problem—dealing with women in intimate relationships—but before going on to that, we should note a few additional points about this approach in therapy.

First of all, it should be emphasized that within a period of two or three years a manual laborer who considered himself a dumb moron, and whose history substantiated that idea, was transformed into a man capable of earning a living in middle-class endeavors and capable of being a successful student in college. He was shifted from being a peripheral person living on the margin of society to being a participating member of reasonably high status. This goal was achieved without any exploration whatever of what was "behind" his problem in the usual psychiatric sense; he changed without insight into his past and without any discovery of the relation between his past and present through anything like transference interpretations. No past traumas were revealed to him or explained as "causal" to his difficulties. His presumably miserable childhood was offered as neither excuse nor explanation for his failures or his poor opinion of himself. In fact, instead of bringing ideas about the past into awareness, the therapy instead made extensive use of deliberate amnesia to keep ideas out of his awareness except upon a planned schedule, and these ideas were not about the past but about his own capabilities in the present.

The therapeutic approach was distinctively Ericksonian and included many tactics appropriate to a learning experience; however, what was learned was not why he was the way he was but how to be different and successful. Perhaps the most remarkable aspect of the case is the fact that the patient did not learn, or did not reach an agreement with Erickson, that he was not feeble-minded until he had accomplished a series of achievements including succeeding in college.

One other important factor should be emphasized; throughout the therapy Erickson used an intricate combination of authoritarianism with the patient at some points, while allowing him almost total autonomy at others. Much of the therapy involved autonomous action by the patient independent of Erickson. In many ways Erickson works as one might with the tractor he used in his example to the patient. He "primes" the patient to get him started and then lets him function in his own way.

SOCIALIZATION AND COURTSHIP BEHAVIOR

While integrating Harold into a more appropriate career position in society, Erickson was also working upon Harold's ability to engage in normal courtship activities. At the beginning of therapy, Harold's relationships with other people were largely limited to his sister and her husband. He had no male friends and totally avoided women. He ate in diners to avoid waitresses, made purchases whenever possible from male clerks, and often walked rather than ride on a bus where there were female passengers. He found it difficult even to tolerate the physical presence of his sister and did so only because she was his sister. His sexual activities were confined to occasional contacts with males with whom he practiced passive and occasionally active fellatio. His sexual partners were preferred with the following attributes: they must be younger than he, preferably of Mexican origin, with long hair, not over five feet four inches tall, and weighing between 120 and 150 pounds. They should have a round face, full lips, narrow shoulders, large hips, a swaying walk, use perfume and hair oil, and have a tendency to giggle readily. Harold knew a number of what he termed "punks" who fulfilled these requirements, and now and then he consorted with them.

Harold had never had an association with a female, had never dated, and insisted that he wanted no part of females. The therapeutic problem of integrating Harold into normal courtship behavior was obviously a formidable one.

Erickson proceeded in a typical manner; he began to offer indirect suggestions that made associations with females more agreeable, and he proposed a series of tasks that led toward courtship behavior. A necessary part of the endeavor was to make Harold more attractive to females by having him become more attractive in dress, living conditions, and career position in society.

Early in the therapy Erickson assigned Harold the task of developing an acquaintance with a total stranger and required him to do this within a week. Harold agreed reluctantly "and he seemed uncertain about whether success or failure was desired" (perhaps because Erickson had just congratulated him for failing the premature algebra course).

In setting up this task for him, I proposed that he walk around some trailer court of his own choosing. Then I maneuvered him into choosing a certain trailer court where another patient of mine lived and whose habits I knew. Harold quite naturally waited until the last evening of the allotted week and then, with dread and uncertainty, began his walk through the trailer court at the specified hour of 6:00 P.M. As he passed one of the trailers, he was hailed by a man and wife sitting in the shade of their trailer. It was their habit to sit there at that hour and to hail passers-by for a social visit. The friendship flourished, and many weeks passed before they learned that they both were in therapy with me. At first almost all the effort to socialize was offered by the man and his wife, but over continued visits Harold became less passive and more responsive.

Although many therapists hope that a lonely patient will find a friend, Erickson prefers to ensure that it happens. He might directly arrange a relationship, or he might require a patient to be at a place where he knows a relationship is most likely to occur; when this happens, it is often thought by the patient to have spontaneously occurred. His next assignment was a more direct requirement. "Some time after the friendship with the husband and wife was well under way, I assigned Harold the task of making still another new acquaintance by giving him an address and telling him to go there and learn well and thoroughly, overlooking nothing, and to visit frequently." It was in this way that Harold met Joe, the handicapped handyman, and developed an important friendship that lasted two years until Joe's death.

By arranging relationships in this way, Erickson manages to avoid the possibility that the relationship with the therapist be a substitute for, and prevent, a more normal set of relationships. The therapist himself provokes other relationships.

The next step in Harold's socialization process was to accept piano lessons in exchange for yard work from the elderly female piano teacher. In this way he experienced a learning relationship with a female and also a relationship in which he was the competent male doing what her ill husband could not do.

Now that Harold was able to associate with a married couple, a male friend, and an elderly female, Erickson required a further step. He suggested that Harold learn to swim at the YMCA and learn social dancing.

To both of these suggestions Harold reacted with violent distaste and emotional distress. Agitated, he explained that women were allowed to use the YMCA pool once a week, and he could not tolerate the thought of immersing his body in water so polluted. And as for dancing, that would require a voluntary touching of women's bodies, and such an idea was intolerable to him. With labored, frightened insistence, he explained anew that he was homosexual, that women were completely disgusting to him, and that he had enough trouble with the world thrusting women forcibly upon him without my adding to it by unreasonable demands.

Erickson was providing two directives at once, one more difficult than the other, so that the patient could reject one and still follow the other. In this case, the suggestion of social dancing was more abhorrent than swimming at the YMCA, an all-male organization. However, it happened that Harold, with some encouragement, managed both activities.

When Harold objected to the swimming and dancing, I offered him an analogy. He was willing to harvest by hand the vegetables growing in a fertilized field and sprayed with insect poison. He knew he could wash both himself and the vegetables and benefit from their food value. In the same way, I dogmatically asserted, anything that happened from swimming and dancing could easily be corrected by water, a bar of good strong soap, and a towel.

Essentially, I summarily dismissed his objections. Then I began to point out that the preferred place to learn dancing was the professional dance studio, where all contacts would be rigidly impersonal. Part of the rationale for these two activities was that he, as a worker, would learn two different physical skills both based upon rhythm.

Harold learned both swimming and social dancing rapidly, and he began to use a certain soap for his ritualistic cleansing afterward. I pointed out that another brand of soap was just as good, but really no better—in fact, both were entirely adequate.

In this way Erickson partly engineered a washing compulsion as a way of encouraging the new social activities. He then began to undermine it, as he often does such compulsions, by unritualizing it; one brand of soap or another will do, one time or another, one amount of washing or another.

While Harold was being required to participate in social activities that involved females, at least impersonally, the therapeutic sessions were devoted to Erickson's way of shifting a patient's ideas and relabeling various aspects of his life.

When Harold appeared to be receptive to sexual understandings, this topic was introduced into the therapeutic sessions. I pointed out that just as I had a diversity of interests and knowledge, he also should have at least a general knowledge of many aspects of human living that were necessary to preserve and continue the species. For example, I said, he clasified himself as a homosexual and me as a heterosexual, but he did this blindly, without really knowing or understanding what either term meant or implied. Then I offered him a factual account of what constituted sexual growth and development, together with an explanation of how differing individuals and cultures approach sexual beliefs and practices. I pointed out that I wanted him to listen and to understand but not to make any effort to modify his own personal views of himself. In this way I offered him the opportunity to modify his views as a spontaneous result rather than a self-imposed effort.

Then I offered Harold a simple, factual, rather academic account of the physiology of sex and its biological importance. Woven in were other ideas such as sexual rhythm, the mating dance of birds, the rutting season of animals, different cultural practices of sexual behavior, and music, dancing, song, and literature on the subject. This led, as I later discovered, to Harold's systematic reading in the library.

I then gave Harold a series of instructions he was not to execute until some time in the future. These cryptic, apparently vague general instructions were repeated to him in a trance state. They were as follows: (a) To discover there are some pretty miserable young people in the world who are just afraid to do things they wish, (b) to look these young people over and speculate why they behave that way, (c) to discover that many young, unhappy people hope, but don't really believe, that someone will come along and help them, (d) to render *a limited number* of those people the help they wanted in a detached, impersonal way.

When I felt it was safe to have him execute this assignment, I instructed him to visit various public dance halls and observe carefully the number of young men who wished to dance but were too bashful and fearful to even try to learn how. Then he was to note the young women, the fat girls, the homely girls, the skinny girls, the wallflowers who looked about hopefully for a partner or desperately danced with each other while eying the young men who were shuffling about too embarrassed to dance.

Harold's reaction to this assignment was not distaste for the task but a startled disbelief that such a situation existed. However, when he first tried to execute the task he suffered an almost paralyzing reluctance, and only after a period of nearly three hours and several false starts did he actually arrive at a public dance hall. There he encountered a group of young men jostling each other and making such remarks as "Ahh, go ahead," "If you will, I will," "Oh, I can't dance," "So what? Maybe some dame there can teach you," "Go ahead," "Ahh, who wants to?"

After Harold had grasped the meaning of this situation, as he later explained, he marched around inside the hall and observed a half dozen girls, obviously wallflowers. They were discouraged but looked up hopefully at him until he paused irresolutely, and then, discouraged anew, they turned their attention to the dance floor, where a number of girls were dancing together. Harold reported, "I took a good grip on myself, marched over, danced one dance with each of about a half dozen of those girls, and then I got out of that place so I could think things over."

Harold made three such visits to dance halls and concluded, "That experience sure taught me that I ain't half as bad as I thought. I ain't afraid to do things." I replied forcefully, "No, you ain't half as bad as you think you are, so why don't you go to the Veterans Administration and have them give you the works in psychological tests to see just how good you are?" Then I immediately dismissed him in a rather startled frame of mind.

Some days later Harold returned, an almost transformed personality. He reported jubilantly that the outcome of the tests indicated he had the equivalent of a high-school education and was qualified to enroll in college. He said, "not bad for a feeble-minded guy," and I answered, "Nope, not even bad for a guy who just thinks he's feeble-minded," and I abruptly terminated the interview. Following this, I refused him several appointments on the ground that he had a lot of thinking to do.

This special assignment is typical of Erickson's approach in many ways. Often he will provide a series of general and rather vague instructions and then later arrange a situation where those instructions will be followed, while the patient has the feeling that he spontaneously made a decision. In this case Harold was advised to observe and offer limited help to some young people; later he was sent to the public dance hall. Once at the hall, he "spontaneously" decided to ask some young ladies to dance, and he experienced a sense of accomplishment. At the same time, the goal of the instructions was to place Harold in a normal courtship situation, have him contrast himself with other males, and let him discover that he was capable of doing what many other males could not. The result was a normal experience Harold had previously missed; attendance at dances and meeting and dancing with strange females.

Harold did not begin a more intimate relationship with a female until later in therapy, while he was attending college, and Erickson did not learn about this relationship until later yet.

During this period Erickson trained Harold in time distortion —the use of hypnosis to affect one's sense of time so that what happens in actuality in minutes can feel subjectively like hours. Partly this was to help him in his academic work. At this time Erickson provided Harold with six sessions of deep hypnosis in which, with the use of time distortion, he had him sit silently and review who he was and what he was and what he would like to be and what he could do. Additionally, he was to review his past in contrast with his future, his actuality as a biological creature with emotional as well as physical forces, and his potentialities as a human personality functioning with a reasonable degree of adequacy in relationship to himself and others. Harold's appearance during these sessions was that of a man intensively engaged in solving problems, some of them pleasant, more of them unpleasant, but apparently all monentous. At the close of each session Harold was quite tired. He was not seen for two weeks after these hypnotic sessions, and then he came into the office to report a "new problem."

Harold's manner was rather tense, and his general behavior seemed somewhat changed and less familiar. He appeared to want information without being willing that I have more understanding of the situation than was necessary. Therefore I received his account passively and was noncommittal on positive matters but rather freely emphatic on negative matters.

His story was that some time previously—just when he did not know, "but it was quite a while ago, maybe a long time ago"—a woman had moved into the apartment next to his. Later he noticed that the woman left and returned to the apartment courtyard each morning and evening at the same time he did. He became painfully aware of this when she began to call a cheerful "Hi, there" or "Hello" to him. This annoyed him, but he did not know how to cope with it except to reply.

Next, the woman began to stop her car and engage him briefly in casual conversation. This distressed him "horribly" because it aroused amused comment from his other neighbors. From them he learned that she was fifteen years older than he, separated from her husband, who was an alcoholic and physically abusive to her, and supporting herself to raise funds for a divorce.

"No real trouble" developed until one evening when, "without any excuse at all," she had "invaded" his apartment with an armful of supplies and proceeded to prepare dinner for the two of them. As her excuse for this "outrageous behavior," she declared that a man ought to have a woman-cooked meal once in a while. Afterward, while she was washing the dishes, she asked him to play some records of classical music. He did so with a feeling of great relief, since it made conversation unnecessary, and "fortunately, after tidying the kitchen," she took her departure. The rest of that evening and until almost daybreak, he had paced the floor, "trying to think but I couldn't get any thoughts."

A few nights later, just as he was about to prepare his evening meal, the woman "just walked in and told me she had dinner ready and waiting in her apartment. There was nothing I could do—I couldn't think of anything to say—I just went over like a little kid and ate. After dinner, she just stacked the dishes and invited herself over to my apartment to listen to more music. That's what we did, and she left about ten o'clock. I didn't get any sleeping done that night. I couldn't even think again. I just thought I was going crazy, and it was awful. I knew I would have to do something and it was something pretty important, but I didn't know what it was. I didn't find out for two weeks. You see, I started avoiding her, but after a couple of weeks I had it figured out. I would cook a dinner for her and that would satisfy her. So that's what I did; only it didn't work out the way I wanted it. It was a good dinner and all that, if I do say it myself. We played records again—she really likes music and she knows a lot about it. She's a very intelligent woman except she's pretty damn stupid in some ways. Anyway, she left about ten-thirty; and as she walked out the door, she leaned over and kissed me. I could have killed her. I couldn't get the door closed fast enough. I just ran into the bathroom and got under the shower and turned it on. I soaped my face thoroughly even before I took my clothes off; I had a hell of a time. I'd soap and scrub, and then I'd soap and scrub some more. That night was really rough. Several times I dressed and went out to the pay phone to call you, but each time I knew I shouldn't call you that early in the morning. So I'd go back and get under the shower and scrub some more. My

God, I was crazy. I knew I'd have to fight it out by myself, but what it was or how I was going to do it I didn't know. Finally the idea came to me that I'd really got the answer all figured out. This was when I had those half dozen or so appointments with you when I got so awfully tired. Something in my head seemed to say, "That's the answer, but it didn't make sense then and it doesn't now. But it did help me to stop scrubbing myself.

"I don't know why I'm here today, but I had to come. I don't want you to say anything, but at the same time I want you to talk to me. But be pretty damn careful what you say. Excuse me for talking that way to you, but I feel that I got to be sure. It's my problem."

Cautiously, I offered a vague general discussion, deliberately designed to be tangential to Harold's own communication. As he relaxed, I pointed out that one ought not to blame or criticize the woman for seeking a divorce; that marriage should entail more than unhappiness and physical abuse; that every human being is entitled to personal as well as physical happiness. Since she was willing to be self-supporting in all regards, she certainly possessed qualities meriting respect, admiration, and liking. As for her friendliness and intrusion upon his privacy, one must recognize that people are essentially gregarious and one would expect her, or him, or all the rest of the human race to seek companionship and to share in common experiences. This could account for her behavior, and even for his acceptance of it. As for meals, since the beginning of history the two best seasonings of food have been the sauces of hunger and of good companionship. Music, too, is primarily best enjoyed as a shared experience. As for that kiss that distressed him, one could only speculate about the possible meaning of so simple a physical act. There is the kiss of love, of compassion, of death, of a mother, of an infant, of a parent, of a grandparent, the kiss of greeting, of farewell, of desire, of satisfaction, to name but a few. Before he could attach any specific meaning to that kiss, he would have to know what manner of kiss it was. This he could learn only by thinking freely and willingly on that subject, without fear of terror but only with a desire to learn. He would also have to be willing to recognize what meaning he wished that kiss to have. As for any personal implication of her behavior or of his, nothing really could be said because neither had given a recognizable definition to their conduct. However, it could be said that he should have no hesitancy about rejecting anything that might in any way be objectionable to him.

After this statement there was silence for about five minutes.

Harold awakened and remarked, after looking at the clock, "Well, I've really got to be moving along, whatever that means," and took his departure.

One aspect of this discourse might be commented upon. Erickson does not in any way attempt to help Harold "understand," in the usual psychiatric sense, the meaning of this experience to him. There are no interpretations about the motherly significance of the woman's being older or other supposedly symbolic meanings of the situation. Therefore there is also no negative sanction against the relationship. It is treated as a real experience with a real woman.

A week later Harold was seen for an hour. He said, "I really shouldn't ask you, but something inside me wants to know how you would think about Jane. So discuss her, but do it carefully, whatever that means. It's some kind of a silly idea I've got, because you don't know her—just the few things I've told you about her. But I still want to know how you think about a woman, but do it carefully, whatever that means." Erickson responded with a discussion of the woman in objective generalities.

Unobtrusively, I mentioned ideas of special significance to Harold. I described Jane as a biological creature who, by endowment, possessed a wealth of traits, qualities, attributes, learnings of various degrees, to all of which she would react in varying ways and which made her unique as an individual. Others of humankind would respond to her in terms of their own capacities and needs. For example, her history of marriage indicated that she was a heterosexual female attractive to the heterosexual male; her employment indicated a capacity to be productive; her seeking a divorce indicated a desire for happiness as a person; his enjoyment of her cooking and companionship indicated that he had found her to be of personal interest.

I also pointed out that any comprehensive therapeutic progress he might wish would include women, not necessarily this individual, as a part of the reality of life. I closed by saying, in the language Harold had used when he first met me, "You sure as hell gotta find out what kinda critter a woman is. You ain't gonna let her sink no hooks into you, and you ain't gonna mess her up or get messed up yourself. All you gonna do is lay the answers right out on the line." I spoke in this way to force him to recognize the contrast between his original and his current status. He left without comment but with a curiously speculative gaze from the door as if he did not know quite what to say.

Harold had not asked for another appointment, but he returned several weeks later and said:

"I'd like to tell it to you my way, but you're a psychiatrist. I owe everything to you, and so I ought to tell it your way and perhaps it will be useful to someone else.

"That last thing you said to me was to lay the answer on the line, and I almost told you I was going to do exactly that. But I realized you weren't the least bit interested in what I could say. You just wanted me to find out for myself who I was and what I was and what I could do. Remember how I stood in the doorway and looked at you for a minute? That's what I was thinking. I knew the answers were going to be laid out one by one. All the way home I knew that, and I felt amused because I didn't know what those answers were. I just knew I'd lay them out one by one.

"After I got home, which was about five-thirty, I was puzzled because I found myself going to the door and looking out as if I expected to see something. It wasn't until Jane drove into her carport that I knew I was looking for her. I went over and asked her to come for dinner. Earlier that morning I had been puzzled at all the things I bought when I went shopping. She accepted and cooked dinner while I played the guitar and sang a duet with a tape recording I had made myself. After dinner, I put on some records and we danced until we felt like sitting down. As we sat on the couch, I told her I was going to kiss her, but first I was going to think about how much I would enjoy it. While I did that, I said, she could get her resistances worked out of her system. She looked puzzled and then started laughing. I realized that what I had said must have sounded pretty odd to her, but I meant it. When she stopped laughing, I took her face in my hands and kissed her first on one cheek, then on the other, and then on her mouth. I like it, but I was so businesslike about it she looked frightened, so I suggested we dance. As we danced, I began kissing her again and she responded.

"That was when other things began to happen to me, and I knew I wasn't ready for that. So I stopped the dancing, played classical music for her, then sang some of the songs I knew and she joined in. She's got a pretty good voice. Then I took her home and kissed her good night. That night I slept like a baby."

At this point Harold was preparing to begin normal sexual activity, and it should be kept in mind how much elaborate preparation had been provided to create an environment where this was possible. Harold could enter more normal courtship activity because he was now dressing properly, living in a respectable apartment, going to college, and working at a good job. He was also able now to share with this woman a knowledgeable interest in music and a knowledgeable interest in cooking. Further, he had had previous experience in social relationships, was able to dance, and was experienced in dancing with females. Finally, his attitude toward women had been reoriented, and he had developed curiosity and a desire to explore.

Harold went on with his account. "When I awakened the next morning, I was glad it was Sunday. I wanted a nice leisurely day just to enjoy life. About three o'clock I went over to see Jane. She was busy making a dress, and I told her to keep at it and I'd have dinner ready for her at six o'clock. After dinner we played classical music and then some popular stuff on my tape recorder. We danced until we were tired and then sat down on the couch. I kissed her and she responded, and we began petting. I was pretty circumspect because I knew that I was just a beginner and probably awkward, so we hugged and kissed, and I learned what a French kiss was. First we'd dance, then we'd pet, and then we'd dance some more. Every time we petted, I'd get a physiological response, and I knew that I wasn't ready to put my answer on the line there. Finally we played some classical records and I took her home, kissed her good night with a lot of feeling for her, and went to bed. I slept well that night.

"I didn't see her for three days. Those were three rather peculiar days because I drew a complete mental blank on those days. I got up Monday morning feeling fine. I thought about Sunday evening and I was pleased. Then I left for my work, and the next thing I knew, the day was over and I was back in the apartment. I couldn't remember a single thing about that whole day, but I had a strong feeling and a good feeling that I had done everything all right at work. Tuesday I left for work planning to inquire discreetly what had happened the day before, and the next thing I knew I was entering the apartment again. I was amused, not troubled, and I wondered what would happen Wednesday. Of course Wednesday evaporated too, but I did find myself bringing in a big load of groceries. What surprised me was the sales check—it showed that I had purchased them in a store I had never been in before. While I was trying to remember that shopping, I must have absent-mindedly walked over to Jane's. I was so surprised when she greeted me that I told her to never mind dressing—she was just wearing shorts and a blouse. I was ready for her, and she could come over and eat dinner."

That night Harold had his first experience with sexual relations, and he experienced it as a curious exploration. He then reported:

"Afterwards we had breakfast, and Jane went to work but I stayed home. I spent all day at home, feeling happy, really happy, for the first time in my life. I just can't explain. There are things you can talk about but you can't put them into words. Thursday was that kind of day.

"We had arranged to get together again on Saturday night, and on Friday I went shopping. On Saturday I cleaned up the apartment, but both days I had no memory of what had happened, except for a comfortable feeling everything had gone well. Saturday afternoon I prepared a darn fancy dinner, and when Jane came in she was dressed in a pretty, feminine dress. When I complimented her, she told me she liked my tie. That was the first I knew I had dressed up too. That surprised me.

"We ate, we danced, we petted. At about ten o'clock we went into the bedroom. It was different this time. I wasn't trying to learn something or to change myself. We were just two people who liked each other a lot making love. Sometime after midnight, we went to sleep. The next morning she fixed breakfast and left, explaining that a friend was coming to visit her for a few days.

"Monday morning I got up early and left for work, not knowing why I went early. It didn't take long to find out. I was driving down the street when it happened. A girl came along towards me on the pavement, and I was so startled I had to pull up at the curb and watch her out of the corner of my eye until she got past. That girl was beautiful, utterly, absolutely, incredibly beautiful—the first beautiful girl I had ever seen. Two blocks further on, the same thing happened again, only this time it was two absolutely beautiful girls. I had a hard time getting to work. I wanted to stop and look at things. Everything was so changed. The grass was green, the trees were beautiful, the houses looked freshly painted, the cars on the street looked new, the men looked like me, and the streets of Phoenix are lousy, just absolutely lousy with pretty girls. It's been that way ever since Monday. The world is changed.

"On Wednesday I wondered what about those punks I used to know, so I drove over to the wrong side of town and looked a few of them up. It was an amazing experience. I must have been pretty godawful sick to have anything to do with those poor creatures. I just felt so damn sorry for them.

"Nothing more happened until Saturday after Jane's visitor left. We had dinner, played some records, and then when I turned the record player off we both felt it was time to have a serious talk. We had a sensible conversation about how we could enjoy each other but it just didn't make sense. I should find a girl my age, and she should think about a man her age. We agreed to break things up but remain friends, and that's the way it is.

"I've been to church, to young people's clubs, I've been sightseeing. Man, I've been alive and enjoying it. I have a future, too. I'm finishing college, I know what kind of career I want, and I know I want a wife, a home, and children.

Harold finished college and found a responsible position that he liked.

V MARRIAGE AND ITS CONSE-QUENCES

       The problems that arise as a consequence of marriage usually involve sexual difficulties, symptoms that handicap or incapacitate one of the spouses, or an apparently unresolvable breach early in the marriage. From the point of view of the family cycle, the goal of treatment is to assist the young couple to a stable relationship and help them make the shift to the stage of producing and rearing children.

       When a newly married person appears with a problem, the nature of the difficulty can look different from different vantage points. If one views only the individual, the problem is different from that of the couple, and yet the marital problem is different from that of the extended family. For example, a young woman was referred to me for treatment because she had developed an involuntary trembling and shaking of her right hand. In the previous year she had undergone extensive and expensive neurological tests, with a final conclusion that the shaking hand was a hysterical symptom. After she had undergone six months of traditional psychotherapy, the shaking hand was becoming worse. Unless something was done quickly, she would lose her job. I was asked to do brief therapy in the hope of relieving the symptom. A few minutes of the Erickson-style hypnotic approach revealed that the trembling could be shifted from hand to hand, yielding the diagnosis of hysteria at considerable less expense that the neurological explorations. The problem of the "cure" remained.

The therapist who had been treating the young woman considered that she faced much the same situation as other young women and that there was something wrong with *her*. But, from a different point of view, the young woman had recently married and the symptom had developed shortly after the marriage.

I brought the young couple together in an interview, and it was evident that the husband was a rather lost young man and the wife was quite protective of him. They had married while he was in the Navy, where he had a position of glamour and status. However, after his discharge he was only a civilian without a job. He could not decide whether to go back to school or get a job, and he was taking no action in either direction. The young wife was supporting him. From this vantage point, the symptom could be seen as serving a function in the marriage. This became more evident when I asked her what would happen if the symptom became worse. She replied that she would lose her job. When I asked what would happen then, she said, "I guess my husband would have to go to work." The symptom therefore served the positive function of moving the marriage toward a more normal state. Given that view, the husband and the marriage should be the focus of therapy.

In such a situation, if only the wife is placed in therapy, there is always a consequence to the marriage. The husband is faced with a situation where his wife is not only in distress but is going several times a week to talk to another man, probably about him. By the very nature of individual therapy, the husband is participating in a triangle with the therapist. In this case the husband felt that his inadequacies as a husband were undoubtedly being discussed by his wife with this successful other man, and he was becoming more uncertain about her loyalty to him. His wife, in turn, was caught between a therapist encouraging her to express her discontents and a husband who behaved as if she would be disloyal if she did.

With long-term individual therapy, other factors enter into the marriage. The wife, as she becomes more attached to the therapist, shifts from the sole commitment to her husband that is part of the marriage contract. Often in such cases the spouse receives the leavings; each new thought and idea of the partner is presented to the therapist, and only later, if at all, is it offered to the spouse. The treatment can become a barrier between the marital couple and erode the marriage by precipitating discontent and perhaps a divorce. Should divorce occur, the individual therapist may feel that his patient has "outgrown" the spouse and that the divorce is necessary, particularly if he has no recognition that his intervention in itself is a major part of the disruption, independent of any "growth." Sometimes the spouse also enters treatment with another therapist, and the marriage shifts to being a foursome. Whatever the benevolent ends of such an arrangement, the longer the treatment continues the more the marriage is "abnormal," in the sense that it is not like the usual marriage. When a spouse is in individual treatment for eight or ten years— I know of one that continued for eighteen years—the later stages of marriage proceed with a bias that prevents normal marital developments. For example, anticipation of childbirth or the rearing of children can be something the wife shares with her therapist as much as with her husband, and the therapist become essentially a paid member of the extended family.

Still a different view of this young woman with the shaking hand can be obtained by enlarging the context to include not only her husband but her family of origin. Her parents opposed her marriage to the young man, and, in fact, forbade it. She decided to marry him anyhow, assuming that once the marriage took place her parents would have to accept it. However, when the young couple had established themselves in their apartment, her mother called and inquired if she were returning home that day. When the wife pointed out that she was married now and had a place of her own, her mother said, "Well, that won't last." The next day the mother asked again if she were coming home and assured her that her room was still ready for her. With persistent regularity, the mother called the girl and commented on the inadequacies of the young man, with full expectation that her daughter would return home. Whatever doubts the wife had about her husband were constantly exacerbated by the mother, and the young husband was living in a context of hostile in-laws. His indecision about a job was partly based upon his overconcern with what would be acceptable to his wife's family, so that his life decisions were inevitably being influenced by this wider family network. In this context his uncertainty can be explained as having a social origin, rather than being a part of his character.

In this larger context the wife's symptoms are part of a conflict between parts of a family and include a difficulty in disengaging from parents and establishing a separate and stable territory with her husband. The previous treatment too can be seen as part of this larger context. The expensive neurological tests, as well as the expensive individual therapy, were paid for by her family. The girl could thereby cost her parents money for the difficulties they were causing and also substantiate their idea that the marriage was a mistake, since it created problems great enough for the girl to require a psychiatrist. The treatment became, as it often does, part of the ammunition in the family struggle, while the therapist remained unaware, or unconcerned, about this aspect of the therapy.

This case also illustrates how therapists can be given credit for resolving a problem that no doubt would have been resolved naturally without assistance. As Montaigne once put it, "When nature cures, medicine takes the credit." Despite the brilliant therapeutic maneuvers, it would appear that the problem was solved independently of the therapy. The young wife became pregnant, which transformed the total context. It was necessary for her to give up her job because of the forthcoming baby, and her husband was forced to go to work to support her. The parents wanted their daughter to return to them, but they did not want her to return with a baby. So they shifted their stance and began to support the marriage rather than oppose it, now that a grandchild was on the way. "Nature" had solved the problem by moving the young couple to the next stage of family development: child producing and rearing. The symptom disappeared, and the young woman and her husband appeared more mature and self-confident.

Many therapists are only beginning to understand that individual symptoms have a function for a young couple in relation to their in-laws. One of the typical problems of a young couple is their inability to pull together when dealing with their families of origin. For example, a wife will not want her husband's family intruding into their lives as much as they do, but her husband will not be able to oppose his parents. In such a situation the wife often develops some type of symptom. In the folowing case that was the situation, and Erickson arranged a more productive symptom.

A woman came to me with a stomach ulcer; a pain that had incapacitated her at work and at home and in all her social relationships. The major issue concerning her was the fact that she could not stand her in-laws visiting her three or four times a week. They came without notice and stayed as long as they pleased. I pointed out to her that she could not stand her in-laws, but she could stand church, and card games with neighbors, and her work. Focusing down on the in-laws, I said, "You don't really like your relatives. They're a pain in the belly *every time* they come. It ought to be usefully developed; they certainly can't expect *you* to mop up the floor if you vomit when they come."

She adopted this procedure and vomited when her in-laws came to visit. Then she weakly and piteously apologized while they mopped up the floor. She would hear them drive into the yard, and she'd rush to the refrigerator and drink a glass of milk. They would come in, she would greet them and start talking, then suddenly she would become sick to her stomach and vomit.

The in-laws began to call up before they visited to find out if she were well enough for them to call. She would say, "Not today," and again, "Not today." Finally she said, "I think I'm all right today." Unfortunately, she had made an error, and they were forced to clean up.

She needed to be helpless, and in this way she saved up all her pain in the belly for the in-laws' visits and had her satisfaction. (She gave up the stomach ulcer and took pride in her stomach. It was an awfully good stomach that could throw the relatives out.) The relatives stopped coming for a couple of months, and then she invited them to come "for the afternoon." They came warily, regularly saying, "Perhaps we had better leave." When she wanted them to leave, all it took was a distressed look on her face and a rubbing of her abdomen. They were quick to depart. She changed from someone who was involuntarily helpless to one who could keep a glass of milk handy in the refrigerator to achieve a deliberate end. Yet there was never a need for an open quarrel. It reminds me of the guest who always dropped in for Sunday dinner and was always served spongecake, and the enjoyment of asking that courteous question, "Will you have some spongecake?" until he finally caught on.

Conservative therapy for a newly married person who develops difficulties is now defined as intruding to produce a change without allowing the intrusion to become built into the system. Sexual problems such as impotence and frigidity often develop during the honeymoon, and often resolve themselves. In many cases when a couple seeks help, it is wiser for the expert to avoid making the issue a pathological one by merely suggesting that their problem is not uncommon and will probably resolve itself. If not, they can always return for treatment. Often a discussion of sex with an authority is enough to solve these early marital problems. This is not necessarily because the young people are given new information but because an authority gives them permission to enjoy themselves sexually when previous authorities have always forbidden that pleasure. This is part of the "initiation ceremony" into the adult world.

When the enjoyment of sexual relations does not occur naturally, the goal of therapeutic intervention is to arrange that enjoyment as well as to stabilize the marriage and assist the young couple toward the child-rearing stage of development. At times, sexual relations do not occur at all, and the marriage lacks not only enjoyment but the possibility of moving to the child-producing stage. Erickson offers example of a case where the complaint was that of the husband.

A young man who normally weighed 170 pounds married a beautiful and voluptuous girl. His friends joked about his impending loss of weight. Nine months later he sought psychiatric advice from me because of two problems. One, he could no longer tolerate his fellow workers joking about his weight loss of over forty pounds. The real problem was something else entirely. The marriage had never been consummated.

He explained that his wife promised each night to have sexual relations, but at his first move she would develop a severe panic and would fearfully and piteously persuade him to wait until the morrow. Each night he would sleep restlessly, feeling intensely desirous and hopelessly frustrated. Recently he had become frightened by his failure to have an erection despite his increased sexual hunger.

When he asked if there could be any help for either himself or his wife, I reassured him and made an appointment for his wife. I asked him to tell her the reason for the consultation and to ask her to be prepared to discuss her sexual development since puberty.

The couple arrived promptly for an evening appointment, and the husband was dismissed from the room. She told her story freely though with much embarrassment. She explained her behavior as the result of an uncontrollable, overpowering terror that she vaguely related to moral and religious teachings. Concerning her sexual history, she exhibited a notebook in which the date and hour of onset of every menstrual period had been recorded neatly. This amazing record disclosed that for ten years she had menstruated every thirty-three days, and the onset was almost invariably around 10:00 or 11:00 A.M. There were a few periods not on the scheduled date. None of these was early. Instead, there were occasional delayed periods, recorded by actual date and with the scheduled date marked by an explanatory note such as "Been sick in bed with bad cold." I noted that her next period was not due for seventeen days.

When I asked if she wanted help with her marital problem, she first declared that she did. Immediately, however, she became frightened, sobbed, and begged me to let her "wait until tomorrow." Finally I quieted her with the repeated assurance that she would have to make her own decision. Then I offered her a long, general discourse upon marital relations, interspersed more and more frequently with suggestions of fatigue, disinterestedness, and sleepiness until a fairly good trance state had been induced.

Then, with emphatic commands to ensure continuance of the trance, I offered a whole series of suggestions with increasing intensity. These were to the effect that she might, even probably would, surprise herself by losing her fear forever by suddenly, unexpectedly, keeping her promise of tomorrow sooner than she thought. All the way home she would be completely absorbed with a satisfying but meaningless thought that she would make things happen too fast for even a thought of fear.

Her husband was seen separately, and I assured him of a successful outcome for the night. The next morning he reported ruefully that halfway home, *seventeen days too early*, her menstrual period began. He was relieved and comforted by my specious statement that this signified the intensity of her desire and her absolute intention to consummate the marriage. I set another appointment for her when her period was over.

On the following Saturday evening I saw her again and a trance was induced. This time I explained that a consummation *must* occur, and I felt that it should occur within the next ten days. Furthermore, she herself should decide when. I told her that it could be on that Saturday night or Sunday, although I preferred Friday night; or it could be on Monday or Tuesday night, although Friday was the preferred night; then again, it could be Thursday night, but I definitely preferred Friday. This listing of all the days of the week with emphasis upon my preference for Friday was systematically repeated until she began to show marked annoyance.

She was awakened, and the same statements were repeated. Her facial expression was one of intense dislike at each mention of my preference. I saw the husband separately and told him to make no advances, to be passive in his behavior, but to hold himself in readiness to respond, and that a successful outcome was certain.

The following Friday he reported, "She told me to tell you what happened last night. It happened so quick I never had a chance. She practically raped me. And she woke me up before midnight to do it again. Then this morning she was laughing, and when I asked her why, she told me to tell you that it wasn't Friday. I told her it *was* Friday, and she just laughed and said you would understand that it wasn't Friday."

I gave him no explanation. The subsequent outcome was a continued happy marital adjustment, the purchase of a home, and the birth of three wanted children at two-year intervals.

The rationale of the ten-day period, the naming of the days of the week, and the emphasis on my preference was as follows: ten days was a sufficiently long period in which to make her decision, and this length of time was, in effect, reduced to seven days by naming them. The emphasis upon my preference posed a most compelling, unpleasant emotional problem for her: since all the days of the week had been named, the passage of each day brought her closer and closer to the unacceptable day of my preference. Hence, by Thursday only that day and Friday remained; Saturday, Sunday, Monday, Tuesday, and Wednesday had all been rejected. Therefore consummation had to occur either on Thursday by her choice or on Friday through my choice.

The procedure employed in the first interview was obviously wrong. It was beautifully utilized by the patient to punish and frustrate me for incompetence. The second interview was more fortunate. A dilemma she could not recognize of two alternatives was created for her—the day of her choice or of my preference. The repeated emphasis upon my choice evoked a strong corrective emotional response: the immediate need to punish and frustrate me temporarily transcended her other emotional needs. The consummation effected, she could then taunt me with the declaration that last night was not Friday, happily secure that I would understand.

Just as a young woman can have difficulty in consummating a marriage, so can a young man. A common difficulty is the inability of a new husband to achieve an erection. Sometimes this can be a surprise on a honeymoon. The man might have had a history of successful sexual relations, but the act of marriage creates a relationship that makes him incapable of performing the act. Sometimes this problem resolves itself; at other times a brief intervention can alleviate the difficulty and save the marriage.

One of my medical students married a very beautiful girl, and on their wedding night he could not produce an erection. Yet he had been rather a man about town and had slept with every chippy in the city. For two weeks after the marriage he could not produce an erection. He tried everything and could not even get one by masturbation. After two weeks of a dismal honeymoon, his wife consulted a lawyer about an annulment.

The young man came to me with this problem. I told him to call up a few friends who knew his bride and have them persuade her to come and see me. She came to the office, and I had the young man wait outside while I talked to her. She was extremely bitter, and I let her tell me the whole disappointing story. She thought she was attractive, and yet there she was completely nude and he was incapable of making love to her. The wedding night can be such an event to a girl. It is a momentous occasion which represents being transformed from a girl into a woman, and every woman wants to be wanted and to be the one and only. It was an overwhelming situation, and so I defined it to her that way.

I asked her if she had thought about the compliment her husband gave her. This puzzled her, since it seemed to be a reversal of what she had been saying. I said, "Well, evidently he thought your body was so beautiful that he was overwhelmed by it. Completely overwhelmed. And you misunderstood that and felt he was incompetent. And he *was* incompetent, because he realized how little capacity he had to really appreciate the beauty of your body. Now you go into the next office and think that over."

I called the husband in, and I let him tell me the whole sad story of the honeymoon. Then I said the same thing to him. I pointed out what a tremendous compliment he had given to his wife. He had a lot of guilt about previous affairs, but here was his incapacity proving to him that he had really found the one right girl, the overwhelming girl.

They drove home to their apartment together, almost stopping the car on the way to have intercourse, and they were successful from then on.

This kind of treatment is essentially crisis treatment in a marriage, and part of its effectiveness is the timing of the intervention. Prompt action at this time can often quickly resolve problems that are resolved only with difficulty if the sexual problem is allowed to become a chronic marital problem. At times the intervention appears to be a permission for success offered by an authority figure, combined with a graceful exit out of the difficulty. There are other variations used by Erickson.

A twenty-four-year-old college-bred bridegroom returned from his two-week honeymoon most despondent in mood because he had been incapable of an erection. His bride went immediately to a lawyer's office to seek an annulment, while he sought psychiatric aid.

He was persuaded to bring his wife to my office and, without difficulty, she was persuaded to cooperate in the hypnotherapy of her husband. This proceeded in the following fashion. I told him to look at his wife and to experience anew and completely his sense of absolute shame, humiliation, and hopeless helplessness. As he did this, he would feel like doing anything, *just anything*, to escape from that completely wretched feeling. As this continued, he would feel himself becoming unable to see anything except his wife, even unable to see me, though able to hear my voice. As this happened, he would realize that he was entering a deep hypnotic trance *in which he would have no control over his entire body.* Then he would begin to hallucinate his bride in the nude, and then himself in the nude. This would lead to a discovery that he could not move his body and that he had no control over it. In turn, this would then lead to the surprising discovery for him that he was sensing physical contact with his bride that would become more and more intimate and exciting, and that *there would be nothing he could do to control his physical responses.* However, there could be no completion of his uncontrolled responses until his bride so requested.

The trance state developed readily, and at its conclusion I instructed him, "You now know that you can. In fact, you have succeeded, and there is nothing you can do to keep from succeeding again and again."

Consummation was readily effected that night. Occasionally I saw them after that as a family adviser, and there have been no sexual difficulties in the marriage.

Although producing an erection can be a problem for a newly married couple, the ingenuity of human beings makes it possible to have difficulty *because* the man easily produces an erection. A wife's dissatisfaction took this form in the following example.

A woman had been married a year and was extremely bitter toward her husband. She explained to me that they could get along all right during the evening, but the moment they went to the bedroom the trouble started. She said, "The second we start for the bedroom he gets an erection. I can undress slowly or rapidly, it makes no difference. He gets into bed with an erection every night. He wakes up in the morning and there it is standing up. It makes me so mad I just find myself quarreling all the time."

I asked her, "What is it you want?"

She said, "If once, just once, he would get into bed and not be able to have an erection automatically. If just once he could let me feel my female power."

This seemed a reasonable request, since every woman has the right to produce an erection and to reduce it. Just being looked at and having an erection happen, or having it happen in relation to the bedroom instead of at her instigation, can be unsatisfactory. So I brought the husband in and pointed out the tremendous importance of this to his wife. I swore him to secrecy about it. He masturbated three times that night, and when he went into the bedroom he really had a flaccid penis. She had a perfectly wonderful time wriggling around and squirming. He was wondering if he could have an erection. What delighted her was that it was just by her movement, never touching him or kissing him, that he got an erection. She really had her female power. Some months later when I visited their city, they took me out to dinner. She's really got female power and is pleased with it, I could see that at the dinner table.

Some women want to enjoy female power, and others find the honeymoon a time when they simply cannot engage in the sexual act. Erickson reports the case of a bride who had been married for a week and was unable to have sexual relations with her husband even though she wished to. She developed a state of extreme panic and locked her legs in the scissors position at every attempt, or offer of an attempt, to consummate the marriage. She went to see Erickson with her husband, haltingly related her story, and said that something had to be done since she was being threatened with an annulment. Her husband confirmed her story and added other descriptive details.

The technique I used was essentially the same as that used in a half dozen similar instances. I asked her if she were willing to have any reasonable procedure employed to correct her problem.

Her answer was, "Yes, anything except that I mustn't be touched, because I go crazy if I'm touched." This statement her husband corroborated.

I instructed her that I would use hypnosis, and she consented hesitantly; again she demanded that no effort be made to touch her.

I told her that her husband would sit continuously in the chair on the other side of the office and that I would sit beside her husband. She, however, was personally to move her chair to the far side of the room, sit down there, and watch her husband continuously. Should either one of us at any time leave our chairs, she was to leave the room immediately, since she was sitting next to the office door.

I asked her to sprawl out in her chair, leaning far back with her legs extended, her feet crossed, and all the muscles fully tensed. She was to look at her husband fixedly until all she could see would be him, with just a view of me out of the corner of her eye. Her arms were to be crossed in front of her, and her fists were to be tightly clenched.

Obediently, she began this task. As she did so, I told her to sleep deeper and deeper, seeing nothing but her husband and me. As she slept more and more deeply, she would become scared and panicky, unable to move or to do anything except to watch us both and to sleep more and more deeply in the trance, in direct proportion to her panic state. This panic state, she was instructed, would deepen her trance, and at the same time hold her rigidly immobile in the chair.

Then gradually, I told her, she would begin to feel her husband touching her intimately, caressingly, even though she would continue to see him still on the other side of the room. I asked if she were willing to experience such sensations, and I said her existing body rigidity would relax just sufficiently to permit her to nod her head or shake her head in reply. I said an honest answer was to be given slowly and thoughtfully.

Slowly she nodded her head affirmatively.

I asked her to note that both her husband and I were turning our heads away from her, because she would now begin to feel a progressively more intimate caressing of her body by her husband, until finally she felt entirely pleased, happy, and relaxed. Approximately five minutes later she said to me, "Please don't look around. I'm so embarrassed. May we go home now, because I'm all right."

She was dismissed from the office, and her husband was instructed to take her home and passively await developments.

Two hours later I received a joint telephone call, and they explained simply, "Everything is all right."

A checkup telephone call a week later disclosed all to be well. Approximately fifteen months later they brought their first-born in with the greatest pride.

Sometimes, although the married couple can perform adequately, something is missing in the sexual act. This was so in the following case.

A college professor came to see me. He had never had an orgasm, he had never had an ejaculation. He looked up the word "ejaculation" in the dictionary. He came to me and asked why the word "ejaculation" was used in relation to male sexual behavior. I asked him, "How long did you wet the bed?" He said, "Until I was eleven or twelve years old."

He said his wife was happily married, they had intercourse, they had two children, so I asked him, "What do you do instead of ejaculating?" He said, "You have intercourse, you enjoy it, and after a while, just as if you were urinating, the semen flows out of your penis."

He had learned that all a penis was good for was peeing, and so he had used his penis maritally to pee into his wife's vagina. He said, "Doesn't every man?" I told him what he ought to do. Every day or every other day, he should reserve an hour for himself. Go into the bathroom and masturbate. In the process of masturbation, I told him, he should identify all the parts of his penis. From the base to the glans, identify all the sensations. He should try not to pee any semen as long as possible to see how excited he could make himself. What little touches and thrills he could add. He should concern himself with the tension, the warmth, the friction, but not the peeing of semen. He should hold off on that. The loss of the semen would mean a loss physiologically of the capacity to go on masturbating.

He thought that was childish and foolish, but he did it regularly for about a month. One night at eleven o'clock he called me up and said, "I did it." I said, "What do you mean?" He said, "Well, instead of masturbating today, I went to bed with my wife and got sexually excited. And I ejaculated. I thought you'd be glad to have me call you and tell you about it." I said, "I'm very happy that you had an ejaculation." At one o'clock he called again; he'd had another.

His wife wanted to know why he called me up to tell me he had intercourse with her. He asked me if he should tell her. I told him it was none of her business. But I later talked to the wife, and I asked her, "Have you enjoyed your marriage?" She said she had. "Has your sex life been good?" She said, "Yes." Then she said, "Ever since my husband called you up in the night to tell you he was making love to me, my sex life with him has been better, but I don't know why."

One of the more common problems of the newly married is an inability to copulate with mutual pleasure because of prudish ideas. Sometimes a brief intervention can shift the relationship so that marriage becomes an opportunity for the young people to enjoy themselves. An example of a procedure of Erickson's illustrates the point.

A bride and groom came to me after less than a month of married life. The bride insisted on seeing me. The groom said his mind was all made up; he was going to get a divorce. He could not tolerate the outrageous behavior of his bride.

He expressed, rather emphatically, an unfavorable opinion of psychiatrists. Finally I said, "Now you've expressed your opinion, and I'm going to speak with equal frankness. You've been married less than a month, and you're talking about a divorce. I don't know what kind of a coward you are, but you ought to see at least one month of your marriage through to the bitter end. So kindly shut up and listen to what your bride has to say to me." He did just that—he folded his arms and set his jaw and listened.

His bride said, "Henry doesn't believe in making love in the right fashion. He wants all the lights off, he wants the curtains drawn, and he wants to undress in the privacy of the bathroom. He won't enter the bedroom unless the lights are completely off. I'm supposed to wear my nighttie and not take it off. All he wants to do is have sex relations in the most simple fashion possible. He won't even kiss me."

I asked him, "Is that right?" and he said, "I believe in having sex relations in the proper manner without getting maudlin over it."

She continued, "He just seems to avoid touching me. He won't kiss my breasts or play with them. He won't even touch them."

The husband responded, "Breasts are utilitarian; they are intended for infants."

I told him that my inclination was to sympathize with his wife, and he probably wouldn't like what I had to say. "Therefore," I said, "you sit there and keep your arms folded and your jaws clenched. Be as angry as you wish, because I'm going to tell your wife some of the things I think she ought to know."

So I told the bride in what fashion I thought her husband ought to kiss her breasts and nurse her nipples. I pointed out *how* he ought to kiss her and *where* he ought to kiss her, and he should enjoy it. As a healthy female, she should enjoy it. Then I pointed out that human beings have an anthropomorphic tendency. They name their guns "Old Betsy," their boats "Stay-Up," and their cabins "Do-Come-In." They have any number of pet names for possessions of various kinds. I said I thought her husband, since he said he loved her, ought to have some pet names for her twins. She looked a little baffled, and I said, "You know they *are* twins," and I indicated her breasts. The twins really ought to have names that rhymed, I said, and I turned to the young man and put the matter to him firmly. I said, "Now tomorrow at your next interview, you will come in with twin names for your wife's breasts. If you don't name them, I will name one of them, and you will be stuck with the name of the other, which will come to your mind immediately." He stalked out of the office.

The next day they came in, and the wife said, "Well, Henry has tried to make love in a much better fashion. He seems to have more understanding, but he says he's never going to name the twins."

I turned to him and said, "Are you going to name the twins? Remember, if you're unwilling to do it, I'll name one with a rhyming name, and you will be stuck with the name of the other." He said, "I'm not going to be undignified about my wife's breasts."

I suggested that he might want to think it over for half an hour while we took up some of the other questions. So we discussed other aspects of their sexual adjustment, as the wife wished.

Finally, at the end of half an hour, I said to him, "Now are you ready with the names for the twins? I'm ready, but I hope you are." He said, "I just defy you." I explained again that I would name one, and the rhyming name would come to his mind immediately. When he again refused, I said to the wife, "Well, are you ready?" She said she was. I said, "I now christen your right breast 'Kitty.' " To the mind of the prudish young man came the rhyming word "titty."

The bride was pleased. They were from out of state, and six months later I got a Christmas card from them. It was signed with their names and "K. and T." The wife wrote me that her husband had turned out to be a pleasing lover and took a great deal of pride and satisfaction in the twins. A couple of years later I visited their town and had dinner with a friend who knew them. He said, "What a pleasant couple they are. I remember how Henry was when they first got married, but he has really become human." Later on I got a card from them and, in addition to "K. and T." there were several other additions to the family. He really learned what a titty was for.

Often in therapy you can use a compulsion in a therapeutic way, which happened in this case. The husband was compulsively avoiding his wife's breasts. I made a compulsive rhyme and he could not escape it. All the compulsion centered on an affectionate name for the breasts instead of an avoidance of them, so his compulsion was just reversed.

Because of the peculiar ability of human beings to be conscious of their acts, behavior that should just happen often becomes a deliberate endeavor, and so the nature of it is changed. A conscious determination to develop an erection, or to have an orgasm, can fall in this category. It is an attempt to produce involuntary behavior by voluntary will, trapping the person in a self-defeating cycle. Sex education is so often offered in a scientific, if not a grim, way that for overeducated people sexual relations can become a technical endeavor. Even the enjoyment of sex can be presented as a duty by well-meaning educators. To force a couple to react sexually in a more human way is worth while as a therapeutic endeavor, and an Erickson procedure illustrates a way of dealing with this problem.

A thirty-year-old university professor attended a university dance and saw a thirty-year-old single woman on the other side of the room. She saw him, and they rapidly gravitated toward each other. Within a month they had planned their future and were married. Three years later they appeared in my office and told their sad story. In telling it, they were extremely prudish and embarrassed, and they used a most stilted and formal wording. In essence, their complaint was that even before marriage they had planned to have a family, and because they were both thirty years old, they felt that there should be no delay of any sort. But after three years they were childless, despite medical examinations and advice. They were both present in the office, and, in telling me their problem, the man said, "In my thinking, and that of my wife, we have reached the conclusion that it is more proper that I give voice to our trouble in common and state it succinctly. Our problem is most distressing and destructive of our marriage. Because of our desire for children we have engaged in the marital union with full physiological concomitants each night and morning for procreative purposes. On Sundays and holidays we have engaged in the marital union with full physiological concomitants for procreative purposes as much as four times a day. We have not permitted physical disability to interfere. As a result of the frustration of our philoprogenitive desires, the marital union has become progressively unpleasant for us, but it has not interfered with our efforts at procreation; but it does distress both of us to discover our increasing impatience with each other. For this reason we are seeking your aid, since other medical aid has failed.

At this point I interrupted and said to the man, "You have stated the problem. I would like to have you remain silent and have your wife state her opinion in her own words." In almost exactly the same pedantic way, and with even greater embarrassment than her husband had shown, the wife voiced their complaint. I said, "I can correct this for you, but it will involve shock therapy. It will not be electric shock or physical shock but it will be a matter of psychological shock. I will leave you alone in the office for fifteen minutes so that the two of you can exchange views and opinions about your willingness to receive a rather severe psychological shock. At the end of fifteen minutes I will come back into the office and ask your decision and abide by it."

I left the office, returned fifteen minutes later, and said, "Give me your answer." The man replied, "We have discussed the matter both objectively and subjectively, and we have reached the conclusion that we will endure anything that might possibly offer satisfaction for our philoprogenitive desires." I asked the wife, "Do you agree fully?" She answered, "I do, sir." I explained that the shock would be psychological, involve their emotions, and be a definite strain upon them. "It will be rather simple to administer, but you will both be exceedingly shocked psychologically. I suggest that as you sit there in your chairs, you reach down under the sides of your chairs and hang tightly to the bottom of the chair and listen well to what I say. After I have said it, and as I am administering the shock, I want the two of you to maintain an absolute silence. Within a few minutes you will be able to leave the office and return to your home. I want the two of you to maintain an absolute silence all the way home, and during that silence you will discover a multitude of thoughts rushing through your minds. Upon reaching home, you will maintain silence until after you have entered the house and closed the door. You will then be free! Now hang tightly to the bottom of your chairs, because I am now going to give you the psychological shock. It is this: For three long years you have engaged in the marital union with full physiological concomitants for procreative purposes at least twice a day and sometimes as much as four times in twenty-four hours, and you have met with defeat of your philoprogenitive desires. Now why in hell don't you fuck for fun and pray to the devil that she isn't knocked up for at least three months. Now please leave."

I learned later that they maintained silence all the way home thinking "many things." When they finally got inside the house with the door shut, according to the husband, "We found we couldn't wait to get to the bedroom. We just dropped to the floor. We didn't engage in the marital union; we had fun. Now the three months are barely up and my wife is pregnant." Nine months later a baby girl was born. When I called on them to see the baby, I learned that formal speech and polysyllabic words and highly proper phrases were no longer necessary in their conversations. They could even tell risqué stories.

The forty-mile drive to the home of the couple in absolute silence made possible, in accord with the suggestions given them, a great variety of much repressed thinking which ran riot in their minds. This resulted in their sexual activity immediately upon closing the door when they reached home. This was what I had hoped. When the couple were questioned about this, they stated that they believed there had been an increasingly greater build-up of erotic thinking the nearer they got to their home, but they said they had no specific memories.

This case history was related in full to an audience of over seventy practicing psychiatrists at Columbia University. Before narrating the case history, I asked the audience if they thought that they could endure listening to some so-called Anglo-Saxon words in relation to a psychiatric problem. The audience were certain they could, and I felt that they could. However, to my astonishment, at the utterance of the key word, the audience actually froze into rigid immobility for a few moments. I noted that my own tone of voice very definitely changed. This was most revealing about the long-continued effects of the learned inhibitions in childhood and their continuance into adult life.

Although with some people Erickson will go out of his way to use shocking words, with others he is equally careful to say something in such a way that the patient only realizes later what he has said. Or he will be extremely cautious with someone who is frightened about discussing something unmentionable. He believes that what is to be done must fit the particular person who comes in and does not attempt to fit all patients into a similar therapeutic mold. He might discuss sex frankly and in a shocking way, as in the previous case, while in another case he might be indirect and let the patient discover that the subject of the discourse is sex. For example:

A married woman came to me reporting a number of fears and a particular anxiety about her hair. She couldn't find a good beauty parlor in town. She'd lie on her right side, on her left side, on her back, and all of these positions meant a difficulty in mussing up her hair. When I wished to talk to her about other things, she would return and talk about her problem with her hair. After she had wasted two hours, I told her, "During this hour you tell me all about your hair and you talk continuously. Because at the end of the hour, I am going to say something that is completely meaningless. I'll listen to what you say, and when you say something that gives me the opportunity to say this meaningless something, I will. As soon as I've said it, I'll open the door and dismiss you."

She talked about her hair, about the wave, the curls, the long wave, the lotions, the shampoos, and so on. At the end of the hour she happened to mention her difficulty in parting her hair. I said, "Look, you mean you would really like your hair parted satisfactorily with a one-tooth comb." I eased her out of the office while she looked at me blankly.

It took her three days to think it over. She told me that all the way home, and the next day, it just didn't make sense at all. "And after three days I began to wonder about my sex life. Then I became more convinced there was a problem there." After that, we got down to work in therapy.

In other cases Erickson will discuss a problem without ever an explicit agreement about the subject discussed. For example, he will talk about the pleasures of eating as a metaphorical way of talking about sex—"Do you like meat rare, or rarely?" He feels that often sexual problems can be resolved without ever being discussed directly. Sometimes, too, if a person is particularly shy and reticent about a problem, he will talk about other matters in such a way that the person finally brings up the unmentionable. For example:

A woman wrote to me that she had a problem she couldn't discuss, and could I do something about it. I suggested I could best help her if she came to see me. She said it would take some months to get up enough courage, but she would do so. Finally she came to see me. She mentioned that she had little self-control. Her sexual relations with her husband were very difficult because of what might happen. Her mother had found it objectionable to take care of her because of an odor. From the emphasis on the word "odor," I knew that her concern was passing flatus. She couldn't really talk about that, so I launched into a discussion of athletic contests. I discussed how it was really something to be able to hit a golf ball three hundred yards. Or to hit a home run over the fence. Swimming a long distance was also really something. Then I mentioned a weight lifter who can pick up two hundred pounds, and I grunted with the effort as I illustrated lifting that weight. She was right there with me in that effort.

Then I told her the body's muscles had the privilege of feeling that they had contracted hard and forcibly and effectively. In the same way, there was a real physical satisfaction in biting down on hard candy. Every child, I pointed out, has learned the absolute delight of swallowing a whole cherry and feeling it go down. She could recognize all those sensations, and she thought it was just a charming dissertation I was giving her. After I mentioned swallowing the cherry, she talked about the things she had swallowed with particular delight. Then I spoke about respecting one's feet by wearing proper shoes, and she agreed one should respect the feet, and the eyes and ears and teeth. I said, "Of course you know that tremendous satisfaction that you have after a good meal when you really feel well stuffed." She was rather plump, and she did like food, one look told you that. I pointed out that the stomach deserves to be pleased, and I inquired whether she didn't think it would be fair and honest to recognize that a rectum could really be pleased by having a good bowel movement. And what should be the consistency of a bowel movement? On a hot day in summer in the desert, you run out of water, and a bowel movement ought to be rather hard and firm because of dehydration. After a cathartic, a bowel movement ought to be rather watery, because the intestine knows what it's doing. The stomach looks at the food it receives and selects what it digests, and the duodenum looks at the food and selects what it can digest, and so on throughout the intestines. And the bowels should look at the cathartic and recognize, "This needs fluid and removal." Then she went to the question "But gas, what is that?" I pointed out that it's a symbiotic thing; the bacteria in the intestinal tract aid in digestion, and they do this by virtue of their own digestion. Therefore there has to be some putrefaction and so a release of gaseous substances. To break down the proteins, you had to get some chemical change. And the rectum should take pleasure in a large firm bowel movement, a large soft one, a long liquid one, or a gaseous one. I also pointed out that there is a time and place for various things. You may eat at the table, but somehow or other—even though it's not against the law —you don't brush your teeth at the table. You don't wash dishes at the table, but in a country kitchen where you have no sink, you put the dishpan on the table and wash right there. It's perfectly all right. But when there's an opportunity, you wash them in the sink. In the same way, there's a good time and place for the function of the bowels. But it must be recognized that the needs of the bowels supersede those of the person. You may be driving a car and need to go someplace, but if you get some sand in your eyes, you'd better stop and tend to the needs of your eyes. Never mind yourself as a person, attend to the needs of your eyes. And one attends to the needs of the various parts of the body and repeats those attentions until one gains the amount of control necessary.

She elaborated on that herself. She went home and cooked herself a big meal of beans. She said later, "You know, it was fun. I spent the entire day making little ones, big ones, loud ones, soft ones." She found that sexual relations weren't interfered with by any concern that she might pass flatus. Now she has a baby.

Although it is "normal" to marry and have children, many people prefer a different way of life and do not marry, or they marry for other purposes. A case illustrates Erickson's way of arranging a marriage of convenience for a couple.

A psychiatric resident in training with me was treating a hospital employee, and he came to me in distress. He said his patient was a homosexual, but he wanted to get married. He asked how to find a girl who would marry him for appearance sake so that he could be part of the community and have a good reputation in the neighborhood.

The resident didn't know it, but I was seeing a girl who worked in the hospital who was a lesbian. She had a similar desire to have a husband for appearance' sake.

I said to the resident, "Suppose you tell your patient to walk along the sidewalk behind the hospital at four o'clock in the afternoon. Tell him that somewhere along the sidewalk he'll meet what he needs."

Then I told the young woman that on the same day at four

o'clock she was to walk behind the hospital in the other direction. I told her she would know what to do.

They were to look out for something on that walk, but they didn't know what. It was just that there was nothing there but each other. In this way nothing was forced upon them. They were free to pass each other if they chose.

The girl was sharper than the man. She came to me and said, "You arranged that, didn't you?" I said, "Yes." She told me, "I knew when I saw him that he was a homosexual, and I frankly told him so. He was so elated. Should I tell him that you know?" I said, "It might be well, in case the two of you want further advice."

They got married and lived respectably. He often went out to a poker club, she often went to a bridge party. After about a year they got a job offer at a hospital in another state. They came to me and asked advice about taking it, and I thought it was a good idea. I knew a physician there, and I wrote to him and said, "Mr. so-and-so and his wife are coming. You will recognize why I'm calling them to your attention. They will need protection and guidance and a cover."

They went to him when they moved, and he told them he'd had a letter from me telling him they were coming, but without saying why. "I think he expected you to tell me why." They sighed with relief—they had the chance to tell him.

They got a four-bedroom home. They often entertained friends. He slept in his bedroom and she in hers, and the other bedrooms were sometimes filled with friends.

Many severe psychiatric problems occur during marriage, and the psychiatry of the past tended to think of the symptom as if it were divorced from the marital context. A problem such as hysterical blindness, for example, was viewed as a response to anxiety and fears in the individual without awareness of the current social context to which the person was adapting. This context was either ignored or considered of secondary importance to the "primary" cause of the symptom, which was the dynamics within the person's intrapsychic life. The more modern view is that symptoms develop as ways of adapting to intolerable situations, and when the situation is resolved, the symptom will have lost its function and disappear. A common intolerable situation arises in a marriage when there are occurrences between the marriage partners that become undiscussable. Although the issue cannot be discussed, it must be dealt with, and a symptom leads to help with the problem. A rather typical case of hysterical blindness demonstrates both Erickson's assumptions about the cause of the difficulty and his way of providing a graceful exit from it.

A mental-hospital employee was referred to me because of a sudden acute blindness that had developed on his way to work. He was led into the office in a frightened state of mind. Hesitantly and fearfully, he told me of having eaten breakfast that morning, and while laughing and joking with his wife, he had suddenly become extremely disturbed by some risqué story she related. He had left the house angrily and decided to walk to work instead of taking the bus as usual. As he rounded a certain street corner, he suddenly became blind. He developed a wild panic, and a friend passing along the highway in a car had picked him up and brought him to the hospital. The ophthalmologist had examined him immediately and referred him to me. The man was much too frightened to give an adequate history. However, he did state that he and his wife had been quarreling a great deal recently; she had been drinking at home, and he had found hidden bottles of liquor. She had vigorously denied drinking.

When I asked what he was thinking about as he left the house, he explained that he was much absorbed in his anger at his wife, feeling that she should not be telling off-color stories. He had a vague feeling of apprehension, believing that he might be heading for the divorce court.

I asked him to trace his steps mentally from his home up to the point of the sudden onset of his blindness. He blocked mentally on this. He was asked to describe that particular street corner, and his reply was that although he had walked around it many, many times, he could not remember anything about it, that his mind was a total blank.

Since the street corner involved was well known to me, I asked various leading questions without eliciting any material from him. Then I asked him to describe exactly how the blindness had developed. He stated that there had occurred a sudden flash of intense redness, as if he were staring directly into a hot, red sun. This redness still persisted. Instead of seeing darkness or blackness, he saw nothing but a brilliant, blinding saturated red color. He was oppressed by a horrible feeling that he would never be able to see anything but an intense glaring red for the rest of his life. With this communication, the patient became so hysterically excited that it was necessary to sedate him and put him to bed.

The patient's wife was summoned to the hospital. With much

difficulty and after many protestations of unfailing love for her husband, she finally confirmed his account of her alcoholism. She refused to relate the story that had precipitated the quarrel, merely stating that it had been a risqué story about a man and a red-headed girl and had really meant nothing.

She was told where her husband had developed his sudden blindness and asked what she knew about the street corner. After much hedging, she recalled that there was a service station on the opposite side of the street. She and her husband often patronized it when buying gas for their car. After still further insistent questioning, she remembered a service-station attendant there who had brilliant red hair. Then finally, after many reassurances, she confessed to an affair with that attendant, who was commonly known as "Red." On several occasions he had made unduly familiar remarks to her in her husband's presence, and they had been intensely resented. After much serious thinking, she declared her intention to break off the affair if I would cure her husband of his blindness, and she demanded professional secrecy for her confidences. Her husband's unconscious awareness of the situation was pointed out to her, and she was told that any further betrayal would depend entirely upon her own actions.

When the patient was seen the next day, he was still unable to give any additional information. Efforts were made to assure him of the temporary nature of his blindness. This reassurance he was most unwilling to accept. He demanded that arrangements be made to send him to a school for the blind. With difficulty he was persuaded to accept therapy on a trial basis, but on the condition that nothing be done about his vision. When he finally consented, hypnosis was suggested as an appropriate, effective therapy for his purposes. He immediately asked if he would know what happened if he were in a trance. He was told that such knowledge could remain only in his unconscious if he so wished, and thus would not occasion him trouble in the waking state.

A deep trance was readily induced, but the patient at first refused to open his eyes or test his vision in any way. However, further explanation of the unconscious mind, amnesia, and posthypnotic suggestions induced him to recover his vision in the trance state. He was shown my bookplate and instructed to memorize it thoroughly. This done, he was to awaken, again blind, and with no conscious knowledge of having seen the bookplate. Nevertheless, he would, upon a posthypnotic cue, describe it adequately to his own bewilderment. As soon as he understood, I awakened him and began a desultory conversation. Upon the posthypnotic signal, he gave a full description of the bookplate. He was tremendously puzzled by this, since he knew he had never seen it. Confirmation of his description by others served to give him a great but mystified confidence in the therapeutic situation.

Following rehypnosis, he expressed complete satisfaction with what had been done and a full willingness to cooperate in every way. Asked if this meant he would confide fully in me, he hesitated, and then determinedly declared that it did.

Inquiry among his fellow workers on the previous day had disclosed that he had a special interest in a red-haired female employee. By gentle degrees, the question of this interest was raised. After some hesitation, he finally gave a full account. Asked what his wife would think of it, he defensively asserted that she was no better than he, and he asked that the matter be kept in confidence.

Immediately, the questioning was shifted to a description of the street corner. He described it slowly and carefully, but he left mention of the gas station to the last. In a fragmentary fashion, he described this, finally mentioning his suspicions about his wife and the red-haired attendant.

I asked if his suspicions began at the time of his own interest in the red-haired girl, and what did he think he wanted to do about the entire situation. He thoughtfully declared that, whatever had happened, both he and his wife were equally guilty, since neither had endeavored to establish a community of interests.

I inquired then what he wanted done about his vision. He expressed fear of recovering it immediately. He asked if this "horrible, bright redness" could be made less glaring, with now and then brief flashes of vision, which would become progressively more frequent and more prolonged until finally there was a full restoration. I assured him that everything would occur as he wished, and a whole series of appropriate suggestions was given.

He was sent home on sick leave but returned daily for hypnosis, accompanied by his wife. These interviews were limited to a reinforcement of the therapeutic suggestions of slow, progressive visual improvement. About a week later he reported that his vision was sufficiently improved to permit a return to work.

Six months later he returned to report that he and his wife had reached an amicable agreement for a divorce. She was leaving for her home state, and he had no immediate plans for the future. His interest in the red-haired girl had vanished. He continued at his work uneventfully for another two years and then sought employment elsewhere.

In some instances, as in this early case, Erickson will resolve a symptom and let the couple work out their marriage on their own. At other times, particularly if they request it, he will intervene and attempt to resolve the marital problems. Sometimes a symptom will appear as a way of avoiding the acknowledgment of an extramarital affair, but often the married couple will come in with an affair as the explicit problem. In the following case, Erickson used one of his many ways of helping a young couple past this difficulty.

A young man brought his wife to me and said, "I'm in love with my wife; I don't want to lose her. She's been having an affair with a friend of mine. I found out about it in a week's time. I love her in spite of the affair. I don't want to lose our two children. I'm sure we can get along, and I'm pretty certain she realizes the folly of her behavior."

I took an hour to verify that the husband was sincere in his point of view. He had forgiven her, and he wanted to keep her. He'd done his own thinking about his marriage and children and had appraised the situation.

So I said to the man, "All right, you go into the next room. Close the door fully. You'll find some books in there to read."

When the wife was alone with me, she said, "I want you to understand that my husband doesn't really know everything. It was more than just a week before he found out."

I said, "You mean there have been more men? How many more?"

She said, "I didn't say that."

"You want me to understand more than your husband understands. How many men?"

She said, "At least two."

I didn't challenge her when she said that, which meant there were at least three. I asked if the man of her first affair was married, and she said he was.

So I said, "Let's be frank and honest and forthright in our discussion. When the first affair broke off, how did the man tell you that he was tired of you as a piece of ass?"

She said, "That's speaking in a very vulgar fashion!"

I said, "Do you want me to speak in the polite terms that he used and avoid the terms he was thinking?"

"He merely said that he guessed he had better return to his wife." Then she added, "The second man called me a piece of ass after three months."

I said, "Now we understand, now we can use polite language."

I talked to her about how her husband thought this affair with the last man had only been in progress a week. Actually, it turned out to be fourteen days. I said, "You mean you decided to let your husband find out about this one, so you're really the one who wants the thing terminated. You must have really been sick of the entire thing to arrange to have your husband discover it so quickly."

When I put it that way, she got all the credit—but she had to live up to the credit. I placed that credit in front of her and shoved her from behind, and she had to support it. But she didn't know I did that. It was just a simple choice of words. She decided to go back to her husband.

Another of Erickson's ways of dealing with an affair is illustrated in the following case.

A young husband, while his wife was visiting in another city, seduced their very homely maid, who was of poor intelligence and had a history of promiscuity. He did it in his wife's bed, and when his wife returned she found out about it and came in to see me, weeping. She could never permit her husband in the house again. She was also in a rage toward the maid.

I saw each of them separately in interviews, and the husband was full of contrition. The maid was equally sorry and also frightened. Then I brought the three of them together in an interview. I maneuvered the conversation so that each had something to say to the other two. The husband had plenty to say to his wife and the maid, because they were both against him. The wife had her objections to make to the husband and the maid. The maid could object to the way husband and wife had treated her. It was a rather dramatic situation, and with all of them there they could really take their feelings out on each other. I demanded that the husband respect his wife's resentment and grief, and I also demanded that she consider how pitifully put upon he must feel. And I let the husband turn on the maid and blame her and let the maid blame him. It was an unlovely situation for everybody, but it salvaged the marriage.

Husband and wife got together and decided to ship that nasty maid to another state, where she had some relatives. I also arranged that the wife force the maid to pack the husband's clothes and carry them out to the front yard so he could go off and live by himself. She threw him out of the house with the maid carrying the suitcases out. Then she had the maid bring them back in, unpack them, and then repack them and carry them out again. In this way I arranged that the wife express pleasure in her power and also arranged that the husband could come back at her bidding. With this arrangement, he could return when she let him, and she decided to let him come back. She told me to notify her husband that he could return. Instead of doing so, I said, "Yes, I can tell him to come back, any third party can tell him to do that, the mailman can tell him." She was tremendously relieved. She wrote the letter to her husband, and the third party, the mailman, delivered it. I didn't wish to be the third party, but I knew there should be one. They got back together with the problem resolved. A couple of years later the maid came back and applied for her job, and they were both righteously indignant.

Like most therapists with a family orientation, Erickson prefers to help a married couple get past a difficulty and remain together. However, if he thinks the marriage has been a mistake, he is likely to agree to a marital breakup. If he evaluates the situation as dangerous, he will actively intervene to encourage a divorce as rapidly as possible.

A couple came from California to see me, and when they sat down together in my office, the man said, "I want you to talk some sense to my bride. We've been married a month, and I have explained very carefully to her that our first child is to be a boy and he is to be named after me. When she asked me what would happen if it was a girl, I told her. I explained that if our first baby isn't a boy, I'm going to shoot her and then shoot the baby."

I looked at the wife, who was frightened, and then I turned back to this angry man and asked him what education he had. He said, "I'm a lawyer. I've got a good practice. And my first child will be a boy. Now talk some sense to her."

He offered this threat as a flat statement in this way, and yet he was an educated man, a practicing lawyer.

I said, "Now will the two of you listen to me. Medically, I don't know of any way to determine the sex of a baby. You have to wait until it's born. The determination of its sex occurs in the first three months of life. After that, there is nothing you can do about the sex. Your wife is a victim of a fifty-fifty chance of having a boy. I don't think she should look forward to a pregnancy that might terminate in nine months with a baby girl and death as her reward. I don't think you should run the risk for nine long months of being a murderer. It just doesn't make sense to me. I'll discuss this with you as many hours as you want to, but I am going to advise your wife to file for a divorce. I think she should go back to California and move to a different town, even take a new name. She should file for a divorce and keep her address a secret. As for you, why don't you go East? Georgia would be a nice place to go. Perhaps you have some friends there. (I picked Georgia out of the air, partly because I had just missed a trip there.) He said, "Oh, yes, I've got some friends in Georgia. I'd like to see them, too." I said, "Well, you go to Georgia directly from here, and I'm sure you can have a pleasant visit there. Your wife will be very glad to get out of the apartment while you're gone."

They came in the next day, which was Sunday, and asked me to go over that discussion again. I did so, and I got an agreement from them that they would do as I advised. She went back to California and later telephoned me from the town she moved to that she was filing for divorce. He telephoned me from Georgia and said he was having a great time with his friends. After the divorce was granted, he called to thank me for my intelligent advice. He said he would think this matter over before he married again; perhaps he was unreasonable. I suggested that in the future he should discuss the entire proposition with any girl *before* a formal engagement.

When the wife telephoned me that the divorce was granted, she said he hadn't contested it. She also told me she had not disclosed her address even to her family. She took his threat seriously, and I think she should have.

With the variety of problems that arrive at the door of a therapist, it is obvious that no one particular method or approach will apply to all situations. It is characteristic of Erickson that his range of responses to problem situations is as wide as the kinds of problems that appear. He can be firm and require certain behavior from a young couple, or he can be amiable and influence them in indirect ways. Most typically, he prefers an approach that "accepts" a person's way of behaving, but in such a way that it can change. If a married couple is fighting, he does not ask them to stop but encourages them to fight. However, he arranges that the fight achieve a resolution of the continuing problem. For example, a couple who always fought with a mother-in-law at the dinner table were required to take her for a ride in the desert and have a fight. To fight in a different setting, and because they have to, shifts the nature of the quarrel and makes it more difficult to continue.

Sometimes Erickson will arrange a fight so that a symptom is no longer used as part of the struggle and so disappears. In the following case, a man suffered from a fear that he would die of a heart attack at any moment, and yet any number of doctors had assured him that there was nothing wrong with his heart. In such a case, the wife does not know how to deal with her husband. She is exasperated by his helplessness and his fear, but also uncertain, since he might have a real heart problem. Usually she oscillates in the way she deals with him, and he in turn dominates whatever happens in the household, since everything is determined by the state of his fears about his heart. Most typically in such a situation, when the husband improves the wife becomes depressed. As she starts to become depressed, he activates his heart fear again, and she responds with helpfulness and also exasperation. In crisis the woman feels useful and has a purpose, but when her husband is well she feels she has lost that usefulness. So it is a contract between them that requires the perpetuation of the fear about the heart. Treating the man alone for the problem can often continue for years without effect.

In such a case, my tendency is to introduce what you could call a vengeful anger. I see both husband and wife, and I usually learn the wife is quite angry. Her husband has dominated her life with his threats of a heart attack, and he moans and groans helplessly. The wife's life is miserable, and so she is motivated once she is sure there is nothing wrong with her husband's heart.

I arranged with such a wife that each time her husband complained of his fear of dying of a heart attack, she be prepared. What she did was obtain advertising material from every mortician in town. She had folders on types of funerals, advertisements for perpetual care, and so on. When her husband mentioned his fear of a heart attack, she would say, "I must pick up the room and arrange it neatly." Then she would distribute the advertisements of the morticians. Her husband would irately throw them away, but she had others she could scatter around the house. He reached the point where he didn't dare mention his heart fear, and it went away. That's introducing vengeful behavior—you're hurting me, and what's sauce for the goose is sauce for the gander. At times she would vary her procedure by adding up his insurance policies.

Approaching it this way forces the husband to deal with his wife without the symptom. She is also forced to deal with him.

differently, and then it is a matter of working on the real issues in the marriage.

In Erickson's approach, there is always an emphasis upon the presenting problem that brings someone into therapy. When a symptom is what the person seeks to recover from, Erickson works directly on the symptom, and through it he makes whatever changes in relationships are necessary. He argues that the symptomatic area is the most important and intense to the person with a problem, and therefore it is in this area that the therapist has the greatest leverage for change. If one member of a married couple presents a symptom, working through that can change the marriage.*

Erickson often considers the problem of early marriage to be resolved when the couple has overcome the presenting symptom and has produced a child. At that point a married couple enters a new phase of development with new problems requiring new solutions.

Sometimes the transition to the stage of having children is held up because the wife or husband is fearful that he or she will not be an adequate parent. Erickson might deal with such a situation by providing the person with a different childhood history, as in the following case. He reports:

In 1943 the wife of one of my medical students approached me, stating, "I have a very difficult problem confronting me and my husband. We are very much in love, and he is in the military service studying medicine and will graduate in 1945. We hope by then that the war will be over. After he completes his service, we hope to have a family, but I am afraid about that. My husband has siblings and comes from a well-adjusted family. I'm an only child. My father is very rich and has offices in Chicago, New York, and Miami. He comes home now and then to visit me.

"My mother is a socialite. She is always attending social affairs in New York or London or Paris or Italy. I grew up under the care of various governesses. They took care of me from the very beginning because my mother could not have her child interfere with her

---

* Occasionally, one finds a case in which both marital partners have the same symptom. A classic case of Erickson's was one of a husband and wife who were both lifelong bedwetters, and he treated the problem by having them both deliberately and simultaneously wet the bed. See Haley, *Changing Families* (New York: Grune & Stratton, 1971), pp. 65–68.

social life. Besides, she insisted that a governess could handle a child much better than she could because governesses were trained. I did not see my mother very often. Before I went to school, whenever my mother came home she would have a big party and I would be trotted out to display my good manners and to recite nursery rhymes for the approval of my mother's guests, and then I would be hurried off the scene. Mother always brought me presents, sometimes a beautiful doll that had to be kept on display on a shelf somewhere, but she never brought me anything that I could really play with. I was just a display object for my mother when she happened to be home. My father was different. When he came home, he tried to make it at times when he could give me a good time. He took me to the circus, to the state and county fairs, to Christmas parties, and he often was home long enough to take me out to dinner at various restaurants, where he let me order anything that struck my fancy. I really loved my father, but his goodness to me made me lonesome for him. As soon as I was old enough, I was sent to boarding schools, and in the summer I was sent to the proper summer camp. Everything was so proper. I was finally sent to a finishing school, where I learned how to toss the conversational ball and say all the right things. The finishing school allowed the class I was in to attend a junior prom at a college. That is where I met my husband. We corresponded and managed to see each other with more and more frequency, and finally my father agreed to our marriage, but my mother looked up my husband's pedigree before she consented to the marriage. She planned a very elaborate wedding and was outraged when my husband and I eloped. I knew I couldn't stand the kind of social affair that my mother would make out of the wedding. She punished me for the elopement by taking off for Paris. My father said, 'Bully for you, kids.' He never really approved of my mother's high-society life. My problem now is that I am very afraid to have children. My childhood was so miserable, and I was so lonely, and my governesses had nobody around to make them discharge their duties properly, and they considered me a pain in the neck. I had no playmates, and I am very much afraid of what I will do to my children. I really don't know anything good about childhood, and I want children, so does my husband, and we both want them happy. My husband has sent me to you to see if you can hypnotize me and allay my fears."

I thought this problem over for several days and then undertook to use hypnosis in a manner I thought would be helpful. The procedure I developed was, first, to test the young woman for her competence as a hypnotic subject. She proved to be a somnambulistic subject and very responsive to all manner of suggestions. In accord with the discovery of her competency as a subject, she was hypnotized and regressed to the age of "somewhere around four or five years." She was given the instruction that upon regression to that age she would come "downstairs to the parlor," where she would "see a strange man" who would talk to her.

She regressed in a satisfactory fashion and looked at me with the open-eyed wonder of a child and asked, "Who are you?" I answered, "I am the February Man. I am a friend of your father's. I am waiting here for him to come home, because I have some business with him. While I am waiting, would you be willing to talk to me?" She accepted the invitation and told me that her birthday was in February. She said her father would probably send her some nice presents or maybe bring them. She talked quite freely at the level of a four- or five-year-old girl who was rather lonesome, and she manifested a definite liking for the "February Man."

After about a half hour visit, I said that her father was arriving and that I would see him first while she went upstairs. After I had left, she should be sure to come down and visit her father. She asked if the February Man would return, and I assured her that he would, and I added that I didn't think he could come until June. However, the February Man appeared in April, in June, and a little before Thanksgiving and Christmas. Between each of these appearances of the February Man, the patient was awakened, and casual waking-state conversations were held.

This therapy continued over a period of several months, sometimes twice a week. She had spontaneous amnesia for the trance events, but in the regressive hypnotic states she was allowed to remember previous visits with the February Man. In the original interview with the patient, I had taken care to make certain of important dates in her life so that the February Man would never accidentally intrude upon some important memory. As therapy continued with her, she was regressed from year to year and there were longer and longer intervals between the February Man's visits, so when she reached the age of fourteen it was possible to meet by "accident" in actual places where she had been at various times in her life. This was frequently done by appearing just a few days before some real memory in her life. As she approached her late teens, she continued her visits with the February Man, evincing definite pleasure in seeing him again and again and talking about teen-age interests.

As I came to learn more about her, I was able, when some new childhood memory was discovered, to regress her back to that age and appear a few days before some really important event of her life and join in her anticipation of it. Or perhaps I would join her a few days later and reminisce.

With this method, it was possible to interject into her memories a feeling of being accepted and a feeling of sharing with a real person many things in her life. She would ask the February Man how soon she would next see him, and when she requested presents, things were offered that were very transient in character. Thus she was given the feeling that she had just eaten some candy or that she had just been walking with the February Man past a flower garden. By doing all these various things, I felt that I was successfully extrapolating into her memories of the past the feelings of an emotionally satisfying childhood.

As this therapy continued, the patient in the ordinary waking state began showing less and less concern about her possible inadequacy as a mother. She repeatedly asked what I was doing with her in the trance state to give her a feeling of confidence that she would know how to share things properly with children of any age. She was always told, in the waking state and also in the trance state, not to remember consciously anything that had occurred in the trance state so far as its verbal meaning was concerned. But she was to keep the emotional values, to enjoy them, and, eventually, to share them with any possible children she might have. Many years later I learned that she had three children and was enjoying their growth and development.

VI
CHILDBIRTH AND DEALING WITH THE YOUNG

The arrival of a child creates mothers, fathers, grandparents, uncles, and aunts and produces repercussions throughout a family system. The child can be a welcome addition or a difficulty, and he can cement a marriage or dissolve one. Usually whatever uncertainties there are about the permanency of a marriage are forced to attention with the arrival of a baby. A new form of commitment is required with the responsibilities of raising a child. Marital contracts also change. The woman who chose a husband she could easily dominate often feels vulnerable at the time of motherhood and wishes for a man who can take care of her. Such husbands are often surprised by new demands from their wives. Mothers-in-law who have been excluded reappear as grandmothers, with new consequences to the married couple. When some type of emotional problems appears, the context is the changing family network.

Often with the arrival of a new baby, it is the mother who begins to manifest symptoms. She becomes depressed, acts strangely, is diagnosed a post-partum psychotic, or behaves in some way that causes concern about her state. When the mother, rather than the total family situation, is focused upon, it is usual to send her to a mental hospital if her upset is extreme. This approach has been considered conservative treatment for the protection of the mother and the child. While incarcerated there, she is helped to understand what is distressing her about becoming a mother. From a family view, hospitalization is a radical intervention in a family, which has unfortunate consequences.

What can be overlooked is the effect of hospitalization in the total family context. Obvious problems can be ignored, such as the question of who is to take care of the new baby while the mother is in a mental hospital. Usually the baby is absorbed into some section of the family; often the husband takes the baby to his family, where it is cared for by his mother. The child is integrated into that family system while the child's mother is isolated from the family. When the mother returns from her psychiatric retreat, she finds that her child is part of another family. It is not uncommon for a mother to have to fight to get back her own child; or she might watch helplessly while it is taken care of by others. When the mother is rehospitalized, it is considered a worsening of her problems around motherhood. It is not noticed that she is rehospitalized when she becomes angry and insists on taking care of her own child, or when she behaves with exasperating helplessness in response to the distrust of her relatives. In such cases the husband is caught between his wife, who had been labeled by experts as mentally ill, and his mother, who has become attached to the new baby. He becomes uncertain what to do when his mother voices the justifiable complaint that she doesn't want her grandchild to be taken care of by a former mental patient. The stigma of mental hospitalization can set the marriage on a deviant course and the treatment compound the problem it is supposed to resolve.

A case can be cited to illustrate the difficulties, as well as the mystery, of a crisis at the time of childbirth.

A woman in her early twenties gave birth to her first child and became extremely upset. She wept and protested that she was worthless and was unable to take care of her new baby. When it was time to leave the hospital, she was still upset, apathetic, and constantly weeping. Her husband took her and the new baby to the home of his family rather than to their own house. While living with his family, the wife began treatment with a local psychiatrist. After a few weeks of unrewarding interviews, she was placed in a mental hospital for a period of observation. According to the referral report, "This was primarily precipitated by her taking ten, or twelve empirin tablets one morning, which gave considerable alarm to her husband and his parents, with whom they continued to live. It was hoped that she and her husband would be able to go to their own home following her return from the hospital, but this was not feasible." After two weeks in the hospital, she showed some improvement, which was "found to be rather an artificial thing which was used to gain the point of getting out of the hospital."

She began individual therapy several times a week, which included several house calls because "of her alleged inability to come to the office." In the interviews she would weep and point out that she was a failure. After four months of unrewarding treatment, the psychiatrist sought another means of dealing with her. He referred her for consultation to two other psychiatrists. One diagnosed her case as a "schizo affective disorder in a rather immature individual," and felt shock treatment might be appropriate since she was not moving in therapy. The other psychiatrist considered her to have a "hysterical character structure with evidence of obsessive compulsive elements," but felt there was a "minimum of psychotic factors." She was also referred to a psychologist for a Rorschach test, and he felt there was "an absence of psychotic features." She gave only three responses to ten cards.

After these consultations, the psychiatrist referred her to me for hypnosis to see if symptom relief could be obtained, or at least a clarification of what was behind her malady, while she continued in individual therapy.

When the wife was interviewed, it was evident that she would be an extremely difficult hypnotic subject. Therefore the use of hypnosis was abandoned (I later learned that on the way to the session she had said to her husband, "No one is going to hypnotize me!").

Since the woman would do nothing but weep, I brought her husband into the session and interviewed the couple together. In this way the wife was encouraged to weep less and to say more— she had to speak to correct what her husband said about her condition.

The husband was a pleasant young man who worked for his father and was bewildered by the state of his wife. He pointed out that even though she said she was incapable of taking care of the baby, she actually could bathe and feed the baby quite competently. The wife interrupted to point out that she could not, and that was why his mother did everything for the baby. She also managed to say that she didn't feel the child was really hers since she wasn't taking care of it. When her husband came home from work, he didn't come to talk to her about their child, he went to his mother and they discussed the baby's activities that day. It was all because she was so worthless and inadequate, she said, with a fresh burst of weeping.

It is possible to see this problem from different vantage points. If only the wife is considered, it would be assumed that because of her past life, motherhood had some special meaning for her that precipitated anxiety and distress when she delivered her child. The treatment would be to help her understand what childbirth meant to her and relate the present situation to her past and her unconscious ideas.

If the view is widened, the husband can be included in the portrait. He was an amiable young man who appeared reluctant to leave his original family and take on adult responsibilities. He worked for his father, and he seemed unable to oppose his mother and support his wife when an issue came up. By becoming incapacitated, the wife had forced her husband to take more responsibility in the marriage. He had responded by turning the responsibility over to his family.

In the larger family context, the young couple was living in an abnormal situation. Their own home was empty, and the mother-in-law was functioning as the mother of the child instead of as the grandmother. The actual mother was becoming more and more isolated from her husband and the family circle, while the husband was returning to his previous role of an unseparated son.

From this wider view, the treatment goal was obvious; the young couple should be in their own home with the mother taking care of her child as normal mothers do. Even if she could not take care of the child, a paid helper would be more appropriate than a relative. An employee can be fired when the mother improves, but a relative is less easy to dislodge.

To resolve the difficulty, a simple procedure based upon Erickson's style of therapy was initiated. Since the wife was defining herself as the helpless one in the situation, the conversation was conducted largely with her husband, while she participated with comments when she objected. The conversation focused upon their future plans, and the husband said that they hoped ultimately to return to their own home. The wife tearfully agreed. When asked, the husband said that he could always take off a couple of weeks from work to help his wife adjust to taking care of the baby when they moved back into their own home. Since the premise was established that they were going to move, the only question was when. Rather abruptly, the husband was asked, "Would it be too soon to move back to your own home this Wednesday?" That was two days later. The husband responded, rather indecisively but agreeably, that he supposed it was possible. The wife stopped weeping and protested that two days wasn't enough time; the house had been closed for months and would have to be cleaned. When asked, the husband agreed that he could take off from work the following day, and in two full days the two of them could have the house ready by Wednesday. The wife became angry and said they could not; the baby's room needed painting, and there was just too much to be done. I told her that they could move in by Wednesday. She stubbornly said they could not. She was told they could. She said angrily that they could not possibly move in before Saturday. A compromise was reached, and they agreed to Thursday, with the wife pleased that she had made her point that Wednesday was too soon. The next three days the wife was so busy cleaning, shopping, and fixing up her home that she did not have time to reflect on the move. The in-laws faced an accomplished fact and could only help in the move.

Instead of taking two weeks off from work to stay with his wife, the husband was back at work within a week. The young mother spent a few days weeping, but she took good care of the child. Within two weeks she had not only stopped weeping but expressed full confidence in her ability as a mother and behaved appropriately. She discontinued psychiatric treatment in an amiable way.

A treatment procedure of this kind raises questions about whether anything has really been solved, even if the mother now seemed normal. What was behind the symptom, and what of the future? The woman continued to be normal, and the baby developed into a happy, healthy child (as it was even during the mother's period of distress). What was "behind" the symptom was never known.

This case illustrates sharply that treatment can go surprisingly quickly if one adopts Erickson's premise that the long-term goal of treatment should be the immediate goal. If the ultimate "cure" is defined as the woman taking care of her own child in her own house with a husband willing to take responsibility, then the treatment should proceed immediately to achieve that end. The goal cannot be achieved as long as the living situation is inappropriate; the problem is to bring about a more normal context of living. To change the social context, one does not necessarily have to treat everyone in a family by bringing all members together, as some proponents of family therapy would suggest. Often intervention through one individual can change the situation, or, as in this case, a couple can shift to a situation of normality, which for this couple was functioning properly in the child-bearing stage; what they needed was assistance to help them through whatever crisis was preventing their transition to that stage.

As a young couple successfully deliver children, they spend a period of years taking care of small children and learning the complex task of becoming parents. Although problems can occur, the most common crisis period is when children reach school age and become more involved with the community. At this time children and parents begin their first steps toward disengagement from each other.

If a child develops problems at this time, it is often because the social behavior that was adaptive within the home is not appropriate for his beginning activities outside. A common problem is the inability of the child to go to school. When this occurs, the problem can be in the home, at the school, or at the interface of home and school. Usually the difficulty is within the family at this stage, but this does not mean that for every child problem the whole family should be put in treatment; however, it does mean that a therapist must be aware of the family context when he intervenes with treatment.

Erickson has developed a variety of procedures for treating children's problems. At times he will bring the parents into treatment, at other times he will merely ask for their cooperation in a certain way, while in many cases he will block the parents out of the treatment and essentially form a coalition with the child against both parents and the wider world.

The crucial importance of "play" in all of Erickson's therapy becomes most evident in his work with children, but it is not play therapy in the usual sense of the term. As with adults, his goal is not to help a child discover how he feels about his parents or what things mean to him but to induce a change; a "play" framework is one way of bringing that change about. Dr. Erickson also uses hypnosis with children, but it should be made clear that it is not the usual kind of hypnosis. He does not use a formal induction of trance but responds to the child on the child's terms and considers this a part of hypnotic technique. An example of this technique is the way he dealt with an accident to his own child. (He often cites incidents involving his own children to illustrate his points.)

> Three-year-old Robert fell down the back stairs, split his lip, and knocked an upper tooth back into the maxilla. He was bleeding profusely and screaming loudly with pain and fright. His mother and I went to his aid. A single glance at him lying on the ground screaming, his mouth bleeding profusely and blood spattered on the pavement, revealed that this was an emergency requiring prompt and adequate measures.

> No effort was made to pick him up. Instead, as he paused for breath for fresh screaming, I told him quickly, simply, sympathetically and emphatically, "That hurts awful, Robert. That hurts terrible."

> Right then, without any doubt, my son knew that I knew what I was talking about. He could agree with me and he knew that I was agreeing completely with him. Therefore he could listen respectfully to me, because I had demonstrated that I understood the situation fully. In pediatric hypnotherapy, there is no more im-

portant problem than so speaking to the patient that he can agree with you and respect your intelligent grasp of the situation as he judges it in terms of his own understandings.

Then I told Robert, "And it will keep right on hurting." In this simple statement, I named his own fear, confirmed his own judgment of the situation, demonstrated my good intelligent grasp of the entire matter and my entire agreement with him, since right then he could foresee only a lifetime of anguish and pain for himself.

The next step for him and for me was to declare, as he took another breath, "And you really wish it would stop hurting." Again, we were in full agreement and he was ratified and even encouraged in this wish. And it was *his* wish, deriving entirely from within him and constituting his own urgent need. With the situation so defined, I could then offer a suggestion with some certainty of its acceptance. This suggestion was, "Maybe it will stop hurting in a little while, in just a minute or two." This was a suggestion in full accord with his own needs and wishes, and, because it was qualified by a "maybe it will," it was not in contradiction to his own understandings of the situation. Thus he could accept the idea and initiate his responses to it.

As he did this, a shift was made to another important matter, important to him as a suffering person, and important in the total psychological significance of the entire occurrence—a shift that in itself was important as a primary measure in changing and altering the situation.

Too often in hypnotherapy, or any utilization of hypnosis, there is a tendency to overemphasize the obvious and to reaffirm unnecessarily already accepted suggestions, *instead of creating an expectancy situation permitting the development of desired responses.* Every pugilist knows the disadvantage of overtraining; every salesman knows the folly of overselling. The same human hazards exist in the application of hypnotic techniques.

The next procedure with Robert was a recognition of the meaning of the injury to Robert himself—pain, loss of blood, body damage, a loss of the wholeness of his normal narcissistic self-esteem, of his sense of physical goodness so vital in human living.

Robert knew that he hurt, that he was a damaged person; he could see his blood upon the pavement, taste it in his mouth, and see it on his hands. And yet, like all other human beings, he too could desire narcissistic distinction in his misfortune, along with the desire even more for narcissistic comfort. Nobody wants a picayune headache; if a headache must be endured, let it be so colossal that only the sufferer could endure it. Human pride is so curiously good and comforting! Therefore Robert's attention was doubly directed to two vital issues of comprehensible importance to him by the simple statements, "That's an awful lot of blood on the pavement. Is it good, red, strong blood? Look carefully, Mother, and see. I think it is, but I want you to be sure."

Thus there was an open and unafraid recognition in another way of values important to Robert. He needed to know that his misfortune was catastrophic in the eyes of others as well as his own, and he needed tangible proof that he himself could appreciate. By my declaring it to be "an awful lot of blood," Robert could again recognize the intelligent and competent appraisal of the situation in accord with his own actually unformulated, but nevertheless real, needs. The question about the goodness, redness, and strongness of the blood came into play psychologically in meeting the personal meaningfulness of the accident to Robert. In a situation where one feels seriously damaged, there is an overwhelming need for a compensatory feeling of satisfying goodness. Accordingly, his mother and I examined the blood upon the pavement, and we both expressed the opinion that it was good, red, strong blood. In this way we reassured him, but not on an emotionally comforting basis only; we did so upon the basis of an instructional, to him, examination of reality.

However, we qualified that favorable opinion by stating that it would be better if we were to examine the blood by looking at it against the white background of the bathroom sink. By this time Robert had ceased crying, and his pain and fright were no longer dominant factors. Instead, he was interested and absorbed in the important problem of the quality of his blood.

His mother picked him up and carried him to the bathroom, where water was poured over his face to see if the blood "mixed properly with water" and gave it a "proper pink color." Then the redness was carefully checked and reconfirmed, following which the "pinkness" was reconfirmed by washing him adequately, to Robert's intense satisfaction, since his blood was good, red, and strong and made water rightly pink.

Then came the question of whether or not his mouth was "bleeding right" and "swelling right." Close inspection, to Robert's complete satisfaction and relief, again disclosed that all developments were good and right and indicative of his essential and pleasing soundness in every way.

Next came the question of suturing his lip. Since this could easily evoke a negative response, it was broached in a negative fashion to him, *thereby precluding an initial negation by him*, and at the same time raising a new and important issue. This was done by stating regretfully that, while he would have to have stitches taken in his lip, it was most doubtful if he could have as many stitches as he could count. In fact, it looked as if he could not even have ten stitches, and he could count to twenty. Regret was expressed that he could not have seventeen stitches, like his sister, Betty Alice, or twelve, like his brother, Allan; but comfort was offered in the statement that he would have more stitches than his siblings Bert, Lance, or Carol. Thus the entire situation became transformed into one in which he could share with his older siblings a common experience with a comforting sense of equality and even superiority. In this way he was enabled to face the question of surgery without fear or anxiety, but with hope of high accomplishment in cooperation with the surgeon and imbued with the desire to do well the task assigned him, namely, to "be sure to count the stitches." In this manner, no reassurances were needed, nor was there any need to offer further suggestions regarding freedom from pain.

Only seven stitches were required, to Robert's disappointment, but the surgeon pointed out that the suture material was of a newer and better kind than any that his siblings had ever had, and that the scar would be an unusual "W" shape, like the letter of his Daddy's college. Thus the *fewness* of the stitches was well compensated.

The question may well be asked at what point hypnosis was employed. Actually, hypnosis began with the first statement to him and became apparent when he gave his full and undivided, interested and pleased attention to each of the succeeding events that constituted the medical handling of his problem.

At no time was he given a false statement, nor was he forcibly reassured in a manner contradictory to his understandings. A community of understanding was first established with him and then, one by one, items of vital interest to him in his situation were thoughtfully considered and decided, either to his satisfaction or sufficiently agreeable to merit his acceptance. His role in the entire situation was that of an interested participant, and adequate response was made to each idea suggested.

This example is so typical of the way Erickson works that it is a vignette of his approach to children or adults. He first accepts completely the patient's position, in this case by saying, "That hurts awful, Robert. That hurts terrible." Next he makes a statement that is the opposite of reassurance. He says, "And it will keep right on hurting." Many people might consider this a negative reinforcement, or a suggestion to continue in distress. To Erickson it is a way of getting together with the patient in a type of relationship that makes change possible, which is his goal. Once he has done this, he can offer a move for change by saying, "Maybe it will stop hurting in a little while, in just a minute or two."

Those who are concerned about "manipulating" people rather than behaving "straightforwardly and honestly" should read this description with some care. As Erickson points out, at no time was the boy given a false statement. It would be far less straightforward and honest to reassure the boy by telling him it didn't hurt, to try to minimize what had happened, or in other ways to dismiss the boy's experience of the situation.

When Erickson calls this a use of hypnosis, it is clear that what he means by hypnosis is not what other people mean. To Erickson, hypnosis is the way two people respond to each other. A deep trance is a type of relationship between two people. Seen in this way, hypnosis does not require a set of repetitive commands, or fixation of the eyes on a device, or any other of the many traditional procedures of hypnosis. In fact, Erickson often prefers to induce a deep trance either by conversation or by a sudden act that precipitates a hypnotic response. An example of a rapid trance induction, totally without ritual, is given in the following case.

An eight-year-old boy was half carried, half dragged into my office by his parents. His problem was wetting the bed. His parents had sought the aid of neighbors and prayed publicly for him in church. They now brought him to the "crazy doctor" as a last resort, with the promise of a "hotel dinner" following the interview.

The boy's anger and resentment were clearly apparent. I said to him, in the presence of his parents, "You're mad and you're going to keep right on being mad. You think there isn't a thing you can do about it, but there is. You don't like to see a 'crazy doctor' but you're here, and you would like to do something but you don't know what. Your parents brought you here, they made you come. Well, you can make them get out of the office. In fact, we both can— come on, let's tell them to go on out." At this point I gave the parents an unobtrusive dismissal signal, and they went out, to the boy's immediate, almost startled, satisfaction.

Then I said, "But you're still mad, and so am I, because they ordered me to cure your bedwetting. But they can't give me orders like they give you. But before we fix them for that," I said, and I *made a slow, elaborate, attention-compelling gesture as I pointed*, "Look at those puppies right there. I like the brown one best, but I suppose you like the black-and-white one, because its front paws are white. If you are very careful, you can pet mine, too. I like puppies, don't you?"

The child, completely taken by surprise, readily developed a somnambulistic trance. He walked over (to the empty floor) and went through the motions of petting two puppies, one more than the other. When he finally looked up at me, I said, "I'm glad you're not mad at me any more, and I don't think that you or I have to tell your parents anything. In fact, maybe it would serve them right for the way they brought you here if you waited until the school year was almost over. But one thing is certain; you can just bet that after you've had a dry bed for a month, you will get a puppy just about like little Spotty there, even if you never say a word to them about it. They've just got to. Now close your eyes, take a deep breath, sleep deeply, and wake up awful hungry."

The child did as he was instructed, and I dismissed him in the care of his parents, who had been given instructions privately. Two weeks later he was used as a demonstration subject for a group of physicians, but no therapy was done.

During the last month of the school year, the boy each morning dramatically crossed off the current calendar day. Toward the last few days of the month, he remarked cryptically to his mother, "You better get ready."

On the thirty-first day his mother told him there was a surprise for him. He said, "It better be black-and-white." At that moment his father come in with a puppy. In the boy's excited pleasure, he forgot to ask questions. Eighteen months later his bed was still continuously dry.

In this case, as in many others, Erickson's induction of trance can appear rather like a sudden and miraculous response. However, it should be kept in mind that the suggestion to hallucinate the puppies was not an isolated statement but had been carefully prepared for by the previous interchange. This interchange included getting together with the boy against the parents, dropping a series of suggestions, and miraculously banishing the parents from the room. The surprise move of pointing to the puppies was the last of several in the interchange which led up to it but which appear unrelated. As in most of Erickson's maneuvers, he elaborately lays the groundwork for what he later does. This ground-work has built into it a number of different possibilities so that he can choose among them when the opportunity arises. He refers to this as "seeding" ideas, so that after a period of uncertainty, when he decides to move in a particular direction, the basis for the move has been arranged.

Erickson describes another case as an example of hypnotic technique. Again this involves no formal induction of hypnosis. A sixteen-year-old high-school girl sucked her thumb, to the exaspera-tion of her parents, her teachers, her schoolmates, the school bus driver, and everyone who came in contact with her. She too was prayed for publicly in church and was required to wear a sign declaring her a thumbsucker, and finally in desperation she was taken to Erickson, even though seeing a psychiatrist was a shame-ful last resort.

Erickson talked to the parents and learned something about the family situation. He also learned that the school psychologist had interpreted to the girl that her thumbsucking was an aggressive act. The parents requested that the therapy of their daughter be primarily based upon a religious approach. Declining this, Erickson made them promise that after the girl became his patient, "for a whole month neither parent would interfere with therapy, no matter what happened, nor would a single word or look of admoni-tion about the thumbsucking be offered." He describes his pro-cedure:

The girl came unwillingly to the office with her parents. She was nursing her thumb noisily. I dismissed her parents and turned to face the girl. She removed her thumb sufficiently to declare she didn't like "nut doctors."

I replied, "And I don't like the way your parents ordered me to cure your thumbsucking. Ordering me, huh! It's your thumb and your mouth, and why in hell can't you suck it if you want to? Ordering me to cure you! The only thing I'm interested in is why, when you want to be aggressive about thumbsucking, you don't really get aggressive instead of piddling around like a baby that doesn't know how to suck a thumb aggressively. What I'd like to do is tell you how to suck your thumb aggressively enough to irk the hell out of your old man and your old lady. If you're interested, I'll tell you. If you aren't, I'll just laugh at you."

The use of the word "hell" arrested her attention completely—

she knew that a professional man ought not to use that kind of language to a high-school girl who attended church regularly. Challenging the inadequacy of her aggressiveness, a term the school psychologist had taught her, commanded her attention still more.

The offer to teach her how to irk her parents, referred to so disrespectfully, elicited even more complete fixation of her attention, so that to all intents and purposes she was in a hypnotic trance. Then in an intent tone of voice, I said, "Every night after dinner, just like a clock, your father goes into the living room and reads the newspaper from the front page to the back. Each night when he does that, go in there, sit down beside him, really nurse your thumb good and loud, and irk the hell out of him for the longest twenty minutes he has ever experienced.

"Then go in the sewing room, where your mother sews for one hour every night before she washes dishes. Sit down beside her and nurse your thumb good and loud and irk the hell out of the old lady for the longest twenty minutes she ever knew.

"Do this every night and do it up good. And on the way to school, figure out carefully just which crummy jerk you dislike most, and every time you meet him, pop your thumb in your mouth and watch him turn his head away. And be ready to pop your thumb back if he turns to look again.

"And think over all your teachers and pick out the one you really dislike and treat that teacher to a thumb pop every time he or she looks at you. I just hope you can be really aggressive."

After some desultory irrelevant remarks, the girl was dismissed and her parents were summoned into the office. They were reminded of the absoluteness of their promise. I said that if they kept their promise faithfully, the girl's thumbsucking would cease.

On the way home the girl did not suck her thumb and she was silent the entire trip. The parents were so pleased that they telephoned to report their gratification. That evening, to her parents' horror, the girl obeyed instructions. The parents also obeyed the instructions not to oppose the thumbsucking. They reported unhappily by telephone the next day. I reminded them of their promise and of my statement about the girl's prognosis.

Each night for the next few evenings the girl was faithful in her performance. Then it began to pall on her. She began to shorten the time, then she began late and quit early, then finally she skipped, and then she forgot!

In less than four weeks the girl had discontinued her thumbsucking, both at home and elsewhere. She became increasingly interested in much more legitimate teen-age activities of her own group. Her adjustments improved in all regards.

The girl was seen again in a social setting about a year later. She recognized me, viewed me thoughtfully for a few minutes, and then remarked, "I don't know whether I like you or not, but I am grateful to you."

There are several remarkable aspects of this case when it is compared with past treatment procedures. A lifelong habit was resolved in a single therapeutic session, which is remarkable enough, but it is even more remarkable that Erickson is so sure of this approach that he can flatly tell the parents that the child will be over the problem in a month. However, he also provides a way out for himself by requiring an activity on their part—their refusal to be provoked and to admonish the girl about her thumbsucking. If they do not carry it out properly, he cannot guarantee the result. Thus both the girl and her parents are forced to behave differently; the girl is forced to deliberately create her own distress, and the parents are forced to tolerate her provocations. As in most such instances, Erickson makes no interpretations about the symptom, he requires that the symptomatic behavior be done deliberately, and he has what is already being done carried to absurd lengths.

In similar cases of thumbsucking, Erickson has presented to the child the notion that the thumb alone is not enough and that he should sit by his parents and suck not only the thumb but each finger as well. Often he has him watch the clock and requires him to suck the thumb and fingers for a set length of time. Transformed into a duty, the thumbsucking loses its appeal. An important part of this procedure is the involvement of the parents in the program, either willingly, as in this case, when they made a promise, or unwillingly, when the child is deliberately setting out to exasperate them with his symptom.

In another case where a problem was resolved in one interview, Erickson used a quite different approach. Hypnosis was not employed, but he would consider that he used a hypnotic technique. The presenting problem was a fourteen-year-old girl who had developed the idea that her feet were much too large. The mother came alone to Erickson and described the situation. For three months the girl had been becoming more and more withdrawn, and she didn't want to go to school or to church or to be seen on the street. The girl would not allow the subject of her feet to be discussed, and she would not go to a doctor to talk to him.

No amount of reassurance by her mother had any influence, and the girl was becoming more and more seclusive. Erickson reports:

I arranged with the mother to visit the home on the following day under false pretenses. The girl would be told that I was coming to examine the mother to see if she had the flu. It was a pretense, and yet the mother wasn't feeling well and I suggested that an examination would be appropriate. When I arrived at the home, the mother was in bed. I did a careful physical examination of her, listening to her chest, examining her throat, and so on. The girl was present. I sent her for a towel, and I asked that she stand beside me in case I needed something. She was very concerned about her mother's health. This gave me an opportunity to look her over. She was rather stoutly built and her feet were not large.

Studying the girl, I wondered what I could do to get her over this problem. Finally I hit upon a plan. As I finished my examination of the mother, I maneuvered the girl into a position directly behind me. I was sitting on the bed talking to the mother, and I got up slowly and carefully and then stepped back awkwardly. I put my heel down squarely on the girl's toes. The girl, of course, squawked with pain. I turned on her and in a tone of absolute fury said, "If you would grow those things *large* enough for a *man* to see, I wouldn't be in this sort of situation!" The girl looked at me, puzzled, while I wrote out a prescription and called the drugstore. That day the girl asked her mother if she could go out to a show, which she hadn't done in months. She went to school and church, and that was the end of a pattern of three months' seclusiveness. I checked later on how things were going, and the girl was friendly and agreeable. She didn't realize what I had done, nor did her mother. All her mother noticed was that I had been impolite to her daughter when I visited that day. She couldn't connect that with the daughter's return to normal activity.

It seems self-evident that this technique is based upon a hypnotic orientation. As Erickson put it, "There was no way for the girl to reject that compliment about her feet, no way to dispute it. 'If she would grow her feet *large* enough for a *man* to see.' The girl couldn't tell me I was clumsy; I was her mother's doctor. She couldn't retaliate in any way. There was nothing for her to do but accept the absolute proof that her feet were small." It is not unusual for Erickson to use hypnosis to arrange that a subject have an idea he cannot reject, and in this case he achieved that end without hypnosis in a social situation.

An important aspect of Erickson's work with children is his basic premise that children are natural antagonists of parents; they are of a different generation, and conflict between the generations must be assumed. This premise is not a comfortable one for people who like to think of parents and children in terms of togetherness. Yet, oddly enough, what often brings parents and children together is an assumption that they represent conflicting interests. As Erickson has said in conversation, "When you are talking to a couple, you can ask what it is they like about each other. When talking to a child, you ask what it is he doesn't like about his parents."

Because of this assumption, Erickson rather typically joins the child against the parents. This does not mean that he sees the child as a victim; it means that for a therapeutic operation it is the best stance to assume in relation to the child. He may at the same time also join the parents against the child, with or without the child's knowledge.

When he joins the child, he might deal directly with the problem or he might communicate indirectly through metaphor. In the following case he talks about certain aspects of muscle control in relation to one subject as a way of influencing a different type of muscle response. This is typical of Erickson's way of inducing change by communicating in analogies, or metaphors.

A mother called me up and told me about her ten-year-old son who wet the bed every night. They had done everything they could to stop him. They dragged him in to see me—literally. Father had him by one hand and mother by the other, and the boy was dragging his feet. They laid him face down in my office. I shoved the parents out and closed the door. The boy was yelling.

When the boy paused to catch his breath, I said, "That's a goddam hell of a way to do. I don't like it a damn bit." It surprised him that I would say this. He hesitated while taking that breath, and I told him he might as well go ahead and yell again. He let out a yell, and when he paused to take a breath, I let out a yell. He turned to look at me, and I said, "It's my turn." Then I said, "Now it's your turn," so he yelled again. I yelled again, and then said it was his turn again. Then I said, "Now, we can go right on taking turns, but that will get awfully tiresome. I'd rather take my turn by sitting down in that chair. There's a vacant one over there." So I took my turn sitting down in my chair, and he took his turn sitting down in the other chair. That expectation had been established—I had established that we were taking turns by yelling, and I changed the game to taking turns sitting down. Then I said, "You know, your parents ordered me to cure you of bedwetting. Who do they think they are that they can order *me* around?" He had received enough punishment from his parents, so I stepped over on his side of the fence by saying that. I told him, "I'd rather talk to you about a lot of other stuff. Let's just drop this talk about bedwetting. Now, how should I talk to a ten-year-old boy? You're going to grade school. You've got a nice compact wrist. Nice compact ankles. You know, I'm a doctor, and doctors always take an interest in the way a man is built. You've got a nice rounded, deep chest. You're not one of these hollow-chested, slump-shouldered people. You've got a nice chest that sticks out. I'll bet you're good at running. With your small-sized build, you've undoubtedly got good muscle coordination." I explained coordination to him and said he was probably good at sports that required skill, not just beef and bone. Not the sort of stuff that they any bonehead could play. But games that require skill. I asked what games he played, and he said, "Baseball, and bow and arrow." I asked, "How good are you at archery?" He said, "Pretty good." I said, "Well, of course that requires eye, hand, arm, body coordination." It turned out his younger brother played football, and was larger than he as were all the other family members. "Football's a nice game if you've got just muscle and bone. Lots of big, overgrown guys like it."

So we talked about that and about muscle coordination. I said, "You know, when you draw back on your bowstring and aim your arrow, what do you suppose the pupil of the eye does? It *closes down.*" I explained that there were muscles that are flat, muscles that are short, muscles that are long—and then there are muscles that are circular, "like the one at the bottom of your stomach; you know, when you eat food that muscle *closes up,* the food stays in your stomach until it's all digested. When the stomach wants to get rid of the food, that circular muscle at the bottom of your stomach opens up, empties out, and closes up to wait till the next meal to digest." The muscle at the bottom of your stomach—where's the bottom of your stomach when you're a small boy? It's all the way down.

So we discussed that for an hour, and the next Saturday he came in all alone. We talked some more about sports and this and that—with never a mention of bedwetting. We talked about Boy Scouts and camping, all the things that interest a small boy. On the fourth interview he came in wearing a big, wide smile. He said, "You know, my Ma has been trying for years to break *her* habit. But she can't do it." His mother smoked and was trying to stop. I said, "That's right, some people can break their habits quickly, others make a great big talk about it and don't do nothing about it." Then we drifted on to other subjects.

About six months later he dropped in socially to see me, and he dropped in again when he entered high school. Now he's in college.

All I did was talk about the circular muscle at the bottom of the stomach closing up and holding the contents until he wanted to empty it out. Symbolic language, of course, but all that beautiful build-up of eye, hand, body coordination. The bedwetting went away without ever discussing it.

Although Erickson discusses various adroit ways of handling difficult problems within his office, occasionally he finds one he just cannot deal with. An example of this kind is the following:

A twelve-year-old boy was sent to me. I knew many of his relatives, so I knew something about the family. His stepmother reported to me that the boy came downstairs one morning with a bicycle chain in his hand. He said to his stepmother, "I want to see you dance." She said, "Are you joking?" and he said, "Oh, no," and he pointed to the baby in the high chair. "You see the baby?" he said, and lifted the chain. He made her dance on the kitchen floor for an hour. His father brought him in to me. I never saw a more utterly vicious child. Finally I told him, "You know, I don't like you and you don't like me, and you're deliberately speaking in intonations that even get under *my* skin. So I'm going to ask your father to pick you up and take you home and have him take you to another psychiatrist." I wanted to beat that kid. His intonations were marvelous for irritating people. It was a work of art that he pulled on me. He knew he was doing it. The father asked me to see him again. I wouldn't.

It is difficult to determine on what basis Erickson decides he cannot treat a child. It seems to be related to whether he can remain sufficiently disengaged from the provocations of the child to work effectively. Evidently his selection is not based upon the severity of the problem or the degree of misfortune in the family situation, as the following case of a difficult child illustrates.

A mother came in and wanted me to take care of her son. She said, "He's a liar, he's a cheat, he governs the house by throwing temper tantrums. And he's got the sharpest tongue imaginable."

The mother was very bitter. She said, "His father is a sexual pervert. I don't know the details of his perversions. Once in a while he comes to bed with me, but he's got a lot of solitary perversions. He uses women's clothes, my clothes, for his perversions. I think he ejaculates on my clothes, since I have to take them to the cleaners. So there's not much relationship between the boy and his father. The father is short-tempered and screams at the boy."

She said the boy was unwilling to come in and see me, but she had told him she would bring him in by force if necessary. She said she'd taken him to other doctors and he just threw temper tantrums and they wouldn't have anything to do with him.

So she brought him in. He was a charming, sweet-faced, soft-voiced boy. He said, "I suppose Mother has told you everything about me."

I said, "She's told me some of the things she knows, but not everything about you. There are a lot of things about you that only you know, and she couldn't tell me a solitary one of those. I'm wondering if you're going to tell me any of *those* things."

He said, "I might not."

I said, "Let's settle one thing right away. I'd rather sit here and waste my time doing nothing with you than sit here and watch you having a temper tantrum on the floor. So what shall it be? Temper tantrum on the floor, or shall we sit here and waste time, or shall we get down to business?"

He said, "Not that way," and smiled. "We can waste time, we can get down to business, and I can still have my temper tantrums." He was a keen, sharp boy.

Yet he's never had a temper tantrum with me. I've had him violently angry. Especially when he threw mud balls and water bombs at the neighbor's house. I asked him to describe the pride, joy, happiness, and triumph he felt when he smashed that water bomb. That infuriated him. I said, "You're willing to have a temper tantrum here; you never have had one, but here's a beautiful chance. Now, what are you going to do, have a temper tantrum or tell me how you felt?" He told me how angry he was.

He improved at home and developed friends. Now he's well behaved at home and school and is enjoying being productive. He laughs at his previous behavior.

Erickson has no set method. His approach is oriented to the particular person and his situation, and he feels that only with experience can one know what to do with a particular child. A part of his success is determined by his tenacity when working with a patient. If one procedure doesn't work, he tries others until one does. He is also willing to extend himself and go to the home or wherever necessary to deal with the patient. The following case illustrates this willingness as well as his insistence that he work with a child in his own way rather than the way the parents prefer.

A nine-year-old girl began to fail in her schoolwork and withdraw from social contacts. When questioned, she would angrily and tearfully reply, "I just can't do nothing."

She had done good scholastic work in previous years, but on the playground she was inept, hesitant, and awkward. Her parents were only concerned about her scholastic rating and asked me for psychiatric assistance. Since the girl would not come to the office, I saw her each evening in her home. I learned that she didn't like certain girls because they were always playing jacks or roller skating or jumping rope. "They never do anything that's fun."

I learned that she had a set of jacks and a ball but that she "played terrible." On the ground that infantile paralysis had crippled my right arm, I challenged her that I could play a "more terrible" game than she could. The challenge was accepted. After the first few evenings a spirit of good competition and rapport developed, and it was relatively easy to induce a light-to-medium trance. Some of the games were played in the trance state and some in the waking state. Within three weeks she was an excellent player, though her parents were highly displeased because of my apparent lack of interest in her scholastic difficulties.

After three weeks of playing jacks, I declared that I could be worse on roller skates than she, since my leg was crippled. The same course of development was followed as with the jacks; this time it took only two weeks for her to develop reasonable skill. Next she was challenged to jump rope and see if she could possibly teach me this skill. In a week's time she was adept.

I then challenged her to a bicycle race, pointing out that I could actually ride a bicycle well, as she herself knew. I boldly said that I could beat her; only her conviction that I would defeat her allowed her to accept. However, she did promise to try hard. She had owned a bicycle for more than six months and had not ridden it more than one city block.

At the appointed time she appeared with her bicycle but demanded, "You have got to be honest and not just let me win. You got to try hard. I know you can ride fast enough to beat me. I'm going to watch you so you can't cheat."

I mounted my bike and she followed on hers. What she did not know was that the use of both legs in pedaling constituted a serious handicap for me in riding a bicycle; ordinarily I only use my left leg. As the girl watched suspiciously, she saw me pedaling most laboriously with both feet without developing much speed. Finally convinced, she rode past to win the race to her complete saisfaction.

That was the last therapeutic interview. She promptly proceeded to become the grade-school champion in jacks and rope jumping. Her scholastic work improved similarly.

Years later the girl sought me out to inquire how I had managed to let her excel me in bicycle riding. Learning to play jacks, jump rope, and roller skate had the effect of bolstering her ego immensely, but she had discredited those achievements considerably because of my physical handicaps. The bicycle riding, however, she knew was another matter. She explained that she knew me to be a good bicyclist, was certain I could beat her, and had no intention of letting the race be handed to her. The fact that I had tried genuinely hard and that she had beaten me convinced her that she "could do anything." Elated with this conviction, she had found school and all it offered a pleasant challenge.

Erickson is willing to use his physical handicaps as part of the therapeutic procedure. Often the extent of his handicap is underestimated: after his first attack of polio, when he was seventeen, he made a thousand-mile canoe trip alone to build up his strength, and after his second attack, in 1952, he took one of the more difficult hikes in Arizona, walking on two canes.

This case of the little girl offers a unique method of trance induction, called the "playing jacks induction." It also offers a portrait of Erickson's willingness to do whatever he feels is necessary to bring about change; if a race down the street on a bicycle is appropriate, he will do it.

It is also typical of Erickson that when parents and child are locked in a struggle in which they are both losing, he arranges a way for them both to win. Often he does this by simply bypassing the struggle and going at the matter differently with the child, as in the following case:

A boy was brought to me who was supposed to be in the seventh grade in school, but he couldn't read. His parents insisted that he could read, and he was deprived in every possible way as they tried to force him to read. His summers were always ruined by tutors. He reacted by not reading.

I started working with the boy by saying, "I think your parents are rather stubborn. You know that you can't read, I know that you can't read. Your parents have brought you to me and they insist I teach you how to read. Between you and me, let's forget about it. I should do something for you, and I really ought to do something that you like. Now, what do you like most?" He said, "Every summer I've wanted to go fishing with my father."

I asked him where his father fished. He told me that his father, who was a policeman, fished in Colorado, in Washington, in California, and even planned to go to Alaska. He had fished all along the coastline. I started wondering if he knew the names of the towns where those fishing spots were located. We got out a map of the West, and we tried to locate the towns. We weren't reading the map, we were looking for the names of towns. You look at maps, you don't read them.

I would confuse the location of certain cities, and he would have to correct me. I would try to locate a town named Colorado Springs and be looking for it in California, and he had to correct me. But he wasn't reading, he was correcting me. He rapidly learned to locate all the towns we were interested in. He didn't know he was reading the names. We had such a good time looking at the map and finding good fishing spots. He liked to come and discuss fish and the various kinds of flies used in catching fish. We also looked up different kinds of fish in the encyclopedia.

Near the end of August, I said, "Let's play a joke on your teachers and on your parents. You've been told you'll be given a reading test when school starts. Your parents are going to be anxious about how you'll do, and so will your teacher. So you take the first-grade reader and you carefully stumble through it. Botch it up thoroughly. Do a better job on the second-grade reader, and a somewhat better one on the third-grade reader. Then do a beautiful job on the *eighth*-grade reader." He thought that was a wonderful joke. He did it just that way. Later he played truant and came over to tell me about the appalled look on his parents' faces and his teacher's face.

If he had read the first-grade reader correctly, it would have been an acknowledgment of failure on his part. But when he misread that and then went beyond the seventh grade to do the eighth-grade reading well, that made him the winner. He could confound his teacher, bewilder his parents, and be the acknowledged winner.

Since most of Erickson's therapy is directive, an important part of the art is to persuade people to follow his directives. One of the many ways he gets people to do what he wants is to begin something and then digress. He describes the procedure in this way:

I do certain things when I interview a family group, or a husband and wife, or a mother and son. People come for help, but they also come to be substantiated in their attitudes and they come to have face saved. I pay attention to this, and I'm likely to speak in a fashion that makes them think I'm on their side. Then I digress on a tangent that they can accept, but it leaves them teetering on the edge of expectation. They have to admit that my digression is all right, it's perfectly correct, but they didn't expect me to do it that way. It's an uncomfortable position to be teetering, and they want some solution of the matter that I had just brought to the edge of settlement. Since they want that solution, they are more likely to accept what I say. They are very eager for a decisive statement. If you gave the directive right away, they could take issue with it. But if you digress, they hope you will get back, and they welcome a decisive statement from you.

Erickson illustrated this strategy with two cases, both of them involving twelve-year-old boys.

Johnny was brought in by his mother because he wet the bed every night. His mother wanted to help him with this problem, but his father did not. The father was a harsh and cold man who accused his wife of "babying the brats too much." When the boy went to his father, he would get shoved aside. The mother tried to make up for the father's behavior. The boy's fundamental reaction was "I want love from my father, he doesn't give it, Mother always steps in and makes it unnecessary for him to give it." Ever since the boy could remember, his father had said that every kid wets the bed, it wouldn't be normal not to, he had done it himself until his late teens. The mother was, of course, fed up with the wet beds and wanted something done about it. Erickson reports:

I had one interview with the father to size him up. He was a loud-voiced man who walked into this office, sat down, and spoke as if I were about sixty feet away from him. He asked me if I didn't know that all kids wet the bed until they got to be about sixteen. That's what he did, that's what his father did, it was very certain I had done it, and certain that every other boy grew up that way. What was this nonsense about curing his boy of wetting the bed? I let the father explain it all to me. He enjoyed the interview and shook hands with me. He said he was delighted to have such an intelligent listener.

When the son and mother came in together, the woman said, "My husband told me he had explained things to you." I said, "Yes, that's right, he explained at very considerable length." Her facial expression said, "Yes, I know." The son had a pained look on his face. I told them, "As far as I'm concerned, I'm going to forget about everything that he said. You don't have to, but then of course you weren't there, you only have some ideas of what he said. I'm just going to forget them because the ideas that you and I and your mother have are important. It's the ideas that you and I have, and that Johnny has, that are important."

You see what that does? I'm tying myself to Johnny first, and then tying it the other way around. First I'm allied with Johnny, then I have mother allied with me. You see Johnny's going to stand by me—because I'm going to forget what his father said, and Johnny would like to forget that. Then I tie mother to me by having her join me in forgetting what father said. This sets father aside, but it's not a hostile putting him aside. I've heard him out, and they know it. Father has come home and told them. I'm just forgetting about it, with no particular anger or distress. Father couldn't be included in the treatment because of his absolute opinions, so he needed to be set aside on this issue.

As I sized up the situation with mother and the boy, it was apparent that Johnny was utterly hostile toward his mother about this bedwetting. He was angry and in a struggle with her about it. I told Johnny that I had a remedy for him that he wouldn't like. It would be an effective remedy, absolutely helpful, absolutely certain to get him over the problem, yet he would not like it—but his *mother* would dislike it *more*. Now what could Johnny do? If his mother would dislike it more than he did, that would be fine. He could put up with anything that made his mother suffer more.

My proposal to Johnny was rather simple. I pointed out to him that his mother could get up at four or five o'clock in the morning, and if his bed was wet she could rouse him. She didn't have to wake him up if the bed was dry. However, if his bed was wet and she roused him, he could get up and sit down at his desk and copy so many pages from any book he chose. He could put in the time from four to seven o'clock, or from five to seven o'clock, copying material. His mother could watch him do that and watch him learning to improve his script. The boy's handwriting was really terrible and needed improvement.

To Johnny it sounded horrible to get up at four or five in the morning—but Mother had to get up first. It sounded unpleasant to have Mother sit there watching him improve his script, yet he only had to do that on mornings when his bed was wet. Nothing more disagreeable than getting up at that hour of the morning—to improve his handwriting.

They began the procedure, and it wasn't long before Johnny didn't have a wet bed every morning; he began skipping mornings. Pretty soon he had a wet bed only twice a week. Then a wet bed every ten days. Mother still had to get up every morning and check.

Finally it was a wet bed once a month, and then Johnny reoriented himself entirely. He developed the first friendships he ever had. It was during the summer, and the kids came over to play with him and he went over to play with the kids. His marks in school that following September were greatly improved. His first real achievement.

Now that was playing mother against son and son against mother. It's that simple idea of "I've got a remedy for you, but you won't like it." Then I digress to the fact that mother will hate it even more. Johnny wants me to come to just what it is that is a remedy. Then he's all for it. Improvement in handwriting becomes the primary goal, a dry bed becomes an incidental, more or less accepted thing. It's no longer the dominant, threatening issue at hand.

Mother, watching her son improve his handwriting, could take pride in her son's accomplishment. The son could take pride in it. When the two of them brought the handwriting to show me, it was just an eager boy and an eager mother showing me this beautiful handwriting. I could go through it page after page and point out this letter "n," this letter "g," this letter "t," and discuss the beauty of the script.

Since Johnny has a dry bed, his father has played ball with him—coming home early from the office. The father's response when the boy stopped wetting the bed was surprisingly complimentary. He told the boy, "You learned to have a dry bed faster than I did; must be you're a lot smarter than me." He could afford to be very generous. He had told me off completely. Besides, it wasn't the psychiatrist who solved this problem for his son, it was the superior brain power he bequeathed to his son. In the family it became a joint achievement that was blessed by the father, and the boy got recognition and acceptance from his father.

Whatever the symptom, whether bedwetting or some other childhood problem, there is usually one adult who is overinvolved with the child, and the therapy disengages that pair from each other. In the previous case a task was given to mother and child, which forced them to become disengaged. In the following case an exasperating problem was relieved by a task for both boy and father.

For two years a twelve-year-old boy had been picking at a sore, a pimple, on his forehead, and it had become a continuous ulcer. His father and mother had resorted to all manner of punishment to keep him from picking at the sore. His schoolteachers and his schoolmates had tried to reform him. Medical doctors had explained about cancer, had bandaged and taped the sore, and had done what they could to keep him from touching it. The boy would reach up under the adhesive tape and pick at it. He explained that he just could not control the impulse.

The boy's mother and father did what they could to stop the boy from picking at the sore, but they disagreed on the value of punishment. The father had gone to extremes, depriving the boy of any number of toys; he had sold the boy's bicycle and had broken his bow and arrow.

Finally the parents brought the boy to me. I had an interview with the mother to learn something about the family situation so I could pick out something to work with. I learned about the values and obligations in the home, including the fact that the boy did chores. They had a large lawn, which he cared for, and a large garden. I also learned that the mother tended to be on the boy's side and that the boy was angry with his father for the various punishments, in particular the breaking of his bow and arrow. I also found out that the boy had a spelling problem; when he wrote he tended to leave out letters in words. I like to check on a child's schoolwork to see what is there.

I had an interview with the boy and his father together, and I focused immediately on how ownership is defined. I picked out the bow and arrow as an issue. Whose was it? The father admitted that the bow and arrow belonged to the boy; they were given to him for his birthday. Then I asked how an ulcer should be treated. We agreed that it should be treated with bandages and medications of various sorts. I asked how would you use a bow and arrow to treat it? How would breaking a bow and arrow be treating an ulcer? The father was very embarrassed, and the son was eying his father with narrowed eyes. After the father had flushed and squirmed quite a bit in this discussion, I turned to the boy and asked him if he did not think he could at least honestly credit his father with good intentions despite his stupid behavior. Both of them had to accept that statement. In this way the boy could call his father's behavior stupid, but to do so he would also have to credit him with being well-intentioned.

Then I asked how much further we should go in discussing medicines that didn't work. Or could we forget about those? I said, "You've had this for two years. All the medicines from breaking the bow and arrow to selling your bicycle didn't work. What shall we do?" The boy had the idea that I should take charge.

I said to him, "All right, I will. But you won't like the way I take charge. Because I'm going to do something that will clear up the ulcer. You won't like it one bit; all you will like is that the ulcer is healed—that you'll really like." I said I wanted him to devote every weekend to curing the ulcer on his forehead—*while his father did his weekend chores for him.* The boy gave a triumphant glance at me and at his father.

We went over the chores and discussed the mowing and raking of the lawn, cleaning up the dog messes, weeding the garden, and so on. I asked who inspected the lawn when the boy did it. Father inspected his work. I said, "Well, on Saturday, in between working on curing your ulcer, because you can't work on it steadily, you can go out and inspect how your father is doing on your chores."

By this time the boy was quite curious about what he would be doing on the weekend to cure his ulcer, and I began the procedure of digressing. In a slow, aggravating, dragging out, shaggy-dog sort of way, I offered the therapeutic plan. When you do this, a patient leans forward wishing you'd come to the point of the whole thing—he wants to know what on earth he is to do. He credits you with being thoughtful, deliberate in your presentation. He knows you're not going to rush things over on him. He's waiting for you to come to the point, and when you finally do he is motivated to accept the plan.

I said to the boy, "I found out that your spelling is very poor. Your spelling is poor because when you write a word you very likely leave out letters."

Then I said, "I think you ought to start curing your ulcer on Saturday morning at about six o'clock. You know you'll take things much more seriously if you get up early in the morning to do it, because it is serious business. Of course, if it's only five minutes to six, you might as well start then instead of waiting until six o'clock. Or if it's five minutes after six you can start—what's the difference of five minutes?"

Then I went on, "Now, you can write with a pen, or you can write with a pencil. Some pencil leads are colored, but ordinary pencil lead would be all right. You could use pen and ink, or a ball-point pen would do. I supposed ruled paper would be best. It could be about so wide, or it could be a little wider, about so wide. I think your father could get you some ruled paper that would be just wide enough."

Finally I broke the news to him. I said, "This is the sentence I think you ought to write: 'I do not think it's a good idea to pick at that sore on my forehead.' I repeated the sentence slowly and carefully and said, "Now, write it slowly, write it neatly, write it carefully. Count each line when you've got it down. Then write the sentence slowly and carefully again. Always check each line and each word, because you wouldn't want to leave out a single letter. You don't want to leave out any of the little parts of healing that take place in an ulcer like that."

I told him I didn't know how long it would take the ulcer to heal. I felt that since he had had it continuously for two years, it really ought to take a month. He could examine it in the mirror every three or four days to see how it was progressing. Not day by day. That way he would be able to find out when it was healed. He might want to write an extra weekend after it was healed.

He was to start at six o'clock in the morning and have breakfast later. I told his mother privately to be sure to be very dilatory preparing his breakfast so he would get a rest there. Every two hours he was to take a coffee break—which was essentially a fruit-juice or water break. Then he could inspect his father's work on the chores and go back and write. I explained that he would have an aching hand the first forenoon, and what ought he do about that? I pointed out to him that at his break he should open and shut his hand rapidly to relax the muscles. This would increase the fatigue, but it would keep the muscles limber. I said that I felt that after dinner he should really be free of the day's work. In fact, I really didn't care if he quit at four o'clock. By making the quitting time a matter of indifference to me, it takes away the punitiveness.

The boy wrote all day Saturday and Sunday every weekend. I had the most tremendous stack of sheets of ruled paper containing that sentence—all written with pride and enjoyment. His father didn't have to urge him at all, and mother and father were astonished at his pride in his handwriting. The one-thousandth writing of that long sentence was beautifully done. I made it clear that the inspection of his writing belonged to me. If he wanted to show it to his parents, that was all right, but I was inspector. I examined every page. I told him I could take a quick, hasty look at each page, and were there any pages he could recall that I should give more than passing attention to? In that way he absolved me from doing a minute examination.

The more the boy wrote, the more justification he had for inspecting his father's work. The more he wrote, the more accurately he had to write. All the dice were loaded in favor of progress. With this approach, I took his compulsive picking away at the sore and had him compulsively write accurately, something in which he could take a wholesome pride.

The father said, "I knew what I had to do. I did the most beautiful job you could ever imagine on that lawn." The boy took such pleasure in discovering a leaf on the lawn. Father got the lawn and garden fixed up thoroughly, the garden fence repaired, all the chores done, and the boy wrote his sentence.

In a month's time the ulcer was healed. A year later there had been no recurrence. That chronic, indolent, horrible ulcer, and yet there wasn't even a scar.

I put that stack of the boy's writing in my case record and asked him how long I should keep it. It would fill one file to the full. He said he thought I might like to keep it for quite a number of months. I asked what I should do with it then. He said, "Oh, it's just wastepaper then."

In these cases Erickson did not deal directly with the conflict between the parents about how to deal with the child, as he sometimes does. On the question of the child used in a war between parents, he has said, "When you correct or cure the child, the parents have got an unfamiliar child. Then they have to go back to their own private war without including the child. He's a stranger now and a pretty self-sufficient one."

Although Erickson will play with children and often joins them against the adult world, he is by no means a believer in raising children in a "permissive" way. He will work with parents to teach them how to play with a child, and he will restrain parents from oversevere and futile punishments. But he will also arrange that parents set firm limits. When a child is misbehaving, Erickson does not help him understand the reasons; he arranges that he behave more properly. Often his ideas sound old-fashioned. For example, if a child will not eat his breakfast and the mother is upset, Erickson will provide her with a procedure to resolve this. He will have her cook the child a good breakfast, and if the child does not eat it, then the mother is to place the breakfast in the refrigerator. At lunchtime she is to bring out the breakfast and offer it. If the child does not eat it, at suppertime she again offers the same meal, and continues with this until the child eats it.

Even when dealing with severely disturbed children, such as an autistic child, Erickson does not approach them as children who need love as much as children who have more power than they can tolerate. He feels that a child's insecurity can come from an uncertainty about what limits are set upon him, and the therapeutic approach is to enforce limits. The problem is to arrange that the parents set the limits, rather than a stranger like a child therapist. With child problems, his focus is upon the family situation as much as it is upon the child.

An Erickson procedure used with children who have behavior problems is illustrated in the following case.

A twenty-seven-year-old mother began to encounter serious difficulty with her eight-year-old son, who was becoming progressively more defiant and seemed to find a new way to defy her each day. The mother had divorced her husband two years previously, for adequate reasons recognized by all concerned. In addition to her son, she had two daughters, aged nine and six. After some months of occasional dating with men in the hope of marriage, she found that her son had become rebellious and an unexpected problem. The older daughter had joined him briefly in this rebelliousness. The mother was able to correct the daughter by her customary measures of discipline through anger, shouting, scolding, threatening, and then an angry spanking followed by an intelligent, reasonable, objective discussion with the child. This had, in the past, always been effective with the children. However, her son, Joe, refused to respond to her usual measures, even when she added repeated spankings, deprivations, tears, and the enlistment of her family's assistance. Joe merely stated, quite happily and cheerfully, that he planned to do whatever he pleased and nothing, just nothing, could stop him.

The son's behavior spread to the school and to the neighborhood, and literally nothing was safe from his depredations. School property was destroyed, teachers defied, schoolmates assaulted; neighbors' windows were broken and their flower beds destroyed. The neighbors and teachers, endeavoring to take a hand in the matter, succeeded in intimidating the child but nothing more. Finally the boy began destroying things of value in the home, especially after the mother was asleep at night, and then he would infuriate her by bold-facedly denying guilt the next morning.

This final mischief led the mother to bring the boy in for treatment. As the mother told her story, Joe listened with a broad, triumphant smile. When she had finished, he boastfully declared that I could not do anything to stop him, and he was going to go right on doing as he pleased. I assured him, gravely and earnestly, that it was unnecessary for me to do anything to change his behavior because he was a good big, strong boy and very smart and he would have to change his behavior all by himself. I assured him that his mother would do just enough to give him a chance to change his behavior "all by himself." Joe received this statement in an incredulous, sneering manner. I said that his mother would be told some simple little things that she could do so that he himself could change his behavior, and sent him out of the office. I also challenged him in a most kindly fashion to try to figure out what those simple little things might be. This served to puzzle him into quiet reflective behavior while he awaited his mother.

Alone with the mother, I discussed a child's demand for a world in which he could be certain that there was someone stronger and more powerful than he. To date, her son had demonstrated with increasing desperation that the world was so insecure that the only strong person in it was himself, a little eight-year-old boy. Then I gave the mother painstakingly clear instructions for her activities for the next two days.

As they left the office later, the boy challengingly asked if I had recommended spankings. I assured him that no measure would be taken except to give him full opportunity to change his own behavior; no one else would change it. This reply perplexed him. On the way home his mother administered severe corporal punishment to compel him to let her drive the automobile safely. This misconduct had been anticipated; the mother had been advised to deal summarily with it and without argument. The evening was spent in the usual fashion by letting the boy watch television as he wished.

The following morning the grandparents arrived and picked up the two daughters. Joe, who had plans to go swimming, demanded his breakfast. He was most puzzled when he observed his mother carry into the living room some wrapped sandwiches, fruit, a thermos bottle of fruit juice and one of coffee, and some towels. She put all these items securely on a heavy couch with the telephone and some books. Joe demanded that she prepare his breakfast without delay, threatening physical destruction of the first thing he could lay his hands on if she did not hurry. His mother merely smiled at him, seized him, threw him quickly to the floor on his stomach, and sat her full weight upon him. When he yelled at her to get off, she said she had already eaten breakfast and she had nothing to do except to try to think about ways to change his behavior. However, she pointed out that she was certain she did not know any way. Therefore it would all be up to him.

The boy struggled furiously against the odds of his mother's weight, strength, and watchful dexterity. He yelled, screamed, shouted profanity and obscenities, sobbed, and finally promised piteously always to be a good boy. His mother answered that the promise did not mean anything because she had not yet figured out how to change his behavior. This evoked another fit of rage from him, which finally ceased and was followed by his urgent plea to go to the bathroom. His mother explained gently that she had not finished her thinking; she offered him a towel to mop up so he would not get too wet. This elicited another wild bit of struggling that soon exhausted him. His mother took advantage of the quiet to make a telephone call to her mother. While Joe listened, she explained casually that she had not yet reached any conclusion in her thinking and she really believed that any change in behavior would have to come from Joe. Her son greeted this remark with as loud a scream as he could muster. His mother commented into the telephone that Joe was too busy screaming to think about changing his behavior, and she put the mouthpiece down to Joe's mouth so that he could scream into it.

Joe lapsed into sullen silence, broken by sudden surges of violent effort, screams, demands, and sobbing, interrupted by piteous pleas. To all of this his mother gave the same mild, pat answers. As time passed, the mother poured herself coffee, fruit juice, ate sandwiches, and read a book. Shortly before noon the boy politely told her he really did need to go to the bathroom. She confessed a similar need. She explained that it would be possible if he would agree to return, resume his position on the floor, and let her sit down comfortably upon him. After some tears he consented. He fulfilled his promise, but almost immediately launched into renewed violent activity to dislodge her. Each near success led to further effort, which exhausted him still more. While he rested, she ate fruit and drank coffee, made a casual telephone call, and read a book.

After over five hours Joe surrendered by stating simply and abjectly that he would do anything and everything she told him to do. His mother replied just as simply and earnestly that her thinking had been in vain; she just did not know what to tell him to do. He burst into tears at this but shortly, sobbing, he told her he knew what to do. She replied mildly that she was very glad of this, but she did not think he had had enough time to think long enough about it. Perhaps another hour or so of thinking might help. Joe silently awaited the passing of an hour while his mother sat reading quietly. When over an hour had passed, she commented on the time but expressed her wish to finish the chapter. Joe sighed shudderingly and sobbed softly to himself while his mother finished her reading.

With the chapter finally finished, the mother got up and so did Joe. He timidly asked for something to eat. His mother explained in laborious detail that it was too late for lunch, that breakfast was always eaten before lunch, and that it was too late to serve breakfast. She suggested instead that he have a drink of ice water and a comfortable rest in bed for the remainder of the afternoon.

Joe fell asleep quickly but awakened to the odors of well-liked foods. His sisters had returned, and he tried to join them at the table for the evening meal.

His mother explained, gravely, simply, and in lucid detail that it was customary first to eat breakfast and then lunch and then dinner. Unfortunately, he had missed his breakfast, therefore he had to miss his lunch. Now he would have to miss his dinner, but fortunately he could begin a new day the next morning. Joe returned to his bedroom and cried himself to sleep. The mother slept lightly that night, but Joe did not arise until she was well along with breakfast preparations.

Joe entered the kitchen with his sisters for breakfast and sat down happily while his mother served his sisters with pancakes and sausages. At Joe's place was a large bowl. His mother explained that she had cooked him an extra-special breakfast of oatmeal, a food not too well liked by him. Tears came to his eyes, but he thanked her for the serving as was the family custom, and he ate voraciously. His mother explained that she had cooked an extra supply so that he could have a second helping. She also cheerfully expressed the hope that enough would be left over to meet his needs for lunch. Joe ate manfully to prevent that possibility, but his mother had cooked a remarkably large supply.

After breakfast, Joe set about cleaning up his room without any instruction. This done, he asked his mother if he could call upon the neighbors. She had no idea what this portended but gave permission. From behind the window curtains she watched him while he went next door and rang the bell. When the door opened, he apparently spoke to the neighbor briefly and then went on up the street. As she later learned, just as systematically as he had terrorized the neighborhood, he canvassed it to offer his apologies and to promise that he would come back to make amends as fast as he could. He explained that it would take a considerable period of time for him to undo all the mischief he had done.

Joe returned for lunch, ate buttered cold thick-sliced oatmeal, helped voluntarily to dry the dishes, and spent the afternoon and evening with his schoolbooks while his sisters watched television. The evening meal was ample but consisted of leftovers, which Joe ate quietly without comment. At bedtime Joe went to bed voluntarily while his sisters awaited their mother's usual insistence.

The next day Joe went to school, where he made his apologies and promises. These were accepted warily. That evening he became involved in a typical childish quarrel with his older sister, who shrieked for her mother. As the mother entered the room, Joe began to tremble visibly. Both children were told to sit down, and the sister was asked to state her case first. When it became his turn to speak, Joe said he agreed with his sister. His mother then explained to Joe that she expected him to be a normal eight-year-old boy and to get into ordinary trouble like all regular eight-year-old boys. Then she pointed out to both of them that their quarrel was lacking in merit and was properly to be abandoned. Both children acquiesced.

The education of Joe's mother to enable her to deal with her son's problem by following out the instructions was a rather difficult task. She was a college graduate, a highly intelligent woman with a background of social and community interests and responsibilities. In the interview she was asked to describe, as fully as possible, the damage Joe had hone in the school and community. With this description, the damage became painfully enlarged in her mind. (Plants do grow back, broken windowpanes and torn dresses can be replaced, but this comfort was not allowed to be a part of her review.)

Next she was asked to describe Joe "as he used to be"—a reasonably happy, well-behaved, and actually a decidedly brilliant child. She was repeatedly asked to draw these comparisons between his past and present behavior, more briefly each time, but with a greater highlighting of the essential points. Then she was asked to speculate upon the probable future of Joe both "as he used to be" and as was "quite possible" now in the light of his present behavior. I offered helpful suggestions to aid her in drawing sharply contrasting "probable pictures of the future."

After this discussion she was asked to consider in full the possibilities of what she could do over the weekend and the kind of role she ought to assume with Joe. Since she did not know, this placed her completely in a passive position so I could offer plans. Her repressed and guilty resentments and hostilities toward her son and his misbehavior were utilized. Every effort was made to redirect them into an anticipation of a satisfying, calculated, deliberate watchfulness in the frustrating of her son's attempts to confirm his sense of insecurity and to prove her ineffectual.

The mother's apparently justified statement that her weight of 150 pounds was much too great to permit putting it fully on the body of an eight-year-old child was a major factor in winning the mother's full cooperation. At first this argument was carefully evaded. The mother was helped to systematically marshal all of her objections to my proposed plans behind this apparently indisputable argument that her weight was too great to be endured by a child. As she became more entrenched in this defense, a carefully worded discussion allowed her to wish with increasing desire that she could do the various things I outlined as I detailed possibilities for the entire weekend.

When the mother seemed to have reached the right degree of emotional readiness, the question of her weight was raised for disposal. She was simply assured that she need not take medical opinion at all but would learn from her son on the morrow that her weight would be inconsequential to him. In fact, it would take all of her strength, dexterity, and alertness in addition to her weight to master the situation. She might even lose the contest because of the insufficiency of her weight. (The mother could not analyze the binding significance of this argument so simply presented to her. She was placed in the position of trying to prove that her weight was really too much. To prove this, she would need her son's cooperation, and I was certain that the boy's aggressive patterns would preclude any passive yielding to his mother's weight. In this way the mother would be taught by the son to disregard her defenses against my suggestions, and she would be reinforced in her acceptance of those suggestions by the very violence of his behavior.) As the mother later explained, "The way that bucking bronco threw me around, I knew I would have to settle down to serious business to keep my seat. It just became a question of who was smarter, and I knew I had a real job to do. Then I began to take pleasure in anticipating and meeting his moves. It was almost like a chess game. I certainly learned to admire and respect his determination, and I got an immense satisfaction out of frustrating him as thoroughly as he had frustrated me.

"I had one awfully bad time, though. When he came back from the bathroom, and he started to lie down on the floor, he looked at me so pitifully that I wanted to take him in my arms. But I remembered what you said about not accepting surrender because of pity but only when the issue was settled. That's when I knew I had won, so I was awfully careful then to be sure not to let any pity come in. That made the rest of it easy, and I could really understand what I was doing and why."

For the next few months, until midsummer, all went well. Then for no apparent reason except an ordinary quarrel with his sister settled unfairly to her advantage, Joe declared quietly but firmly that he did not have "to take that kind of stuff." He said he could "stomp" anybody, particularly me, and he dared his mother to take him to see me that very evening. At a loss what to do, his mother brought him to the office immediately. As they entered, she declared somewhat inaccurately that Joe threatened to "stomp" my office. Joe was immediately told, disparagingly, that he probably could not stomp the floor hard enough to make it worth while. Irately, Joe raised his foot and brought his cowboy boot down hard upon the carpeted floor. He was told, condescendingly, that his effort was really remarkably good for a little eight-year-old boy and that he could probably repeat it a number of times, but not very many. Joe angrily shouted that he could stomp that hard fifty, a hundred, a thousand times if he wished. I replied that he was only eight years old, and no matter how angry he was he couldn't stomp a thousand times. In fact, he couldn't even stomp hard half that number of times, which would only be five hundred. If he tried, he would soon get tired, his stomp would get littler and weaker, and he would have to change off to the other leg and rest. Even worse, he was told he couldn't even stand still while he rested without wiggling around and wanting to sit down. If he didn't believe this, he could just go right ahead and stomp. When he got all tired out like a little boy, he could rest by standing still until he discovered that he could not even stand still without wiggling and wanting to sit down. With outraged and furious dignity, Joe declared his solemn intention of stomping a hole in the floor even if it took a hundred million stomps.

His mother was dismissed with instructions to return in the "square root of four," which she translated to mean "in two hours." In this way Joe was not informed of the time when she would return, although he recognized that one adult was telling another a specific time. As the office door closed upon his mother, Joe balanced on his right foot and crashed his left foot to the floor. I assumed a look of astonishment, commenting that the stomp was far better than I had expected of Joe, but I doubted if he could keep it up. I said that Joe would soon weaken, and then he would discover that he couldn't even stand still. Joe contemptuously stomped a few more times before it became possible to disparage his stomp as becoming weaker.

After intensifying his efforts, Joe reached a count of thirty before he realized that he had greatly overestimated his stomping ability. As this realization became evident in Joe's facial expression, he was patronizingly offered the privilege of just patting the floor a thousand times with his foot, since he really couldn't stand still and rest without wiggling around and wanting to sit down. With desperate dignity, he rejected the floor-patting and declared his intention of standing still. Promptly he assumed a stiff, upright position with his hands at his sides, facing me. I immediately showed him the desk clock, and I commented about the slowness of the minute hand and the even greater slowness of the hour hand despite the seeming rapidity of the ticking of the clock. I turned to my desk, began to make notes in Joe's cased record, and from that I turned to other desk tasks.

Within fifteen minutes Joe was shifting his weight back and forth from one foot to the other, twisting his neck, wiggling his shoulders. When a half hour had passed, he was reaching out with his hand, resting some of his weight on the arm of the chair beside which he was standing. However, he quickly withdrew his hand whenever I seemed about to look up to glance reflectively about the room. After about an hour, I excused myself temporarily from the office. Joe took full advantage of this, and of several repetitions, never quite getting back into his previous position beside the chair.

When his mother knocked at the office door, I told Joe, "When your mother comes in, do exactly as I tell you." She was admitted and seated, looking wonderingly at Joe as he stood rigidly facing the desk. Signaling silence to the mother, I turned to Joe and peremptorily commanded, "Joe, show your mother how hard you can still stomp the floor." Joe was startled, but he responded nobly. "Now, Joe, show her how stiff and straight you can stand still." A minute later two more orders were issued. "Mother, this interview between Joe and me is a secret between Joe and me. Joe, don't tell your mother a single thing about what happened in this office. You and I both know, and that's enough. O.K.?"

Both Joe and his mother nodded their heads. She looked a bit mystified; Joe looked thoughtfully pleased. On the trip home Joe was quiet, sitting quite close beside his mother. About halfway home Joe broke the silence by commenting that I was a "nice doctor." As the mother later said, this statement had relieved her puzzled mind in some inexplicable way. She neither asked nor was given any explanation of the office events. She knew only that Joe liked, respected, and trusted me and was glad to see me occasionally in a social or semi-social fashion. Joe's behavior continued to be that of a normal, highly intelligent boy who now and then misbehaved in an expected and warrantable fashion.

Two years passed and Joe's mother became engaged. Joe liked the prospective stepfather but asked his mother one demanding question—did I approve of the man? Assured that I did approve, there was then unquestioning acceptance.

In an undefined world where intellectual and emotional fluctuations create an enveloping state of uncertainty that varies from one mood and one moment to the next, there can be no certainty or security. Joe sought to learn what was really strong, secure, and safe, and he learned it in the effective way one learns not to kick a stone with a bare foot or to slap a cactus with the bare hands.

VII MARRIAGE AND FAMILY DILEMMAS

When a married couple reach the middle years of marriage, their difficulties have often become habitual patterns. Sometimes the children are involved in their struggles, but often the presenting complaint is an acknowledged marital problem. A typical issue offered at this time is a power struggle between husband and wife over who should be the dominant one in the marriage. It is in the nature of all learning animals that they organize in a hierarchy, and a continual question in marriage can be who is first and who is second in the hierarchy of a marital relationship. Some couples manage flexibility on this issue; at times and in some areas the wife is dominant, at other times or in other areas the husband is, and in many situations they function as peers. A marriage in difficulty is usually one where the couple is able to function only in one way and there is discontent with that way. Sometimes, too, one of the spouses makes paradoxical demands on the other. Often a wife wants her husband to be more dominating—but she'd like him to dominate her the way she tells him to.

When married couples are caught in a power struggle of this kind, it can continue for years although neither spouse wants it. As part of this struggle they will use a wide range of behavior, including symptoms, as ammunition in the situation. Erickson has developed a variety of procedures for resolving marital conflicts that have become embedded as habitual, cyclical behavior. Two cases illustrate two quite different approaches to what is essentially the same dilemma. A married couple in the restaurant business together are in an unresolvable power struggle in the marriage, which takes the form of who should manage the restaurant. In the first case, Erickson resolved the problem by interviewing only the wife; the husband was not directly included.

This man, let's call him Mr. Smith, was in his fifties and had run restaurants all his life. He started out with a hot-dog stand in high school. During all the years he had a restaurant, his wife put him through his daily catechism about the restaurant. This had begun when they were engaged and continued right on through the marriage. As she reported it, she felt compelled to check each day by going down to determine whether he was running the restaurant correctly. Her checking on him made him furious, yet he let her do it. She would spend about two hours there checking on everything and having him recite his report on what he had purchased and what arrangements he had made.

She said she didn't want to dominate her husband in this way, and she would do anything to be able to stop doing it. Since she felt helpless about this and compelled to do it, I decided to utilize that feeling of compulsion by having her apply it to herself and shift it from him. I assigned her the task of quizzing her husband, as she was doing, but she was to make a written list of the questions she always asked. Then she was to frame a parallel list of similar questions about her own activities. After she quizzed her husband, she was to go off and quiz herself about what her own activities had been. She should pose questions as if from her husband and then answer them. Just as she would ask him about the stock of this and stock of that in the restaurant, she would ask herself about the stocks in the home. She would reply, "I ordered seven quarts of milk for the household, I bought two loaves of bread," and so on.

The husband was still being quizzed, but this was always followed by her taking the husband's role—except that she literally asked his questions herself and had to answer all the questions. She had the whole management, and yet she was merely in a recitative role.

She reacted predictably; she got fed up with the whole procedure and stopped questioning her husband every day. The last time I saw her was quite a while after the treatment ended. She told me she only goes to the restaurant when she is with some friends and is going there to eat. She never queries him, and she never reports on the household. But she runs that fifty-thousand-dollar house to his complete satisfaction.

What is typical about this case is the way Erickson arranges that someone with a compulsion go through a compulsive act that overcomes the difficulty. What is unusual is the way the husband is used in the treatment without ever being involved. The wife who has managed her husband is managed into the task of managing herself managing him managing her and drops a procedure of many years' duration, which has angered her husband and produced distress in the marriage. It is also typical of Erickson that he determines the husband's competence in running the restaurant before he relieves the wife of the task of supervising him.

In another quite similar case, Erickson dealt with husband and wife together. He resolved a long-term marital conflict by a simple instruction that forced a change because of the nature of the situation.

This husband and wife had been running a restaurant business together for many years and they were in a constant quarrel about the management of it. The wife insisted that the husband should manage it, and he protested that she never let him do it. As he put it, "Yes, she keeps telling me I should run the restaurant. All the time she's running it she tells me I should do it. I'm the bus boy, I'm the janitor, I scrub the floors. She nags at me about the buying, she nags at me about the bookkeeping, she nags at me because the floor needs scrubbing. I really should hire someone to scrub the floor, but my wife can't wait until somebody comes in and applies for the job. So I wind up doing it myself, and then there's no need to hire someone to do it."

The wife took the reasonable position that she wanted her husband to take care of the restaurant because she would rather be at home. She had sewing she wished to do. And she would like to serve her husband at least one home-cooked meal a day with special foods he liked. Her husband replied, "That's what she says. You can hear it, I can hear it. But she'll be in the restaurant tomorrow morning!"

I learned that they locked up the restaurant in the evening at about ten o'clock, and they opened at seven in the morning. I began to deal with the problem by asking the wife who should carry the keys to the restaurant. She said, "We both carry the keys. I always get there first and open up while he's parking the car."

I pointed out to her that she ought to see to it that her husband got there half an hour before she did. They had only one car, but the restaurant was just a few blocks from their home. She could walk there a half hour later. When she agreed to this arrangement, it solved the conflict.

Discussing this couple with some colleagues, Erickson put the matter as simply as that. Having the woman arrive a half hour later than her husband resolved the problem. Since this solution seemed more obvious to him than to his audience, he went on to explain.

When the husband arrived a half hour before his wife, *he* carried the keys. *He* opened the door. *He* unlocked everything. *He* set up the restaurant for the day. When his wife arrived, she was completely out of step and way behind. So many things had been set in motion by him, and he was managing them.

Of course, when she remained behind at home that half hour in the morning, it left her with the breakfast dishes and the housework to do before she left. And if she could be a half hour late, she could be thirty-five minutes late. In fact, what she hadn't recognized when she agreed to the arrangement was that she could be forty minutes or even an hour late. In this way, she discovered that her husband could get along at the restaurant without her. Her husband, in turn, was discovering that he could manage the restaurant.

Once the wife yielded on that half hour in the morning, then she yielded on going home early in the evening and preparing a bedtime snack for him. This meant he took over the task of getting the restaurant in shape for the night and closing up.

The wife also was learning to manage the house, which was a more important activity to her. In their final arrangement she stayed home, but she was available for the cashier's desk or some other position if an employee was sick or on vacation. At other times she didn't need to be at the restaurant, and she wasn't.

When discussing the case, a colleague pointed out that this wasn't the individual problem of the wife; the husband had been busy inviting his wife to take charge in the restaurant, and it was therefore a game in which both people were involved. Erickson agreed but said that helping the husband discover his involvement was not necessarily relevant to bringing about a change. As he put it, "I couldn't feel I would get anywhere by telling the husband he was inviting his wife to manage him into mopping the floor, and so on. He wouldn't have understood that. But he did begin to understand that he was in charge of the place for a whole half hour. And he was perfectly comfortable being in charge."

Often it is difficult to get a wife to make a change of this kind and stick to it, particularly when she is a woman who likes to manage. Commenting upon this, Erickson pointed out that the wife was willing to accept the idea and follow through on it because of the way it was put. *She* was asked to *see to it* that her husband arrived a half hour earlier than she did. She was put in charge of the arrangement and so was willing to accept it.

Often when a therapist is dealing with a couple, he finds that their contract is that the wife will determine whatever is to be said in the room. Just getting the husband's view of the problem is difficult, because the wife does not allow him to talk but helpfully talks for him whenever he is asked a question. Asking the wife to be quiet so the husband can have his say is often successful, but sometimes the wife will not be restrained by such a request. Erickson has different ways of dealing with such a "dominating" woman.

When I ask a husband for his point of view and the wife interrupts even when I ask her not to, then I usually find some action that will quiet her. For example, I will do it this way. I say to the wife, "I still want your husband's point of view, and you keep right on talking. I know it is because of your eagerness to help me understand. But do you happen to have a lipstick?" Of course she usually has a lipstick, and I ask her to take it out of her purse. Then I say, "Now, this will seem ridiculous to you, but suppose you hold that lipstick like this"—I show her that I want her to hold it with the tip just gently touching her lips. "Now keep it right there, just touching. I'm going to ask your husband some questions, and I want you to notice how your lips want to move. I think you'll find it very interesting." A woman can get quite fascinated watching the quivering of her lips on that lipstick. By doing that, I've given her a legitimate use for her lips. She doesn't quite understand it, but she finds it amusing.

When a woman is so dominating that she excludes her husband from the raising of their child, Erickson will join her in such a way that he persuades her to see to it that her husband is more involved.

When I face a woman who is truly overdominant in her marriage, I compliment her and show my appreciation of her competence. When that is set, I raise a questioning doubt. I express my inability to understand how a woman of her intelligence could neglect using the competency of her husband. Then I point out to her that biologically a man is quite another order of creature from the female. His philosophy of life is different, and his physiological functioning is different in relation to children.

A woman's one complete sexual act takes about eighteen years to complete. She must receive the sperm, carry the unborn child for nine months, and nurse the child, and all of this involves transformations in the body of a woman. She must take care of the baby, teach it, nurture it, educate it, and guide and protect it through the long years of childhood. Biologically, the woman is oriented to that task. When my dominant woman listens to that, she has a legitimate excuse for accepting her dominance in child rearing. Yet as surely as she accepts that legitimate excuse, she lays herself open to the responsibility for using every favorable influence in the environment. Among the favorable influences is that husband of hers, who represents another order of biological experience, of biological learning. Her child must live in a world of men *and* women and deal with both sexes. Therefore the child must have an adequate awareness of the biological character of both sexes. The dominant woman is literally made to realize that she must utilize those innate, inherent things in the biological structure of her husband for the sake of the child.

At one time Erickson was told about a wife who so dominated her husband that if she answered the telephone for him and the person wouldn't say who it was, she would simply hang up. She acted as if all communication with the husband must be cleared through her. When asked how he would deal with the man who was allowing this to happen, he said he would prefer to deal with the wife.

I would see the wife alone, and I would approach her in a roundabout way about the importance of the integrity of the self. There are certain things an individual must keep secret from other people, even from intimates. I'd point out that there is no reason why a wife should announce to her husband that her first menstrual day has begun. It's of importance to him, but still it's a private, personal thing. Then I would discuss the contacts one makes that should be kept secret. No woman should train a husband not to keep from her the secret of his Christmas present to her, or of his birthday present. It should be a secret that he is having his sister-in-law quietly buy her a gift. Or it should be possible for a neighbor's wife to make sure secretly that he will have his wife at the church meeting to be elected president of the group. There are so many secrets that are essential to the integrity of one's living. We even keep secrets from ourselves. How many men actually know which trouser leg they put on first?

I would let the woman know you can have full knowledge of everything, but that won't be comfortable knowledge. This makes it her responsibility to have comfortable knowledge for herself and to provide areas of significant privacy for her husband.

Although one of the more common problems is the struggle between a husband and wife over the wife's being too dominating, it also happens that conflict arises when the husband is too dominating. Clearly the problem is not merely how marriage "ought" to be but the conflict of the particular couple over this matter. Often couples manage two kinds of agreement simultaneously; they pretend the husband is in charge, while the wife actually is in charge of most areas of family life. Each marital pair suffers from the myth that it was different two generations back. For example, we have the idea that fathers were stronger and more dominant figures during the Victorian period. Yet our information on the structure of the family at that time is largely hearsay. An anecdote may illustrate the kind of mythology with which we live. I once began to inquire among a few elderly people who were raised in Vienna at the turn of the century about what their families were like. I was interested in what sort of family climate was evident in the time of Sigmund Freud, when he viewed the father as such a powerful, castrating figure. A Viennese woman informed me that in her family her father was a very powerful figure when she was young. She added, "We weren't even allowed to sit in Father's chair." Curious, I asked her how her father managed to keep the children out of his chair. She replied, "Oh, Father didn't do that. Mother did. She told us that if we sat in Father's chair we would get pimples on our bottoms." It would seem that her father was at least given the credit for being the power in the family.

At times in these middle years a wife enters therapy protesting that the marital problem is caused by her husband's being too dominating and never letting her have a say in any matter. Two of Erickson's cases illustrate his way of handling this problem, both when it is a gross and explicit domination and when it takes a more subtle form.

A woman reported to me a serious problem with her husband. They had been married a number of years and had saved their money to buy a house, an important event in their lives. However, now that they were prepared to select a house, the woman's husband had insisted that she was to have no voice in the matter. The choice of house and the selection of furnishings were his domain. She reported that he had always been tyrannical, but on this issue of the house she felt she must do something because it was important to her to have a say in what kind of home they would choose.

There are a number of possible therapeutic interventions for a problem posed in this way, ranging from treating the woman in relation to her problem of feeling helpless to bringing in husband and wife and helping them clarify their communication with each other. Erickson tends to focus upon the specific presenting problem and to resolve it in the most efficient and economical manner.

I arranged to have the husband come in for an interview and saw him without the wife. I discussed with him who should be the boss in the family, and we agreed absolutely that the man should be the boss. We also agreed that if a house is being bought, the man should have the final say on what kind of house it should be and how it should be furnished. During the interview I shifted to a discussion of the kind of man who is *really* the boss in his family. When I aroused his curiosity about what kind of man that was, I suggested that a man who was really the boss was a man who was powerful enough to allow his underlings a say in minor matters. In this way I persuaded him to take charge at a higher level while *allowing* his wife to be in charge of details. We arrange that he select twenty plans of houses and twenty plans of house furnishings, and he allowed his wife to choose among *his* plans. The result pleased the wife, and it pleased the husband, since he was really in charge of the whole arrangement.

Approaching the problem in this way, Erickson expanded the relationship between husband and wife so that there was more room for both of them to deal with one another amiably.

In another case of a tyrannical husband, the problem was of a different kind because the husband was so benevolent.

A husband and wife had been married for quite a period of time and were in a constant battle that could never be quite expressed. He had grown up in a wealthy New England family where everything had been done for him. He was an extremely meticulous man who had to do everything just right, and his life was rigidly governed according to the correct code of etiquette. The wife had been raised on a farm and was accustomed to a casual life, with picnics, camping, and the enjoyment of spontaneous activities.

The husband benevolently and protectively arranged everything in their life together, and the wife developed a tremendous resentment that she could not express because what he did was always proper and benevolent. The resentment came out in their sexual life in an unfortunate way. She was cold toward him, and he had premature ejaculations. She would get sexually hungry, and he would have a premature ejaculation, leaving her unsatisfied. When he was able to control his ejaculation, she was definitely uninterested in sex and would submit unwillingly and yawn during intercourse.

I approached the problem by dealing with different areas of their life together. I chose such issues as their problem in enjoying dinner at a restaurant, the kind of flowers he brought her, and their wedding-anniversary celebrations.

The wife liked to go out to dinner, and the husband enjoyed taking her, but a trip to a restaurant always turned into an absurd endeavor ending with both of them discontented. Supposedly he would take her anyplace she wanted to go, let her select whatever she wanted to eat, and so on. Somehow it always worked out that she never went to the restaurant she wanted to go to, she never sat at the table she would prefer, and she never got the food she wanted. Yet she always had to admit that it was a nice restaurant and a nice dinner, and everything was wonderful. But she would go home full of fury and feeling helpless. Her husband always offered her the opportunity to correct him, but in such a way that she could not.

The problem became evident in a joint interview I held with them. At her suggestion that she didn't get to choose what she wanted in a restaurant, he protested, "Believe me, I wouldn't do anything like that. I certainly wouldn't want to deprive my wife in any way." He then explained to his wife that the situation wasn't really as she described it, until finally she agreed in my presence that he didn't behave in that way.

I asked him if he would be willing to take his wife out to dinner in such a way that she could surprise him with the choice of restaurant. He agreed, since of course he wanted to do the proper thing. So when they came in the next time, I had arranged in advance a set of instructions for them to follow. He was to drive, and his wife was to read the instructions to him. Taking a city map, I had listed the streets he would drive. Starting from their home, he would go so many blocks down one street, turn left so many blocks, turn right so many blocks, then a certain number of blocks north, and so on. Then he was to turn in at the first restaurant on the right, which happened to be a restaurant we'll call the Green Lagoon. She had previously mentioned that restaurant as one she hadn't been to, along with a number of others. Actually, the path I outlined for them took them around the city and back within a few blocks of their house, where the restaurant was located.

My instructions included not only the drive to the restaurant but what to do when they entered. They had to walk past the first booth, walk past the table on the right-hand side, go over to the row of booths against the wall, around another table, and ultimately sit down at a particular table. The waitress brought the menus, and I had given the wife careful instructions. I pointed out that the waitress would give her the menu first and then give him one. As he was examining his menu, which he always read thoroughly, she was to say, "Let's trade menus." This seems a simple thing, and yet it changed his whole orientation. She was making choices from *his* menu. When he asked her what she wanted, she told him to order filet mignon, medium rare, the chef's salad with Roquefort dressing, and so on. He kept looking at his menu and closing it, and asking her what he might order for her. This extremely meticulous man felt that *his* menu was in her hands, and therefore he must think of ordering from that one through her.

The dinner proved to be quite a pleasant one. He thought it was delightful that those directions worked out so precisely to bring them to the Green Lagoon. Such a meticulous man appreciated this as a work of art. The next time they went out to dinner, he took over the situation, saying they had such a good time driving in that ridiculous way. "Let's drive the same sort of way and see what restaurant we wind up in." Then he repeated the same drive for a considerable distance and finally said, "Let's drive ten blocks more and stop at the first good-looking restaurant we see." (I had forbidden their going to restaurants they had been to before.) His wife saw one and said that it looked like a nice one, and he turned in. It was a big place, he had no pattern set up, and his wife immediately announced her wishes as she had at the Green Lagoon, and they had another enjoyable dinner. He hadn't understood how he was tyrannizing his wife, but he did understand that for the first time she really enjoyed something with him and told him so. He had never had that kind of gratitude, and it encouraged him to continue a new way of having dinner with her.

One of the major changes that came about with this couple occurred because they were about to have a wedding anniversary. Always before, the husband had arranged an anniversary party, which the wife disliked but could not oppose. She told me what he would do. He would arrange an ornate cake, have the proper people there, see that the proper toasts were made with the right vintage of champagne, and so on.

I saw the husband alone and told him that, with this wedding anniversary coming up, it would be delightful if he should surprise his wife. He should give her a surprise that would be absolutely unforgettable. I outlined the surprise while he stared at me with horror. I told him to rent a pickup truck and buy sleeping bags and other camping equipment, bacon and eggs, hot dogs and hamburgers, and similar food. He was to buy his wife some Levi pants and rough shoes, getting the measurements from his sister-in-law. I told him to drive into the yard that afternoon of the anniversary and tell his wife, "Here are your clothes. Put them on. You've got a surprise coming." He did just that, and their wedding-anniversary breakfast was over a campfire after a night sleeping in the back of that pickup truck out in the desert. I had also told him to do some mountain climbing the next day, cook another meal, and then get in that truck and get lost.

Again, he did just that. He told his wife that instead of driving back to town, he was going to take a road at random even though he didn't know where it went. They had a delightful ride. From then on he and his wife camped weekends all summer. She thoroughly enjoyed that anniversary. She had missed all the picnicking and camping of her past.

Now the husband looks me up about three times a year to review his adjustments and his wife's adjustments. She comes in about twice a year, just to review things. I know some schools of therapy would recommend that a couple with these buried resentments should express them to each other and work through them. My own view is that it is best to bypass the issue when one can. If the house is uncleanable, don't try to clean it; move out into a new one.

In the case of a power struggle between husband and wife, Erickson is quick to act if he feels there is danger involved. He does not believe that one should not intervene in people's lives, or merely offer advice, particularly when there is a risk to survival. For example, one mother who came to him with her child talked about her husband, and Erickson told her to leave town, not even going home to pack. She did so, and the husband later came in to see him, angry that Erickson had arranged for the wife to be where he could not find her. However, the husband admitted he had bought a gun to kill her. Later Erickson brought the wife and husband together in his office to resolve the problem.

A part of Erickson's confidence in his approach to patients is the sureness of his own moral posture. He has definite ideas about how people should behave, and yet at the same time he is tolerant of the various ways of living there are in this culture. His moral position is not rigid; yet he does not also continually question it as many liberal intellectual therapists do.

Usually Erickson's moral position is not based on an abstract idea but upon what will cause life to be most enjoyable. Sometimes, when one spouse seems to be taking advantage of the other, he moves to make a change.

One of my patients had a wife who had been married fourteen times previously. He thought she had been married twice before. I liked the guy. He was a nice, strong character. He felt his strength, but he didn't want to exercise it on his nice, sweet, mistaken, neurotic wife, who couldn't be blamed because she had had two unhappy marriages.

I saw the wife alone, and she wasn't going to tell me about the fourteen previous marriages, but somehow she "spontaneously" did so. She made me promise not to tell her husband. I pointed out that her husband had been awfully patient and kind with her. He had allowed her to forge checks, and he had made good on them. She lost her temper and wrecked the car, and he had paid for it. She chased out with other men repeatedly. I told the woman that her husband was now trying to make up his mind whether he ought to stay with her. I asked her, "Don't you think you ought to tell him about the other twelve marriages that you haven't mentioned?" She said, "No!" I replied, "Well, that's your answer and *stick to it*."

Of course she told her husband. She couldn't take orders from men, and I had given her an order to "stick to her decision." She showed me up by telling him.

When he found out about all the previous marriages, the man took a different attitude. He asked her, "How many times in your previous marriages did you commit forgery?" She told him. "How many times did you run out with other men?" She told him. He said, "All right, I married you and I'm in love with you even if you're a louse. Any more forgery, any more running out, and I'm going to get a divorce. I'll have the good grounds that you withheld vital information from me."

The wife straightened out. She was afraid of losing that fifteenth husband.

When dealing with a married couple, Erickson usually manages to avoid siding with one against the other, considering this an important general rule except in those cases where violence or total uncooperativeness is involved. Sometimes he will see the spouses individually and sometimes together. Often he makes this decision in his waiting room. He says:

> When a married couple arrives, I go in to see them and almost invariably I ask, "Which of you wants to see me first, or do you want to see me together?" Then I watch their facial and head behavior.
>
> When I see them looking at each other as if to say "Won't you please come in with me?" then I invite both of them in. If the husband looks at me in almost shocked horror and points to his wife with a gesture that indicates she is the one to come in, then I look over at her to see if she is pointing at him in the same way. If so, I invite both of them in. If he points to her and she looks expectant, I take her first.
>
> Now and then a husband says, "Before you see my wife I want to see you," or the wife might say the same thing about seeing me before her husband does. I don't always abide by their wishes. Sometimes I say, "All right, but suppose for my better understanding I see both of you together for five or six minutes. Then I'll see one of you." I do this because if they are too dictatorial about whom I should see first, they're trying to take charge—so I take charge. Then when I see them together I might prolong the time to fifteen or twenty minutes, but almost always I abide by the five or six minutes. Then I send one of them out, and I might say, "Now I'll see one of you for five or six minutes." I always limit it, and I give myself the opportunity to reconstitute the procedure.

Sometimes one of the spouses refuses to come into the office to deal with a marital problem; often this is the husband rather than the wife. Different therapists handle this problem in different ways. Usually a direct request to the reluctant spouse brings results, but when it doesn't, Erickson has one way of bringing in a spouse that seems unique.

> A husband brought his wife to see me, saying that he was tired of paying fees to a psychoanalyst three times a week for five years when his wife was worse off than when the treatment started. He told me he wouldn't talk with me, he just wanted me to deal with his wife and do something about her.
>
> I saw the wife for about seven hours before I managed to get him in to see me. I used a procedure I often turn to in such cases. I talked to his wife, and in each session I would bring up something

her husband might disagree with, saying, "I don't know how your husband would feel on this particular subject." Often it would be something that the husband would feel I was not understanding properly. After each interview with me the husband would pump his wife about what happened in the session, and each time she would mention this question I had raised about some minor point. After those seven sessions, he gave her orders to make an appointment for him. He had to come in to straighten me out, and then I could deal with both of them.

There are times when Erickson feels it is essential to see both husband and wife together, and he describes the situation in this way:

> When you have a husband and wife who are extremely suspicious as well as angry at one another, you need to see them together. You define your role immediately. If the husband pours out a lot of suspicious stuff, which he might do very subtly, I turn to the wife and say, "And he actually believes that and he's sincere in his statements, isn't he?" The wife thinks, "He's on my side," and the husband thinks I'm on her side. So then I say to the husband, "Now for courtesy's sake let's hear a few comments from your wife." She will then retaliate with less subtle suspicions and accusations. Because she's been put on the defensive. Then I turn to the husband and I make exactly the same remark about how she really believes that and is sincere in her statements. Then the wife suddenly realizes that I'm on her side but on her husband's side, and he reacts that way too. I give them just time enough to absorb this and say, "Now, you've come to me for help. You certainly want me to see both sides of this sympathetically so that we can reach the actual truth. And I'm certain that both of you are unafraid of the actual truth." In this way I define the actual truth as *my* view of it. Each thinks I'm on his or her side, and then they find I'm on the side of the actual truth with their wholehearted cooperation.

> Generally I feel I should manage to be on the side of both parts of the marriage, but now and then I take an entirely different attitude. If the complaint starts from the most vociferous one, and I see how unreasonable that person is going to be, I turn to the other and say, "He really sincerely believes all of that. He's convinced of it. Now, you know that a great deal of what he says, perhaps all of it, probably just a great deal of it, is not soundly based. You want him to know fully everything that is soundly based, and you want him to discard what isn't. Just as he wants to discard everything that doesn't really fit."

In this way I have justified the vociferous one, and I've asked for an absolutely objective attitude by the other. Yet the vociferous one has been told he's going to reject all that isn't so, and he's got to agree all the way along. Now, this sounds as if I were deliberately directing and controlling. Actually, all I'm doing is making it possible for the person to alter his own thinking and his own views. I'm merely pointing out, "Here are a few dozen other roads to travel that you didn't notice on the map."

When a couple is having difficulty talking about something they feel guilty about, Erickson will restrict their communication in such a way that talking about guilty material is appropriate.

Sometimes when I am seeing the husband and wife together, I restrict the wife from looking at her husband, and I restrict the husband from looking at his wife. They feel that restriction quite strongly. Their tendency is to sneak a look at each other to see how the other is taking it. But that's a naughty thing to do, according to their thinking. And so they bring out more material than they ever thought of bringing out. You see, they need to do something, they can't quite do it, and yet they've got to do something. Because they can't sneak that look, they have to communicate verbally. Since they feel guilty about occasionally sneaking that look, they express ideas and thoughts that carry a burden of guilt. It is a guilt-producing situation, and so they communicate guilts. However, with this situation you have to watch out that they don't use it for vengeance or to start recriminations. "He wouldn't take me out to dinner." You don't want that sort of thing. It's just faultfinding.

Erickson is willing to restrict communciation within the room in various ways, and either in or out of the room he is quite comfortable about requiring strange and inappropriate behavior to achieve some end. At times his approach can be like the therapy of the absurd. He might tell a patient to drive thirty-five miles out into the desert and find a reason for being there. He can also encourage absurd behavior within a marriage.

Once I presented him with the problem of a young couple who were expressing a common problem in an extreme form. The husband was unable to initiate behavior; he expected his wife to lead in whatever he did. As a particular illustration, on Saturday when the wife cleaned house the husband would follow her from room to room watching her dust and vacuum. This irritated the wife, but she did not know what to do about it; everywhere she went in the house there was her husband standing around watching her work. Her husband said he liked to watch her work. Erickson explained how he would deal with this problem. He would see the wife alone and instruct her to do her work as usual the following Saturday. As she finished vacuuming each room, with him following her, she would say, "Well, that's done," and go on to the next room. When she had completed her cleaning, she was to take the dust bag of the vacuum cleaner and go back over the rooms. In each room she was to make a pile of dust here and there on the clean floor. When she had piled the dirt throughout the rooms, she should say, "Well, that's that until next Saturday." Then she would refuse to discuss it with her husband. According to Erickson, her husband would be unable to follow her again, and they would have a fight during the week over an important marital issue.

When Erickson wishes to start a fight between a married couple who are being too nice, he might approach the problem gently or he might introduce something absurd. To deal gently with it, he will say, "If you were a less tolerant woman, and if you were a less tolerant man, what do you suppose would be the things you would disagree with your spouse about?" In this way the couple is pushed a step further toward expressing disagreements.

Discussing how to produce a fight in a more extreme way, Erickson says, "A fight can be started by the introduction of anything that is incomprehensible. Ask a child to polish your shoes, and when he gets through with them deliberately splash water on them. Then foolishly say, 'It spots them, doesn't it?' That feeling of being at a loss is a disagreeable feeling and leads to action. Or ask that a button be sewed on, and when it is reluctantly done pull it off and say, 'It really was tight, wasn't it?' If you undo something done and do something incomprehensible, it is so destructive."

Sometimes Erickson does not provoke a fight between a married couple but instead encourages them to go on fighting in their usual way. To have a fight under duress forces a change in the nature of the fighting. This technique of encouraging people to behave in their usual ways is typical of Erickson and appears to grow out of his ways of encouraging resistant behavior when hypnotizing someone. An example of how he encourages a couple to do what they have been doing but in such a way that change can take place is the way he dealt with a drinking problem of a married couple. He reports:

A husband and wife came to see me, and the wife was a pretty bad alcoholic. She was a secret drinker. Every day when her husband came home from the office she would be drunk, and they would have a nightly battle as he raged around the house looking for the bottle. She was mad because he hunted for it. It became a game of skill to find the bottle as well as a nightly fight.

I found out that his idea of a good weekend was to lean back in an easy chair and read *Business Week* or the *Wall Street Journal* or a book. Her idea of weekend enjoyment was to go out in the yard, work with the flowers, and when nobody was looking slip up to her mouth that bottle of whiskey hidden in the ground. She really enjoyed gardening; she also enjoyed the whiskey.

With the two of them in the office, I pointed out that every evening he laboriously tried to find the hidden bottle and she took a gleeful pleasure in hiding it. I told them to continue with exactly that procedure. He was to hunt for the bottle and she should hide it. But if he couldn't find it, *she was entitled to empty it the next day.*

I let them play that little game for a while. It isn't a good game, but he didn't like that hunting and she got too much joy out of it. However, the procedure *robbed her of the privilege of hiding the bottle secretly.* It became a purposeful hiding, not that guilty, shameful, sneaky hiding. It took some of the joy out of it. They had the most astonished facial expressions when I suggested that she hide the bottle and that as a reward it was his if he found it and hers if he didn't. But they had been doing that for twelve years anyway.

The next step was to have him buy a trailer and take her up to Canyon Lake and go fishing—without whiskey. I picked out boating as a recreation because I had found that she was raised in a lake region and she *hated* lakes and fishing. He hated fishing too.

I pointed out to them that being out on the water alone in a small boat without whiskey would keep her sober, which would be good for her health. It would be good for her husband to be out in the open getting some fresh air instead of sticking his nose in a newspaper in sluggishness and inertia.

Predictably, they began to use the trailer, but not to go fishing in a boat. They went camping on weekends, which they both enjoyed. She sobered up and stayed sober, and they began to enjoy themselves. They camped each weekend in all the available areas and gave up their battle.

This case illustrates an additional technique that is typical of Erickson. The married couple in this case was asked to get a trailer and go fishing on a lake. Erickson wanted them to change their pattern of weekend behavior; instead of their staying at home avoiding each other and drinking, he wanted them out in a new weekend activity. However, he chose fishing on a lake—which neither one liked. They chose another alternative *within the framework* he had established and began to go camping on weekends, which they both enjoyed. In this way the couple made a "spontaneous" choice about how to spend their weekends differently.

Besides encouraging people to behave as they usually behave, Erickson will also anticipate some change in them by having them prepare for that change. The change is more likely to take place if the people are doing those things that would only be done if the change had taken place.

Another way of dealing with a drinking problem illustrates this approach. Since he assumes that a severe problem such as drinking involves more than one person, Erickson usually works with the family in such cases. He has found, as have others, that the spouse of an alcoholic can react negatively when the alcoholic quits drinking, often forcing the drinking to continue. Erickson will anticipate this reaction as a way of changing it. He says:

> When an alcoholic quits drinking, his wife no longer has a chance to nag him. Often she feels lost and without purpose in life. One way I sometimes deal with this is to see the alcoholic husband and wife together. I ask him to define the problem situation for me. He'll say something like, "I don't think I'd be an alcoholic if my wife didn't nag me all the time." My comment to the wife is, "I doubt if you really nag him; I expect you express your legitimate regret that he drinks excessively. And that has used a lot of your energy in the past. As he improves, what are you going to use that energy for?"
>
> I persuade her to wonder about that. But by putting it that way, I give the husband an opportunity to watch her to see that she uses her energy in those other areas. And he has to stop drinking so that she can have that energy to use in other areas. You always tie the two in together, but you never tell them that. When you commit her to use her time and energy elsewhere, you're committing him to give her the opportunity.
>
> I'll point out, "Each morning you wake up with a certain allotment of energy. During the day you use it up, and by bedtime you're tired. You want to go to bed and replenish your supply of energy. When he stops drinking, how are you going to spend that energy during the day?"

Sometimes I take the same approach with the whole family, since there is always a reaction in the family when an alcoholic improves. I might ask the daughter as well as the wife, "When your father ceases to be an alcoholic, just how are you going to spend that time you spent in the past wishing he wouldn't drink, or avoiding him, or hammering away at him to mend his ways?" I've had school children say, "Well, I can put it in on my geometry." I've had a wife say, "Now I'll have a chance to do some committee work at church."

Not only do many young people today get involved in a variety of drug trips, but their parents become hooked on their own types of drugs. One of the most common is tranquilizers. Unlike many psychiatrists who see medication as a way of quieting and stabilizing people, Erickson views it as an inappropriate way of life. Sometimes he is given the task of unhooking someone from some sort of drug. He comments:

I don't prescribe tranquilizers for people. Often my problem is to get someone off tranquilizers. When someone asks me for a prescription for tranquilizers, if I merely refuse they will go to some other physician and obtain them. Therefore I don't refuse them, but somehow I don't provide them.

For example, a woman came to me and asked me rather desperately if I would give her a prescription to continue the tranquilizer she had been taking. I said, "Yes, certainly," and began to search my desk. "I have my prescription book right here," I said, and searched the top drawer and couldn't find it, searched the second drawer, explored the top of the desk. I stir myself actively in such cases, but I can't locate the prescription book, and meanwhile we have begun to talk. Somehow or other, at the end of the interview, she gets out and we've both forgotten about the prescription for a tranquilizer. If she's been accumulating any, she has to delve into her stored-up supply, because I continue forgetting in the next interviews.

When I forget, and she forgets, then her failure to remind me causes her to think between sessions, "I must remind him," instead of going to some other physician. But obviously it is innocently forgotten on my part, and unintentionally forgotten by her. That way I keep her requests centered on me.

Sometimes when someone is hooked on tranquilizers and I have to provide some, I offer the samples the drug companies send me. I point out that this will save them exorbitant prices. Therefore they get tranquilizers only from me, and I can control how few and how infrequently they take them.

Sometimes Erickson uses what he calls a normal cure for a tranquilizer addict. In the following case he reports using such a cure on a rather severe problem.

A physician discovered that a woman had liver damage from tranquilizers and telephoned me from his city and asked if I'd be willing to take her on as a patient. If a leaf fell from a tree or a scrap of paper dropped on the floor, she needed to take a tranquilizer. When she came in with her husband, her appearance suggested that she would like to be regarded as a normal person. I could see that if I indicated that she was neurotic, she would become hostile and reserved, no matter how much she cooperated with me. She wanted to be treated as normal. She had been in psychiatric treatment several times a week for reasons quite unclear. As I talked with her, I learned that she had a degree in music and her husband, who seemed a levelheaded man, had a doctoral degree in the sciences. Since she had a primary interest in classical music, I told her that any remedy for her tranquilizer problem should have a fairly classical character. Something that would last her throughout the years.

I pointed out that from her appearance, from the way she wrapped her legs around each other, and the way she wrapped herself up in her arms, she clearly had been taking too many tranquilizers and was suffering the results. I said I had a variety of tranquilizers that I was certain she would like and that her husband would approve. I said they would be extremely beneficial, but she'd have to do quite a bit of work preparing herself to take these tranquilizers. Then I told her what kind they were. I said that every time she felt a compelling desire to swallow a tranquilizer, she had to sit down and verbally and emphatically say aloud every obscenity and profanity she knew. She thought that was a good idea, and so did her husband. She reacted to my advice by feeling that there was nothing really wrong with her that wouldn't disappear as soon as the tranquilizers inside her were excreted. They went out happily and I set an appointment to see them again.

When I suggested obscenities and profanities, I explained that she had held back an awful lot of them throughout her childhood, and life must have been a living hell for her as a kid and as a teen-ager. She agreed with me. She told me various details about her mother's barging in her first year of married life, mother's demands, mother's expectations and arbitrary ways. I pointed out that classical profanity had been going on since the days of the cave man and had been found effective. She enjoyed talking to me and adopted this solution. It was a normal solution to a normal problem.

At the next visit of the couple, I asked, "What other problems do you think you need to talk about?" They agreed with me that the dead past was better buried and thought about intelligently.

INTERVIEWING THE FAMILY AS A GROUP

It is generally conceded that family therapy, defined as interviewing the family members together, began in the early 1950s. Many therapists chose this procedure at about that time, and Erickson was one of them, but his family work is not well known, since he has published little on his family-treatment procedures. Although his therapy is very much oriented to defining psychopathology as a family problem, he does not routinely bring in the whole family group for an interview. When he does do so, he works in his own particular style, which is quite different from the approach of other family therapists. For example, when a whole family is brought together, sometimes it is the mother who is dominating and defensive, preventing others in the family from expressing what they have to say. Many family therapists deal with this problem by asking the woman to be quiet, usually unsuccessfully, or they put up with her intrusions, or they break up the family into subsections so that other family members have a chance to be heard. Erickson approaches such a problem in a rather different way.

A father came to see me to ask if I'd be willing to see his family. He came secretly without letting his wife know. He said he was miserably unhappy, and his sons were getting into trouble with the law. Later, when he brought the family in, it was clear that the mother was the kind of woman who thought it wasn't necessary for the others in the family to speak; she would take care of that.

I told the mother that she must prepare herself for an utterly unusual situation. I had her place her hands in her lap, and I asked her to feel those hands very carefully, and to keep looking at them while she kept her thumbs just about one-quarter inch apart. I told her that she should watch her thumbs closely and not let them move closer together or farther apart. I said she would have an exceedingly hard struggle keeping her mouth shut, but she was to do that no matter what someone else in the family said. I wanted her to have the last word later on, I assured her, but right now I just wanted her to focus on her thumbs and not speak. Then I turned to the husband and told him to keep his mouth shut, and I told the first son and the second son to keep their mouths shut. Then I told the baby of the family, the least important one, the one whose opinions were least momentous, to start voicing his opinions of each of the other members of the family. They listened to him tolerantly, especially the mother, although she curled her lip, because that was just the baby talking. Yet once the mother accepted that, she was also affirming the right of the second son and the first son to talk, and of course her husband's right to talk as well. She had to listen attentively, because to have the last word she would have to answer what was said. Now and then I'd raise the question, "Are you really listening, Mother?" She couldn't speak without moving her thumbs, so each time she started to I would point to her thumbs and she would be quiet and listen again. Holding the thumbs like that is so unimportant, but before she can do anything she's got to undo that, and there's no reason why it should be undone.

In this way, it's possible to restrict the communication in the family so that they are motivated to become more communicative. It's just a temporary restriction. Because if you listen to little Johnny, and then to medium Willy, and then to big Tom, each motivates the other to be more communicable, because he's entitled to it. When mother's turn came to talk, she literally had to tell everything, since she had the last word. In the ordinary situation she could talk by the hour and never succeed in saying anything. But in that situation she had to have plenty to say on every point that the others had mentioned. An amazing amount of information can be brought out by that simple arrangement.

This procedure is typical of Erickson's preference for engaging someone in a struggle on *his* ground rather than that of the other person. The woman was an expert at talking, but not at holding her thumbs a certain distance apart. Trapped into that endeavor to prove to Erickson that she could do it, she found herself cooperating in letting others in the family talk, which was Erickson's goal.

When Erickson is working with the total family group, he likes to define each of their positions geographically and then shift them from one chair to another.

He has other ways of encouraging a family to talk in ways that he considers productive.

When someone in a family group isn't talking and I feel he or she should, I'll begin to bring him out. I'll turn to the person and say, "I don't know how many things have been said here that you think should be stated differently." Then I'll turn to the others and let them talk. Later I'll turn to the person and say, "There are undoubtedly some things that you feel really need restating." The third time around I'll say, "Have you decided which of those first things need to be stated differently?" and before the person can answer I'll frustrate him by turning away and talking to the others.

Frustration of speech is the way to encourage someone to talk. Sometimes with a person who has an emotional problem about being able to speak, I'll ask, "What is your name, how old are you, what town did you come from, what baseball team do you want to support?" Each time the patient struggles to answer and begins the mouth movements to get under way, the next question is asked. They tend to speak impulsively. With a patient who wants to be mute, you ask a question, just start a pause, and don't give him a chance to respond. With the next question you wait, but not quite long enough. You're so earnest, and it frustrates them until finally they say, "Will you shut up? The answer is . . ." They've got to let loose of their way and get hold of something new, and the something new is what you're presenting.

Sometimes in the first interview it is necessary to help someone talk. People come to tell you about their problems and yet are reluctant to discuss them. One way to deal with this is to say, "This is your first interview with me. You tell me you want to talk about some very painful things. In other words, I judge there are some things you'd rather not tell me. I think you ought not tell me those things you just can't endure telling me. Tell me the things that you can, with the least amount of pain. Be sure you hold back the things you can't bear to tell me." The person starts to talk, and at the end of the hour will say, "Well, I've told you all the things I can't bear to tell you." What they do is select. They think, "Can I dare tell this or not? I'm free to withhold it, but I guess I can tell this one." They always vote in favor of telling. They postpone the telling, but that's what withholding is.

With a married couple you can approach the matter in a similar way. You say, "Now, I want to hear both your stories. But there certainly are things that you're going to withhold. You're going to withhold them because you'd rather let your wife tell me than tell me yourself." In this way you're actually saying, "Would you rather tell me or do you want someone else to?" It's a facing of reality. Sometimes someone says there is something he would rather not tell me and I shouldn't pry. I reply that if he tells me spontaneously, he shouldn't accuse me of prying. He usually talks about it spontaneously.

Another variation on encouraging people to communicate by asking them to withhold is to give simple instructions to the family.

I will see mother, father, and son together and ask them to be very sure not to tell something that they don't want the other person to learn about. In other words, I make each of them very watchful of what he says. But while they are each watchful of themselves, they also become extremely watchful of each other. Mother will watch her own statements, but she's going to see how father and son betray themselves. What comes out are resentments, not merely recriminations. In this way you take over what they are going to do anyway, but out of your range of activity. You send them hunting where you want them hunting. It also prevents an alliance against you if you don't want that.

Although at times Erickson will see the whole family in a group together, or a married couple together, he often prefers to change a family problem by working with one individual while occasionally seeing the others in the family. When he does allow a problem to be "worked through," it is by carefully arranging how it is to occur. Such an arrangement is described in the following case, which also illustrates Erickson's view of what understanding has to do with change. He does not have enthusiasm for "insight," and comments on it in this way. "Helping a patient understand himself, become more aware of himself, has nothing to do with changing him. Most psychiatrists make people more self-aware but never get the patient to become aware of what he can *do*. It is irrelevant to know why a person does what he does. If you look over the lives of happy, well-adjusted people, they have never bothered to analyze their childhood or their parental relationships. They haven't bothered and they aren't going to."

However, Erickson does see a certain kind of understanding as useful. As he puts it, "When you can force people to get beyond the immediate confines of an emotional configuration and look at something objectively, they get a different view and then there is nothing they can do about that new understanding they develop. They have to accept a change." The following case illustrates this point.

I had been seeing a wife who was having a series of affairs. Her husband ostensibly did not know about them. She told me she wanted her husband to become aware of the affairs so they could either break up their marriage or re-establish it on a sound basis. I told her I would see her husband at one o'clock on Saturday afternoon, and I wanted her to leave town and not come back until Sunday morning.

When her husband—let's call him Gerald—came in, he began to tell me in a repetitious way what a nice, sweet wife he had. He just couldn't understand why they had conflict with each other or what the trouble was. ·

He talked about their life together, and he said that every time he had to go out of town on a trip, his wife got lonesome and so one of his friends dropped in. He was pleased that a friend came over, because he didn't want his wife to be lonesome. He mentioned that a friend had left a tube of toothpaste on the bathroom sink. Another time he noticed a discarded razor blade there which was of a different make than his own.

He talked about the visting friends as if they had come on Saturday, left at dinnertime, come back on Sunday, and left at dinnertime. Friend and wife had listened to records together and talked.

He talked about his adjustments with his wife and their constant quarreling and friction. Then he would mention that his wife had pubic lice, from her social-service work in a poor section of town. He'd comment that when he returned from one trip, there was a breakfast food at home of a different kind from the usual, and that there would be leftover breakfast dishes that looked as if his wife had eaten two breakfasts.

He began talking at one o'clock, and finally at six he remarked, "You know, if my wife were any other woman, I'd say that she was having affairs."

I asked, "In what way does your wife differ from other women?"

He said, "My God, my wife *is* any other woman!" At this point he became quite upset, yelled, waved his arms, and proceeded to go over the same details again. The toothpaste in the bathroom, the razor blade, the breakfasts. He identified every detail in that new context.

All afternoon I had been hoping he would say something that would allow me to ask that kind of question. That's why I let him repeat his story over and over again, looking for some little remark so that I could yank him outside that constricted configuration. Once he recognized that his wife was "other women," there was nothing he could do about that new understanding.

I made an appointment for him and his wife the next day, and I saw them together. I said to his wife, "Now, you keep very quiet. Your husband has something to say." Since she had been out of town, they had not talked together, and I did not want them to talk together now. I wanted her to just listen.

The husband went through the entire story detail by detail. Coldly, deliberately, he identified the toothpaste tube, the razor blade, the dishes, the items on the grocery bill when she had cooked something special for a boy friend, and so on. The wife sat there mute, obviously upset and distressed. She was amazed at the acuity of his unconscious recognition. Gerald also made some errors in his statements about what must have happened, and she had to accept those errors because she had to be quiet. I didn't want her to defend herself or she would transform the situation. She wanted to defend herself, but her emotion went into the idea, "I might as well take that disgrace as well." She was punishing herself with the weapon her husband was offering.

When he finished what he had to say, I told his wife, "You go out into the other room and I'll ask your husband what should be done next." I talked to him alone. He had received the passive acknowledgment by her silence and knew it was all true. He said, "What should I do?" I said, "You've got a lot of thinking to do. Do you want to continue your marriage, do you want a divorce, or do you want a separation?" He said, "I love her very much. I'd like to put all of this in the past." I told him, "That's an impulsive utterance. Suppose you come back here a week from now. In the meantime, don't see your wife. Do all of your own thinking by yourself."

He went home, and she went to a hotel at my suggestion. I set an appointment for her in a week's time, and an appointment for him. I happened to set the appointments at the same time, but they didn't know that; each was expecting just to see me. So they came in unprepared.

When they came in, I asked the question the husband would have asked if he had thought of it. I said, "Before we begin the interview to determine your future, there's one question I want to ask: You've been living at a hotel this past week. Has your bed been occupied only by you?"

She replied, "I was tempted several times, but I figured that my husband might want me back. I knew I wanted to come back, and I didn't want to gamble for a few minutes' pleasure."

They did little discussing of the affairs, so I had to ask the personal questions. I asked some of him and some of her. I said, "What about your good friend Jack?" He said, "He used to be a good friend, but he'll get the go-by next time I see him." I asked his wife, "What about Bill?" There were a half dozen college men she was having affairs with, and I noted the ones her husband emphasized and asked him about those, and I asked her about the others. They were disposed of.

I wanted the confrontation in my presence because I didn't want an argument where they would go back to previous patterns of behavior. He would think, "If I had said this . . ." and she would think, "If I had answered that . . ." Then it's a reaffirmation of past patterns. With the confrontation, the separation, and the confrontation again, there was no possibility of an argument until this red-hot situation had cooled down. It wasn't too difficult to keep them from dwelling on the past—I wanted to know about the future, not the past. Is this a termination of your relationship or the beginning of a new one? If it's termination—period. If it's a new relationship, what do you want out of it?

The two of them went back together, and the problem of affairs did not come up again. A year later when I saw them, they were saving money and planning children, which they later had. For a number of years I met them socially. Once some years later I was talking with him and he reminisced about marriage. He commented, "That was about the time I discovered my wife was just another woman," and he said it with amusement in his voice.

Although some marital problems are clearly a part of a struggle in a marriage, others can appear as a symptom in an individual. Many symptoms of an individual are obviously a product of a marital situation and are dealt with by Erickson in such a way that the symptom and the marital problems are both resolved. The way he works is often so subtle that a detailed presentation of a case is in order here.

A patient came in because of choking spells, gasping spells, all-gone feelings in her chest, the fear that she could not survive another half hour. When did these choking spells, gasping spells develop? She said any time of day or night. But it wasn't long before I discovered that they tended to develop before bedtime. I also found out that they developed at noontime, in the evening, at lunchtime, when friends came in to visit, if risqué stories were told. And so I let my patient think that she was separating her symptomatology from the bedroom by relating it also to casual visits from neighbors, casual social groups. But I always managed to get her to think of some risqué story a next-door neighbor told, some risqué story that was told at a social gathering. Usually I objected to the patient's telling me the story. Let's put an inhibition on the narration of the story. The purpose would be to get the inhibitions out and working, but to inhibit something else; let's inhibit the story, the narration of the story, rather than inhibit her breathing. There is no sense in trying to deprive her of her pattern of using inhibitions. Give her lots and lots of opportunity to use inhibitions. And so I let her inhibit herself from telling me the stories, but I *instructed* her to inhibit herself. She would not have told them to me anyway, but I merely took that over. Then I pointed out to her that this choking and gasping just before she went to bed must have made preparation for bed difficult. Did the steam from the shower bath aggravate her choking and her gasping? She had to think about that, but what she didn't know was that she was thinking about herself in the nude. And I was enabled by that question to get her to think about herself while in the nude without asking her to go through the process of undressing. So she was doing that for me as she studied that. Then I asked her if stepping from the shower out onto the bath mat—that sudden change in temperature from the warm, moist air of the shower into the relatively cool air of the bathroom—did that sudden change of temperature on her skin aggravate her breathing in any way, increase the choking or the gasping? If it did, would drying herself with the towel and rubbing her body improve it, lessen it, or what did it do? The woman is thinking about herself, rather extensively, in the nude out in the open in the room, not behind a shower curtain, and she is discussing that openly with me.

Then the next thing I wanted to do with her was to raise the question of what in the *bedroom* could possibly cause that choking, gasping, and painful feeling in her chest. Because she would develop that maybe an hour or an hour and a half before bedtime. Therefore it was the psychological anticipation of something in the bedroom. Something *in* the bedroom! Not something going to be in the bedroom, but something *in* the bedroom.

I assume her problem is related to the bedroom by virtue of that extreme, laborious way in which she smoothes down her dress and tucks her feet very carefully under the chair, holds herself rigidly and primly, the high-necked blouse she is wearing, the hair pulled straight back in a completely prim fashion, the fact that I know she's got only one child. Her entire manner is one of extreme and rigid, prudish modesty. All of her behavior suggests that—I don't know if it is so or not. But she is rigidly, primly modest, and she chokes and gasps every night.

Already in the discussion I've offered, she has faced the fact that she is nude out in the middle of the room, and a strange man is discussing her bare skin. It's been done so quickly and so easily, but it is a fact, it has already been done. That is going to teach her that she is going to face a lot of issues among other things in the bedroom. Now, very, very probably somewhere in the interview I have mentioned that undoubtedly she has this symptomatology when she is visiting her mother or father, when she is visiting friends —signifying right then and there that it isn't necessarily related solely to *her* bedroom, concealing the fact that I am aware of the fact that it might possibly be related to her husband. I am helping her to conceal any awareness of the possibility of its being related to her husband. But I *am helping* her to *conceal*. Then what are the things *in* the bedroom? Well, you know there are windows with drapes, there are the chairs, and there's the dresser. The question I asked her with very great interest was "Do you have your hope chest there?" Do you see how a hope chest embodies or symbolizes all of the hesitancies or uncertainties that a nubile girl has about marriage and about sex and every possible uncertainty, every possible inhibition? Fortunately, she did have her hope chest there. I didn't know it, but I wanted to know for a certainty.

When she mentioned the hope chest, I inquired if it was made out of cedar completely, or was it one of these lovely cedar-lined chests, or was it a combination—cedar-lined, cedar exterior, plywood? I've forgotten what it was. She told me what a lovely chest it was, and then I asked, "About how long have you been married?" "About twelve years." I said, "There have been lots of changes in your hope chest, especially after your daughter was born." "A lot of changes in your hope chest"—no further specifications, no further analysis. But a tremendously long pause, a thoughtful pause giving her every opportunity at the conscious level as well as the unconscious level to think of all the changes since that hope chest first became a reality; there had been twelve years of married life.

What else is in that bedroom? Of course there is a carpet. *Of course* there is a carpet. Do you recognize what that statement is? It's a most emphatic emphasis on the obvious. Of course there is a carpet—it's obvious there is a bed. But I have mentioned that bed so emphatically by saying of course there is a carpet. So that bed is as good as named and described. And of course there are all the other things—remember, I mentioned the dresser and the drapes and the chairs. My patient has an awareness of the other furniture, and I made an incomplete mention of things. It's an interrupted, incomplete task and my patient knows this. My patient is not really going to be interested in the mention of the bed. So I have met my patient's need not to mention the bed. But there is still a need to mention it; that's why she's come to me. Now, with that uncompleted task of mentioning the bedroom furniture, I finally achieved it by saying, "*Of course* there is a carpet." That "of course" means, "Well, it's a bedroom, you don't have to name everything in the bedroom." Now my patient knows that I am going to inquire into bedroom behavior. What do psychiatrists do? My patient is a college graduate. Sex has got to come out. I have got to ask what you do in the bedroom. And I ask her, "You know, in hanging up your clothes for the night, do you put them on the back of the chair, on any particular side of the room?" I'm actually talking about which side of the bed she undresses on—the right side of the bed or the left side of the bed or at the foot of the bed. But I'm not really talking about that. I'm talking about where she hangs up her clothes. For example, do you put your blouse on the back of the chair or the arm of the chair? As if that were an important question, and it is an important question; the word "back" and the word "arm" have crept into the inquiry and nobody has noticed it except the unconscious, because of that sensitivity. Because here is a woman I suspect of having a sexual conflict of fears or anxieties. And so we go into this question of where she puts her clothing when she has taken it off. And then my question relates back to the bathroom again. I really don't know what your metabolism is. Some people want to sleep very warmly in bed at night; they want pajamas and they want blankets. Other people like to sleep with a minimum of night clothes; some women really like these abbreviated nighties, they really do. Some of them like abbreviated pajamas, and some like long pajamas or long nighties. It is usually a function of how the skin reacts to a temperature change. We are still talking about getting into bed in relationship to body temperature, skin feelings, degree of covering. Then I can comment to the effect that one of the problems in marriage is often a difference in the physiological reaction, a matter of body temperature when sleeping. Sometimes a husband wants lots of blankets, and sometimes he doesn't want any. When a husband and wife agree physiologically, it isn't necessary to put one blanket on one side of the bed and two blankets on the other side. But I have mentioned disagreement between husband and wife and difficulties in their adjustment. She replied that Joe liked to sleep in the nude and she liked to sleep in a very long nightie. I've got my information very, very painlessly—by the process of cultivating every one of her inhibitions.

Next I spoke to her about different patterns of sleep. Some people sleep very soundly, some very lightly, and some very restfully. I don't know what the effect of this choking, gasping, is upon your sleep pattern. But I would like to have you think about the sleep pattern of your daughter and your husband, and then speculate upon your own pattern of sleep. She told me that her daughter could sleep through an earthquake. The house could burn down, and the daughter would still sleep. I pointed out, "You know, if you had a second or third child, you'd undoubtedly note that they had different sleeping patterns. Incidentally, was your daughter a planned child and do you want only one child, or would you really like to have a larger family?" When I ask was your daughter a *planned* child, are you interested in having an *only* child, would you really want additional children, what am I actually asking about? Did they plan sex relations very definitely, are they still having planned systematic sex relations? And yet it's a casual inquiry that you could expect from a good friend. Her statement was that the child was a planned child, that they desperately wanted more children, but that it didn't seem to work—"*it* didn't seem to work." So she is mentioning, quite directly, sexual relations. Then I switched immediately to this matter of a *long* nightgown. "Do your feet get cold at night?" Now we all know what cold feet mean. "And does anything in particular seem to intensify your choking and your gasping? For example, when your husband kisses you good night. Does that increase your choking or your gasping?" She said, "We don't kiss good night because he always wants to hug me when he kisses me good night, and I can't stand that pressure around my chest." I offered my sympathy about that and pointed out that it would, of course, interfere with love-making too, wouldn't it? But, you see, that's a tangential observation. What we are really talking about is kissing good night, and I make the tangential observation that difficulties of hugging would interfere with intercourse. By bringing it out that way, I have given her a face-saving explanation, and she can tell me very quickly and very easily. I've told her how to defend herself in explaining sexual difficulties. I much prefer *my* method of defending herself in her sexual difficulties than anything she can think up, because that places the situation in my hands. If it had come out in a different way, she might have said there were no difficulties in intercourse. So I've got this matter of difficulties in sex relations brought out. My statement then is essentially this: You know, sooner or later I really ought to go into this matter of your sexual adjustment with your husband; I suppose we might as well do it now. I am not certain how much detail we'll need, but I would say that anything that is particularly unusual in your mind ought to be enough to discuss. Now, I don't know whether you enjoy sex or have difficulties in having orgasms. I suppose your chest complaint interferes quite a bit with satisfaction. But I wonder if there is anything in particular that *you* might think I would consider unusual or different. She said, "Well, I suppose you will laugh at me when I tell you that I always undress in the dark."

First I asked her to think in terms of her own thinking; then I asked her to think in terms of her purposes in coming to me. Well, she's used to her own thinking, it's utterly, completely safe. So she starts thinking in those safe terms, and then I ask her to start thinking in terms of her purpose in coming to me. It was she who came to me and that was a safe thing because *she* decided to come to me. So she tells me that, and then she asks me not to laugh at her. I asked if she thought that anything that governed a person's behavior over twelve years of married life was anything to laugh at. She said no. And I said the words "governed her behavior through twelve years of marriage." What is her behavior through twelve years of marriage? It is a beautiful summary of twelve years of sex relations. So I asked, "Is your husband sympathetic with this extreme modesty of yours?" He wasn't. "Do you blame your husband for being impatient with your extreme modesty, or do you recognize that he *is* a man? And that he is going to think and behave like a man."

Here I've got a very crucial thing about her behavior. A woman who has to undress in the dark—this tells me that her husband would like to have the light on, he'd like to watch his wife undress. Therefore I add, "Of course you do the same when you are home alone, isn't that right?" Which is doing what? She can't really admit that she's so afraid of her husband, and I don't want the woman to humiliate herself by confessing that she was so unwilling to enter into the marriage relationship. Because she is going to condemn herself, and she is already condemning herself frightfully. So I pointed out that of course she does that even when she is home alone.

I had mentioned the drapes earlier, and now I know this much about her undressing behavior; therefore I go back and inquire about the drapes. I find that they are very special drapes; that she has window shades, Venetian blinds, and drapes all on the same windows and that she has got very special waterproof drapes over the bathroom window, which is frosted glass. After I had all of this material, so safely, I asked her, "Speculate on the most horrible thing that you could possibly do in relationship to getting ready for bed. What could be the most horrible thing you could possibly do? Just speculate on it, don't tell me, just speculate on it. I think it's going to open a whole new view of what your problem is, but I'm not at all sure of it. But don't tell me about it, because I want you free to speculate on the most horrible thing you could do in relationship to getting ready for bed." She sat there and thought, and flushed and paled, and while she was flushing I said, "You really wouldn't want to tell me, would you? Then she has got to be sure if she really wouldn't want to tell me, which is literally nothing more than an instruction—"Elaborate that fantasy, whatever it is. Dress it up, because you really wouldn't want to tell me." Finally she burst out laughing and said, "It's so horribly ridiculous that I almost would like to tell you." I said, "Well, be sure that you really would like to tell me, but if it is as funny as that I would like to know." She said, "Joe would drop dead if I came into the bedroom in the nude dancing." I said, "We ought not to give him heart failure." *We ought not to give him heart failure.* Do you see what that does? We are going to give Joe something but we aren't going to give him heart failure. There is my foundation laid very quickly, very effectively. I have told her that she is going to do *something.* Then I tell her that of course you know that Joe really wouldn't drop dead of heart failure if you came into the room in the nude dancing, but you can think of a lot of other things he'd be doing. She said, "Yes," with trepidation. I said, "Of course, you could fantasy entering the bedroom that way. You know what you can really do—you can undress in the dark, get in the nude, and your husband has the lights off usually, isn't that right? Because he is a considerate man, isn't he? You can enter the bedroom dancing in the nude in the dark and he won't even know about it." Can you see what this is going to do to her attitude toward sex? I was literally telling her *you can* carry out this ridiculous fantasy. *You can* find it amusing. *You can* experience a lot of feelings within yourself very, very safely. So I've got her in the process of actually dealing with her own reality, her own feelings. And then of course the double bind—I told her I didn't think she ought to do that "too soon." I cautioned her very strongly not to do it tonight or tomorrow night or even next week. But the week following that—I don't know whether it happened the first part or latter part of the week.

She asked me what the sense was of really engaging in such a childish thing. I told her there was one way of finding out. While her daughter was at nursery school and she was alone in the house, why not darken the house and actually discover for herself the niceness of a sense of complete nudity. Then I went on to discuss the pleasure of swimming in the nude. People seldom realize what a drag a bathing suit is until they can feel the water slipping not over a bathing suit but over a nude body. Swimming is so much more pleasurable. And if she had any doubts about it, she really ought to take a tub bath wearing a bathing suit. She would discover what a handicap clothing was. Then I asked her what type of dancing she liked. Well, she likes round dancing—she has done square dancing—she takes in a little ballet. She enjoys it. Incidentally, she does a great deal of knitting, embroidery, crocheting, dressmaking. She makes potholders and scarves for Christmas presents. She likes sewing. I asked her then, when I found that out, did she make her own nighties? I pointed out to her that she ought to make her own nighties, at least "run up one." I used that same phrase sometime later. That's a dressmaker's term—to run up a dress, run up a blouse. At a later interview I spoke of letting her nightie run up to her neck, and still later run up to the head of the bed. She *did* do that nude dancing, she enjoyed it. She told me about it. She said it was the first time in her life she had ever really enjoyed entering the bedroom. She said she went to sleep giggling and her husband wanted to know what she was giggling about.

How do little children feel when they have done something they consider ludicrous and daring? They giggle to themselves. Especially when it's something ludicrous and daring that they can't tell people about. They giggle and giggle and giggle—and she went to sleep giggling, and she didn't tell her husband, and she didn't go to sleep choking and gasping. She couldn't possibly anticipate going to bed choking and gasping with that tremendous sense of the ludicrous, the daring, the embarrassing thing accomplished. She had plenty of inhibitions about telling her husband, she had plenty of inhibitions about showing off for her husband. She had plenty of inhibitions and they were all laughable. Then I pointed out to her, "You know, when you were full of giggles like that, your husband must have wondered. It was really unfortunate that you didn't have some love-making, because you were certainly in the mood for it then with all those giggles." You should have seen that awfully thoughtful look in her eyes. Yet it was just a casual comment on my part. Then I asked her what else she ought to do. Did she really enjoy that sense of physical freedom? And *where* did she have her nightie when she danced into the room in the nude? She said, "I was using it as a scarf, and before I got in bed I slipped it on."

I began to deal with her directly about sex by asking, "How do you feel about sex relations with him? You know, we really ought to get down to the hard, cold facts of your maladjustments. Just as soon as you think you can discuss your sexual maladjustments, let me know. Let me know directly or let me know indirectly. I don't care which it is, and if I'm too stupid to recognize an indirect mention of it, be sure you make me pay attention." At the very next interview she said, "I'd like you to tell me all about sexual relations —how a man should behave and how a woman should behave." Then she gave me a very adequate account of her own frigidity, her own fears, her own anxieties, that choking and gasping behavior. The way she choked up at the thought of penetration, at the thought of defloration. Her own choking and gasping behavior, Joe's own awkwardness and clumsiness, his own uncertainties, and his own fears. Then she later told me about the rigid, stupid teachings her mother had given her and her own inhibited behavior throughout high school and college; avoidance of any incidental sexual learning. Never able really to think through it. She wanted to know what an orgasm was and to have me describe it to her— what should a woman's orgasm feel like? I told her that every woman has her own individual orgasm. "I can only describe to you what various women have told me—that doesn't mean very much. It has to be experienced and it has to be developed. Now, what are the things you want me to do to ensure your sexual behavior with your husband? You've used this choking, this grasping for a long time to ensure against it. Now suppose I insist that you use this choking and gasping behavior for something else entirely, something different?"

How many patients resent your taking their difficulty away from them? How many bottled chronic appendices are there in the family treasures? Have you ever listened to someone tell you, "This is the appendix the doctor took out. Do you know how many attacks I had of appendicitis?" They treasure their problem, but they want to treasure it safely. What I was saying to her was, "Let's put your choking and gasping into a specimen bottle of some kind—and you can have it, it's yours." She told me what she wanted her choking and gasping behavior for. She said, "There is a couple that have been friends of ours for a long time, and I don't like them. They always come and they always want drinks and they always drink too much. They always find fault unless we have the best whiskey. Joe likes them. I don't like them. Joe always ignores one particular thing. He ignores the fact that the man, whenever he gets the chance when his wife is out of the room, always mentions that he saw a good-looking blonde recently. I know that he is stepping out on his wife. I want to get rid of them. I don't want them to be friends of ours." Every time that couple came to call, she had a choking and gasping episode, and now she is rid of them.

Now Ann is very, very free in discussing sex. She goes to bed in the nude; after sex relations she put on her nightie. She likes to sleep in her nightie, she likes to make love in the nude. Sex relations three times a week, four times a week, sometimes Saturday night and Sunday morning, Sunday night. Sometimes when they are alone and her daughter goes to visit a friend on Sunday afternoons. Perfect freedom. She modeled some negligees, short nighties for her mother in her husband's presence. Mother sat there in frozen horror. Ann said, "You know, I felt sorry for Mother because I knew exactly how she was feeling and I wish she wouldn't feel that way."

This case illustrates the elaborate care with which Erickson will sometimes protect patients from facing issues before they are ready to do so. He will carefully manage the interviews so that the person is not confronted with an idea that cannot be tolerated. Yet he is also flexible enough to confront patients and force issues upon them if he feels that is the best approach for that particular person. The following case illustrates a confrontation approach. It also represents the economy and efficiency with which he deals with problems as he grows older. The case is that of a family with several members, each with a quite severe problem that has resisted previous therapy. Erickson reforms the family members rapidly, using a direct approach with each member. As is typical in therapy with a family orientation, if the therapist can produce a change in one family member or family relationship, the odds are that he will be successful with the next one he focuses upon.

A man came in and said, "I've got a vicious headache. I've had that headache since I was seven years old. I've managed to get through grade school, high school, and college, and in spite of that headache I built up my own business. I'm doing very well, but I have a headache all day. I've gone to hundreds of doctors, had hundreds of X-rays; I've spent countless thousands. They tried to tell me that it's all in my head. And I know it is, but they don't mean it that way; they mean I'm crazy. I finally decided to come and see you because you're a family counselor and the family does have a lot of difficulty. I expect you won't insult me. Another reason I'm here is that I find I've developed a drug addiction. I can't get along without cocaine and Perkodan.

I let him tell me the entire story. Then to his surprise, I summarized this way: "You've had this headache since you were seven years old. You've had it daily. You've gone to bed with it at night. You've awakened in the morning with it. You had it the day you were married. You had it the day that each of your six children were born. You had it when each child learned to walk. You had it when each of your six children entered kindergarten. And are you an honest businessman? Do you really think that you're an ethical and honest businessman?"

He was rather astonished. I said, "There are various kinds of honesty. It isn't related just to money, to material things. Because you told me the story that you've been keeping a seven-year-old kid's headache for years and years. Why in hell don't you let that seven-year-old kid *have* his headache? What's a grown man like you doing, hanging on to a little kid's headache for thirty years?"

He tried to explain, but I could only understand that *he* had kept a seven-year-old kid's headache, and I really cussed him out for that.

He was honest in business. He had to defend himself on a matter of business. He had to agree with me. It's awfully hard to agree and disagree at the same time.

He had to agree that he was honest in business, which was important to him. And to place a statement about honesty in business on the same level as accusing him of keeping a little kid's headache—you can't put them on the same level. And he had no way of disputing me.

If it hadn't been framed that way, starting first with the business, it wouldn't have been an effective thing to say about the headache. You have to start it in such a way that they have no way of countering you.

He left the office very angry with me. He noticed at dinner-time that he didn't have a headache. But he knew he'd have it when he went to bed. And he knew he'd want his dose of medicine. But he didn't have the headache, and he didn't want his Perkodan. But he knew he'd have the headache when he awakened, and he'd hunger for the drug. He was rather surprised when it didn't happen.

He came in to see me on February 26, and on April 17 he came in and very apologetically, in an embarrassed fashion, said, "I'm afraid you were right. I was hanging on to a little kid's headache. I've waited and waited. I've waited daily ever since that first day, and now I've finally decided that I haven't got a drug addiction, I haven't got a headache."

I said, "Well, it took you a long time—from the twenty-sixth of February to the seventeenth of April—to decide that you didn't have a headache. Rather a slow learner, aren't you? There's something else. You mentioned your family not being very happy. Tell me, what kind of misery did you inflict on your wife, what kind of miserable shrew did you make out of your wife, and how many of your six children have you damaged?"

He said, "Well, the oldest boy isn't very manageable. The next one is a girl, and she's very much overweight. The next one is a boy, and he's fourteen years old and still in the first grade. We've spent thousands of dollars trying to teach him how to read. The next boy had a harelip, and he doesn't speak clearly. The other two are yet too little to show how much damage has been done."

I said, "Now that you know all the damage you did by hanging on to a little kid's headache, you'd better send your wife in. You know that I can correct your dishonesty. Now send your wife in and let me correct some of the damage you did to her. Have her bring the fat girl and the fourteen-year-old boy who's in the first grade."

I spent four hours telling that woman, in very impolite terms, that she was the supreme shrew and she ought to be ashamed of herself. She was appalled. She tried to defend herself. I kept insulting her. The girl and the fourteen-year-old boy tried to defend their mother to me. I told the girl, "Now you stand up and turn around. How old are you, and how much do you weigh, and do you realize you look like the south end of a northbound horse?"

The girl was so furious she left the office. I told the fourteen-year-old boy, "Now, when you get home, I want you to take a newspaper and just copy one hundred words from it. One from this place and one from that place on the next page, and so on. Never words that are close together, but from a hundred different places."

I turned to the mother and said, "As for you, Mother, you just think of how you've changed from a nice, sweet, pretty young girl into a nagging, quarreling, screaming shrew. You really ought to be ashamed of yourself. You're old enough to know better." After four hours of that tirade, mother finally said, "I'm not going to take any more of this insulting," and she rushed out of the office. She lived fifteen miles way. She got in her car, and you could see the smoke boiling out of the car as she pulled away from the curb. After about the time it took to travel fifteen miles, the telephone rang. It was her voice, and she was panting. She said, "I ran all the way from the garage to phone you. I was halfway home before I realized that you told the truth. I was just burning up all the way until it dawned on me that everything you said was the truth. Now, when can I have my next appointment with you?"

I gave her an appointment for the next day, and I said, "Bring your husband in, and bring your fourteen-year-old boy. See to it that he's copied the one hundred words."

Both parents arrived, and I said, "Now, can you estimate how many thousands of dollars you spent on that private school and on the psychologists and special teachers for remedial reading and so on?" The father said, "Well, the county is paying part of that, because the school board feels obligated to have a boy learn to read. So they're paying two-thirds of the cost. It's costing us over a hundred dollars a month."

I said, "Well, let's see what the boy copied. Isn't it astonishing that he recognizes capital letters, small-case letters, that he recognizes the beginning of sentences, even putting a period after a word that was the last in a sentence. You know, I think the boy can read and is concealing the fact from himself as well as from you. If you'll turn the boy over to me, I'll get him through the eighth grade. This is April, school ends the last of May. I'll give the boy June in which to discover for himself that he can read. On July first, if he can't read from the eighth-grade reader, I'll take over the education. Cancel the contract you have with the special school. And plead with the principal of the elementary school to give the boy an eighth-grade diploma. They'll be glad to get rid of the kid. I'll see the boy." I set a date to see him alone.

When he came in, I said, "Bill, walk from there to there. Now walk backwards from there to there. Now walk sideways to the right, sideways to the left. Walk toward me, forwards, now walk toward me backwards, walk away from me forwards and away from me backwards." When he'd done that, I said, "You can now graduate from the eight grade. You can walk. You can't dispute the fact that you can walk. Now, you live fifteen miles from here. Beginning tomorrow you will pick up the right foot and put it ahead of the left foot, and then the left foot and put it ahead of the right foot, all fifteen miles from home until you get here at nine o'clock. When you get here, you can sit in one of the rooms, you can have a glass of water. Bring a sandwich with you. And you can read until four o'clock. I don't care what you bring with you to pass away the time. But be sure it isn't anything you play with."

One day he demonstrated that the battle was won by coming

in to me at four o'clock to say, "Can I stay another hour? Fractions are very interesting." He had brought schoolbooks with him. He entered high school.

When he first came, he couldn't throw a ball; he hadn't learned how. He hadn't ever played with the other children, he just stood and looked on. He entered high school that September, because I had explained to him, "Now, Bill, you can keep walking fifteen miles here every morning, arriving at nine o'clock. And when you walk home fifteen miles, you'll be tired enough to go to bed. Your mother will furnish you an adequate dinner; you'll be hungry enough to eat, and tired enough to go right to bed. You can do that September, October, November, December—that means Thanksgiving Day, Christmas Day, every Sunday—January, February, March, April, May, June, July, August, September, October, November, December, and so on. For as many years as you want to. Or you can enroll in high school and pray that you pass all examinations."

He enrolled in high school, passed with C and B grades, and he turned out for the tennis team and made it the first semester. He's now a senior in high school.

The father had a return of a headache once in May when a business proposition went wrong. His wife called me and said her husband had his headache back again. I said, "Have him call me up when he comes home." He did, and I asked, "How far is it to your office?" He said, "Eleven miles." I said, "Be sure you start early enough in the morning so that you can walk to your office; the fresh air will cure your headache."

The fat daughter got married. She ran away from her husband twice in the first six months. She locked him out of the apartment. Once he forcibly broke down the door. Then in his absence she went home to mother. Mother said, "A six-months-old marriage, two runaways, one lockout, one broken-down door, a third runaway back home. That marriage is no good." She took her daughter back to the apartment and had her pack up everything. She wrote a note that she would not see her husband again. The mother brought the girl to me and said, "You've straightened out the rest of us. What about my daughter?"

I said, "Sit in the next room. Don't close the door too tightly." And I turned to the daughter and said, "Tell me about your husband." For about three-quarters of an hour I listened to her tell me how wonderful her husband was, how much in love she was, how all their quarrels were nothing more than momentary flashes of temper, and all was sugar and honey."

At the end of three-quarters of an hour the mother came in and said, "I've been listening as my daughter told you how wonderful her husband is," and she turned on her daughter and said, "And you know what you've said to *me* about him. I think I've been the biggest damn fool in the world. I think I poked my nose in where I had no business to poke it. I'll take you home. You're not going to discuss your marriage with your father or me. You're not going to use the telephone to discuss it with your father-in-law. You can stay in our home as long as you wish, but you're going to resolve the marriage all by yourself. Either you are married or you are divorced. There'll be no interference from your father or me. We'll let you eat and sleep at home, but you won't get any money for anything else."

The girl had been so absorbed in her own thinking that she hadn't noticed I said "Not too tightly" when I told the mother how to close the door.

But that arbitrary manner of dealing with them. The mother asked, "Why on earth did I ever let you get away with what you pulled on me?" I answered, "You were in trouble, and you knew it, and you knew I knew it. You could find no excuse for the trouble you were in. You knew you ought to get out of it. You take medicine. You don't know what kind it is, but you swallow it because the doctor prescribed it. That's why you did what I said."

VIII WEANING PARENTS FROM CHILDREN

One of the comforts of life is the fact that human problems continue to be the same over the centuries, and so we have a feeling of continuity. Yet we also learn to think about old problems in new ways and so have the opportunity to change. A new idea came into the world in this century, and this book, particularly this chapter, is an attempt to communicate the new possibilities for solving old problems that have come about because of it.

Let us examine the way a problem was defined and a cure attempted by the great hypnotist Anton Mesmer one hundred and fifty years ago, and compare it with the approach of the contemporary hypnotist Milton Erickson today.

Writing in the eighteenth century, Mesmer reports:

> I undertook the treatment of Miss Paradis, aged eighteen. . . . She received a pension, being quite blind since the age of four. It was a perfect amaurosis, with convulsions in the eyes. She was moreover a prey to melancholia, accompanied by stoppages in the spleen and liver, which often brought on accesses of delirium and rage so that she was convinced she was out of her mind.

Mesmer took the young lady, along with other patients, into his home and treated her with the assistance of his wife as well as others.

> The father and mother of Miss Paradis, who witnessed her cure and the progress she was making in the use of her eyesight,

hastened to make this occurrence known and how pleased they were. . . . Mr. Paradis . . . began to be afraid that his daughter's pension and several other advantages held out to him might be stopped. He consequently asked for his daughter back. The latter, supported by her mother, showed her unwillingness and fear lest the cure might be imperfect. The father insisted, and this dispute brought on her fits again and led to an unfortunate relapse. However, this had no effect on her eyes and she continued to improve the use of them. When her father saw she was better . . . he demanded his daughter with some heat and compelled his wife to do likewise. The girl resisted. . . . The mother seized her daughter angrily from the hands of the person who was assisting her, saying: "Wretched girl, you are too hand in glove with the people of this house!" as she flung her in a fury head first against the wall.

Later the father politely asked to be allowed to take his daughter to a home in the country for a rest and Mesmer reports:

Next day I heard that her family asserted that she was still blind and subject to fits. They showed her thus and compelled her to imitate fits and blindness.*

Mesmer, thinking within the context of his time, considered the problem to be Miss Paradis. Because his unit of observation was the individual, Mesmer viewed the family as peripheral to the girl's problem. They were a hindrance to his treatment, and a puzzle to him because they did not welcome his success in helping their daughter to change.

If we go forward in time a hundred years, we find Sigmund Freud thinking about a similar problem in the same way.

I took a young girl—many years ago—for analytic treatment; for a considerable time previously she had been unable to go out of doors on account of a dread, nor could she stay at home alone. After much hesitation the patient confessed that her thoughts had been a good deal occupied by some signs of affection that she had noticed by chance between her mother and a well-to-do friend of the family. Very tactlessly—or else very cleverly—she gave the mother a hint of what had been discussed during the analysis; she did this by altering her behavior to her mother, by insisting that no one but her mother could protect her against the dread of being alone, and by holding the door against her when she attempted to leave the house. The mother herself had formerly been very nervous,

* J. Ehrenwald, *From Medicine Man to Freud* (New York: Dell, 1956), pp. 268–74.

but had been cured years before by a visit to a hydropathic establishment—or, putting it otherwise, we may say she had there made the acquaintance of the man with whom she had established a relationship that had proved satisfying in more than one respect. Made suspicious by her daughter's passionate demands, the mother suddenly *understood* what the girl's dread signified. She had become ill in order to make her mother a prisoner and rob her of the freedom necessary for her to maintain her relations with her lover. The mother's decision was instantly taken; she put an end to the harmful treatment. The girl was sent to a home for nervous patients, and for many years was there pointed out as an "unhappy victim of psycho-analysis"; for just as long I was pursued by damaging rumors about the unfortunate results of the treatment. I maintained silence because I supposed myself bound by rules of professional secrecy. Years later I learned from a colleague who had visited the home and there seen the girl with agoraphobia that the intimacy between the mother and the wealthy man was common knowledge, and that in all probability it was connived at by the husband and father. To this "secret" the girl's cure had been sacrificed.

Like Mesmer, Freud thought his problem was the young lady and that the mother was interfering with the treatment for her personal ends, possibly with the father's collaboration. Speaking of families in this same discussion, Freud says:

In psycho-analytic treatment the intervention of the relatives is a positive danger and, moreover, one which we do not know how to deal with. We are armed against the inner resistances of the patient, which we recognize as necessary, but how can we protect ourselves against these outer resistances? It is impossible to get round the relatives by any sort of explanation, nor can one induce them to hold aloof from the whole affair; one can never take them into one's confidence because then we run the danger of losing the patient's trust in us, for he—quite rightly, of course—demands that the man he confides in should take his part. Anyone who knows anything of the dissensions commonly splitting up family life will not be astonished in his capacity of analyst to find that those nearest to the patient frequently show less interest in his recovery than in keeping him as he is . . . the relatives . . . should not oppose their hostility to one's professional efforts. But how are you going to induce people who are inaccessible to you to take up this attitude? You will naturally also conclude that the social atmosphere and degree of cultivation of the patient's immediate surroundings have considerable influence upon the prospects of the treatment.

This is a gloomy outlook for the efficacy of psycho-analysis as a therapy, even if we may explain the overwhelming majority of our failures by taking into account these disturbing external factors! *

Both Mesmer and Freud felt they knew what to do with an individual patient, but they did not know what to do with the relatives, even when Freud conceded that treatment could fail if one did not successfully deal with the family. Each of them was working with a young lady and each of them found that when they produced improvement the parents reacted against them and took the girl out of treatment. Trying to explain this puzzling behavior of the parents, each therapist sought an explanation according to his interests. Mesmer felt that the parents of Miss Paradis were concerned about the loss of her pension and also suspected there might be a political plot against him. Freud sought the explanation in the attempt to conceal the mother's immoral sexual behavior. Faced with a similar problem, other therapists would explain the situation on some other basis. Yet what has been discovered in this century in hundreds of cases is the fact that this type of response by parents to the improvement of an adolescent with a severe problem is typical. The explanation cannot be in terms of finances or immorality in each case; there is a more general factor operating here. When a child approaches the age when it is appropriate for him to leave home, the "problem" is not the child but the crisis stage the family has entered. Dealing with relatives is essential to the treatment because they are *the* problem. Both the Mesmer and the Freud case reported here would be viewed by many family therapists as typical problems of the stage of family life when children grow up and begin to leave home. At that time new problems appear, old problems become more extreme, and a therapist who is intervening in the situation is not dealing with an individual but with a phase of family life where difficulties can take a variety of forms.

---

* Sigmund Freud, *Introductory Lectures on Psycho-Analysis* (New York: Norton, 1929), pp. 385–86. Freud's personal solution for his inability to deal with the family is a curious one. He says, "In the years before the war, when the flux of patients from many countries made me independent of the goodwill or disfavour of my native city, I made it a rule never to take for treatment anyone who was not *sui juris*, independent of others in all the essential relations of life. Every psycho-analyst cannot make these stipulations" (p. 386). Such a stipulation essentially eliminates everyone involved with other people in any dependent way.

Earlier in this work there was an emphasis upon the dilemma of the young person who is attempting to detach himself from his parents and establish a life of his own. For this to happen, the parents must disengage themselves from the child, and this aspect of the problem will be emphasized here. Not only is the human being the only animal with in-laws, but he is the only one who must go through the extraordinary shift from taking care of his children to dealing with his children as peers. When the children become grown and set out toward an independent life, major changes must occur in a family.

What Mesmer and Freud lacked was the idea that "symptoms" are contracts between people that serve many functions, including protective ones. Not only will parents resist improvement in a disturbed adolescent child, but the child will resist improvement if something is not done about his family. The more extreme his behavior the more possible it is that catastrophe can arise in the family with his change. Once one grasps this point of view, a variety of possible approaches to resolving the situation become evident. A therapist might undertake crisis treatment and bring together the whole family at this time of instability, or he might intervene through mother, through father, through child, through extended kin, or through all approaches simultaneously. He is most likely to fail if he tries to stabilize the situation by hospitalizing or prescribing drugs for the child. He is most likely to succeed if he keeps the focus upon the whole family and moves the child out toward a normal living situation while continuing the child's involvement with the family.

Erickson has a variety of ways of dealing with crisis at this stage of family life. His way of working with one young woman and her parents can be contrasted with the approach of Mesmer and Freud. He describes the way he dealt with the problem:

A young woman was brought to me by her father. She was an acute schizophrenic. The father stayed the first week to see that his wife didn't come to take the daughter home. Then I saw the mother. I arranged that the daughter stay here in town while her parents went back to the Coast.

The young woman was overweight; her thighs and hips were horribly fat. She also had a style of withdrawal, with a vague sort of fantasy formation, apart from this world. She had no coordination of tactile sensations with the visual. She could feel the arm of the chair, but not quite find it visually.

According to her, from earliest infancy her mother had hated her. Her mother used to take advantage of her father's absence to spank her as an infant. She was told by her mother that she was hideous and homely, that she had no future, that her father was no good and selfish. Her mother insisted that she had been beautiful and having this miserable baby had ruined her looks. My problem was to teach the girl to recognize the fact that she was a pretty girl. And that she did not have to overeat. I expressed curiosity about the beautiful thighs inside that wrapping of blubber.

I talked to the mother about her daughter. She hadn't wanted a baby, and when she got pregnant she didn't like it and neither did her husband. The mother impressed upon the girl what an undesirable child she was. In fact, she would laugh when the little girl was in the bathtub and call her a fat and hideous child. When I talked with the daughter about her mother, I called the mother a fat slob. I asked her why in hell her father shouldn't go screwing around with a fat slob of a wife like that who yelled and screeched and beat up a child that was a product of what should have been a happy sexual relationship. When I said that kind of thing, the daughter would tense up. When I had her sufficiently tense, I would distract her. I would ask, "Is your elbow comfortable on the arm of that chair?" I would get searching behavior then. I'd say, "Yes, you can't really find the arm of the chair—except with your elbow. Since you can find it with the elbow, you can really enjoy it. Your arm can find the arm of the chair, and you can find your arm." So I developed more and more her ability to feel.

I would distract her when she tensed up over the criticism of her mother to mobilize her emotions. I didn't want her to get her emotions roused up and then let her try to dissipate them in her own way. I could mobilize them, distract her, and her emotions were right where I wanted them. Then I could offer another criticism of her mother, intensify her emotions, and distract her again. I would say that if her father wanted a mistress when his wife denied him sex, I didn't see why that wasn't all right. I had her emotions mobilized and she could attach them to her father's needs and her father's rights. All her emotional intensity went into the right of her father to have intercourse with any woman he chose, including mother. Actually, of course, the father had *never* stepped out, but the mother had taught the daughter to believe that he had. By building up her emotions and then mentioning her father's rights, I was leading her to become protective of her father and inclined toward his rights I wanted her to identify with her father. It was difficult for her to identify with her mother except in fatness and all the wrong things. But her father was a good man, and when she started defending his rights, she started to identify with all the good things about him. You start defending my rights and what happens? You become my ally, you become part of me.

Given this description, it appears that Erickson is focusing only upon the daughter as other therapists might do who ignore the family context. Insofar as the daughter is triangulated with her parents, she cannot achieve autonomy without a disruption of the parental lives. With improvement in such cases, parents typically take the child out of treatment, develop problems themselves, and often divorce. It is not a matter of the daughter's perception of her parents, but their real life reactions when she changes and is no longer a vehicle of communication between them. However, Erickson does not merely deal with the daughter. While working with her, he continues a relationship with the parents that helps them survive the daughter's improvement. As he says, continuing his description:

I told the father to separate from his wife and live in a different place. Now and then his wife would get agreeable and he would go home and have sexual relations with her. He would stay with her a week or two weeks at a time if the situation was agreeable. The mother was an excellent golfer and in many ways a marvelous companion. I arranged that the mother call me regularly while I was treating her daughter. She used me as a sort of father figure who would talk harshly but impersonally with her. When she'd do something wrong, she'd call me and tell me about it, and I would whip her over the telephone. So I kept in contact with the parents while seeing the daughter.

I did a lot of work with the girl teaching her the goodness of her body underneath that wrapping of blubber. I could praise her body, tell her how attractive it was; it was still completely wrapped, covered not only by her clothes but also by a layer of blubber. She hadn't seen the beauty of her body, and I was talking about it—so it was a rather remote thing about which I could talk freely. I gave her a good narcissistic appreciation of her breasts, her belly, her thighs, her mons Veneris, her labia, the soft inner skin of her thighs underneath that layer of blubber. I was so interested in finding out what that pretty girl was underneath that wrapping of blubber. She's married now, happily so, and going to have a baby this summer. She married a nice young man of whom I approved. The girl asked me, "Should I invite my mother to the wedding?" She was afraid her mother would come and throw a weepy, hysterical scene. That she would denounce the girl and her bridegroom and the groom's parents and her father. Yet she felt she ought to invite her mother. I said, "You lay it on the line to your mother. Tell her to sit down, shut her trap, and listen to you. Then with absolute intensity you explain to your mother that she's welcome to come to the wedding, and to be *your* definition of a good mother—well behaved, well poised, and courteous." The girl really did lay it on the line, and her mother was terrified. Mother behaved herself in an excellent fashion.

Erickson's approach to this case is clearly one of getting a family past a developmental phase. Rather than focus upon the girl and have her parents take her out of treatment when she improved, he focused upon the situation of the parents as well. Simultaneously, he dealt with the deficiencies of the girl, established a continuing relationship with the mother and father that supported them, and reorganized their marriage by having the father move out and then move back upon his own terms. Instead of letting the parents separate spontaneously as the girl improved, which happens in many cases, Erickson arranged the separation, moved the girl out and established her in a marriage, and then put the parents back together again on a new basis.

Unlike many family therapists, Erickson did not work with this family by bringing them together regularly as a group. Sometimes he does this and sometimes he does not. In the early days family therapists often assumed that parents and child should continue to live together while therapy focused upon clarifying their communication with each other and helping them to reach understanding. When this approach failed, many family therapists shifted to a strategy of moving the child out into a normal setting (rather than a mental hospital), such as an apartment or boarding house, while continuing family-therapy sessions. Merely having the family talk together while the child remains at home never resolves the crisis of the child's moving out. Erickson learned to prefer an approach that did not focus upon bringing about togetherness in this situation. In a conversation in 1958 he objected to the idea of keeping the child within his family "so he can learn to handle his parents differently." He said, "Can a young person live within that kind of family and really learn to handle his parents differently? He's had a lifetime in which he learned how *not* to deal with them successfully. He's learned such a wealth of ways, so many tiny skills, of not dealing well with his parents. I usually arrange to get the young person separated while I go on dealing with the parents."

Sometimes Erickson will see the whole family together and shift the way child and parents deal with each other, although more often he prefers to see them separately and only occasionally together. An example of how he dealt with a relatively mild problem by seeing the whole family together illustrates how he quickly forces parents and young adult to deal with each other in more mature ways and with respect.

A father, mother, and daughter came in to see me and I saw them together in my office. The other children in the family were essentially adults and away from home. This last daughter was adolescent and stormy as could be. The parents were equally stormy, and the three of them were unable to listen to each other.

When I saw the situation, I told them to sit down and said I wanted them to talk one at a time. I said that while one person was talking, the other two were to keep their mouths shut. I encouraged a full and biased account of the situation from the father and the mother and the daughter. I don't remember the order in which I had them speak—sometimes I vary it. But in this particular case, I let the daughter have the last say.

Each one expressed his feelings while the other two listened. Then I said, "All right, let me think." In a couple of minutes I turned to the daughter and said, "I want you to take five or ten minutes, you can watch the second hand on the clock there. Think over in your mind everything you want to say to your parents— pleasant, unpleasant, indifferent—and go over the order in which you want to say it. Do this frankly, flatly, honestly. Now, I'll watch the clock too. It should take about ten minutes. I think you can get all the *thinking* done in that length of time. Then you'll know just how you will handle the next ten minutes."

Now, presumably I was having her think to prepare what she was going to say, but actually I was altering the situation. I said, "At the end of ten minutes you'll know what you're going to do and how you're going to do things in the next ten minutes." The girl altered in that fashion.

At the end of ten minutes, she said, "I've said everything I wanted to say to them; they just haven't listened. But they know what I've said and so do I. No sense repeating it." I told the girl, "Would you mind going and waiting in the other room?" She left and I turned to the parents. "How does your daughter's statement coincide with your own thinking? She says that she has said everything there is to say, you didn't listen, and there's no sense in repeating it." Then I said, "Now you both stay quiet and think that over. At the end of five minutes you'll know how you're going to handle the next five minutes." I had given the girl ten minutes, but I gave the parents only five as my concession to them that they were adults.

After five minutes they said, in essence, "When you actually stop to think over all the stupid things we've been saying, all the futile emotions you can have, you notice that no one has any respect for anyone else. Certainly not one of us showed any respect for each other here in this office. You were the only one who seemed to have any respect."

I said, "Do we need to tell your daughter what you think?" They said they thought she knew it just as well as they did.

I called the daughter back in and said, "Your parents think you might as well all go home. They say they know what they ought to do, and that you know what you ought to do. They say they think you're as intelligent as they are."

I saw that family only that once. But I know from other sources that the girl got along all right.

One of the problems in weaning parents from their children is the concern, benevolence, and overprotectiveness that prevents child and parents from shifting to a relationship more like peers. The most destructive parents are not those who treat a child badly but those who are so overindulgent and protective that the child cannot be allowed to move toward independence. The more benevolent and helpful the parents are at this stage of life, the more difficult is the therapeutic task of weaning child and parents from each other. A case that did not go well illustrates a typical problem.

A physician called me up and asked if I would see his son, who was a high-school youth who had been an ever increasing management problem. They had bought him a car, a stereo set, a color TV; they had given him a very generous allowance, and the boy had just become increasingly demanding, selfish, and destructive of the entire family.

I said I would at least interview the boy in the presence of his mother and father. They brought him to me. I told the boy to sit down and keep his mouth shut, I wanted to hear all the worst things about him that his father and mother could say. They reluctantly told me about his misbehavior. As they talked, the kid looked at them with a gratified expression on his face. I asked him, "Is that a fairly accurate story?"

The boy said, "Hell, no, they left out a lot of stuff because they're too ashamed to tell about it. I ripped up my mother's panties, I jacked off in front of them, I said all the four-letter words I could think of, I dumped urine over the dinner. You know what my old man always did? He gave me a five- or ten-dollar bill, and my mother cried."

I said, "Well, your parents want me to take you as a patient. I'm not your father, and I'm not your mother. I'm also not your equal physically. But one thing you'll find out about me is that my brain is a lot stronger and quicker than yours. Now, if you want to be my patient, you've got to agree on certain things. I'm not going to be the least bit kind like your father and mother. They want to go on a vacation trip. They'll be gone for two weeks, and while they're gone you can stay here and be my patient. You'll live in a nice motel near here. The rent will be a hundred and forty-five dollars a month, and you can order whatever meals you want. You can live the life of Riley. But each day you will see me for an hour or two. We'll find out if you can withstand various and numerous things I'll say to you, calmly and objectively. I don't think you'll like any one of those things that I'll say. Now, do you want to see if you can put up with me for two weeks while your parents are on vacation?"

He said, "I can give it a good try. But besides the rent and food, what about spending money?"

I said, "We'll be reasonable about that. I'll tell you how much spending money you can have, and that's all you get. Your father won't like it, perhaps you won't like it. But you can have twenty-five dollars a week, not one cent more, and no credit cards and no debts."

He said, "Well, it would be fun to see what you think you could do."

I turned to the parents and said, "He's agreed to it. Now you start your vacation trip, and at the end of it drop in and see how he's doing." So they left.

The boy did a lot of reading the first few days, good reading. He talked to me about books and we discussed what he wanted out of life. He could have the fun of making his parents miserable, but what in hell could he do after they were dead? What would he be prepared for? How much money would his father leave him, if any?

After a few days he said, "You know, spending that amount of money for one room with one bed doesn't make sense. I'm going to hunt up an apartment, and I'm going to get a job." So he found an apartment to share with two young men. They were both in their late teens, both employed, and they were working hard to earn money to go to college. They didn't drink or use drugs. He moved in with them, decided to look for a job, and got one.

About three days before his parents were to return, he said to me, "The hell with it. After all the damage I've done to my parents, I'm not going to amount to anything. I'm not going to see you any more."

For the next two days I had difficulty in getting the boy to come in, but he came under duress. Then I arranged that he arrive the next day when his parents returned. His parents came in, and I said to him, "Now, you give your parents a proper greeting." He used a four-letter word. I said, "Take off your shoes and socks, go in the next room and sit on the floor, and think this situation over."

I talked quietly with the parents and told them, "You've handled that boy so that it has become a contest." I reported all the good things the boy had done, named the books he had read, said he had actually secured work and held the job a couple of days. Then he had the realization that his parents were about to return and he would be confronted with the same old nonsense. He rebelled, and I had to have him brought to the sessions. I said I wanted to wash my hands of him.

The parents tried to tell me he was a good boy at heart. Perhaps they had been too generous, too forgiving. I said, "Well, I can't handle him now. And I'm going to let you find out in the very worst way how stupidly you have handled him."

I had the boy sit across the room from his shoes and socks and said, "You're going home with your parents. Now get over there and pick up your shoes and socks. Return to your chair and put them on." The boy sat there and looked defiant.

There was utter silence in the room. I waited and waited and waited and waited. Finally the father walked over, picked up the shoes and socks, and gave them to the boy. His wife said, "Oh, no, not that!" When he asked what she meant, she said, "No matter what, you always give in, you weaken, you do things."

I said to the boy, "Now what would you like to do? I don't want an intentionally misbehaving smart aleck on my hands. If you want to cooperate, I'll cooperate with you. Or you can go home with your parents and think over the emptiness of your future. I think your future is the boys' vocational school, prison, or a mental hospital, and it's not far off."

He said, "Well, I'll go home with my parents and be more independent. I won't use the family car, I'll walk. I'll get a job, and I'll sell off a lot of my stuff so I'll have my own money.

I said, "All right, suppose you go back to the motel and pack. I'll talk to your parents a while." After he left, I said, "You've heard your boy's statements." The father said, "I think it's wonderful." The mother said, "Are you sure he means it?" I told them, "He means to promise you the world on a platter, and he'll repeat those promises each time in glowing words. But he won't do any of those things. He has friends on drugs and friends who are thieves; he might join them." The mother said, "I don't think it will be that bad. He'll keep his word."

The boy didn't follow through on any of the promises. He became more and more disturbing to the parents and they finally had him committed to the state mental hospital. The boy called me up from the hospital and asked if I was willing to accept him as a patient. I said I'd be willing but he'd have to be as serious about it as I would be. He stated that after he had spent a few weeks there in that lousy place with those lousy people, eating that lousy food, he'd really be ready for therapy.

His parents came to see me and said they'd ruined their son. I pointed out that they had two other children, and were they going to be as indulgent with them. They said they weren't.

Later I got a phone call from the father saying they wanted to thank me for all I did for them and had tried to do for the boy. They said they were going to handle the other two children correctly. The father has referred other patients to me.

The boy called me a few weeks later and said he was getting out of the hospital in a few days, and would I accept him as a patient. I said I would, and he knew the terms. He had the satisfaction of giving me the hope of seeing him, and I never heard from him again.

I saw no hope for the boy, but I saw hope for the parents in one way. If they completed sacrificing that boy, they would then be forced to treat their remaining kids in the right fashion. I gather from people who know them that that has been happening.

In this case Erickson focused on the boy and did less with the problems of the parents than he usually does. He attempted to directly disengage the boy into a normal and productive life, and that failed. Whereas in other cases Erickson might work through one or both of the parents to move the boy out, in this case he did not. Whatever function the boy's misbehavior had in the marital and family situation was not dealt with, and Erickson found himself in a situation similar to that of Freud and Mesmer, where the family was seen as a handicap in the treatment of the child rather than as the problem to be treated.

A special aspect of this case was the entanglement of the boy and the father. Usually when a child is disturbed, one of the parents is locked with the child in an overindulgent way. The other parent is more peripheral. The treatment usually shifts the more peripheral parent to a more central position to break up the overintense relationship of the other parent. In most cases it is the mother who is overprotective and overinvolved with the child and the father who is peripheral. In this case it was the physician father who was too intensely involved with the child. It might be said that the overprotection of the boy by the father was matched by the boy's protection of the father, which took the form of declining to leave him. Erickson did not intervene in such a way as to shift that relationship.

Often Erickson works directly with the child and disengages him from the family successfully. Sometimes the approach he uses is to have the young adult look at his parents critically and think for himself about where he wishes to go in life. The parents are not ignored but are dealt with as peripheral to the child's real interests. That approach was taken in the following case:

A girl from a New England family was brought to Phoenix by her mother to see me. The girl had been through an unfortunate experience. She was in an auto accident and a friend was with her. Out of this incident she received some minor injuries, but four different families became involved in suing each other. The girl was also given two operations I told her I didn't feel were necessary, and she spent a period of months talking with a psychiatrist about her childhood, which I also didn't think was necessary. He referred her to me because he didn't feel she was making any progress and because she was suffering pain with no organic cause, which he had been unable to influence even with hypnosis.

She came into my office in a woebegone, dejected way, with her left arm in a sling, obviously crippled for life. She was living as a handicapped person who could not leave her parents, and yet there was really nothing physically wrong with her.

Therapy was essentially in the form of a casual social visit. I managed to get the girl to think critically about her parents, about her younger sister, about whether she had really learned anything at the expensive private school she went to before she started college. She hadn't really thought critically about her life before, or what she wanted to do with it. I pointed out that the auto accident had left her with some bruises and a couple of pointless operations, and what did she really want? To remember the past, or to think about the next fifty years and what she wanted from them? I told her the future ought to provide her a number of things; no quarrels with parents, no lawsuits. She ought to think about what she would enjoy. She began to talk about marriage and said her sister had married a young man against her parents' wishes and was now going to have a baby. She said her parents were getting reconciled to this. I asked her why a father and mother should have to get reconciled to the idea of their daughter's growing up and getting married.

At the end of one of the sessions—it was Easter time—I asked her if she had ever heard of a New Englander enjoying swimming in the winter. I told her to try the pool when she went back to the motel.

The girl's mother came in and said, "I don't know what you've done with my daughter. She's swimming, she's diving, she's enjoying herself. She isn't the girl I reared." I agreed with the mother that she wasn't.

After nineteen hours of treatment, including some two-hour sessions, the girl and her mother went back home. Before they left, I told the mother to talk to her husband and drop the nonsense about the lawsuit over the automobile accident. It should be settled out of court or dropped.

The girl returned to college, and the mother wrote me and asked if I would be willing to see the rest of the famiy in treatment. I wrote that if they proved to be the caliber of their daughter, I'd be delighted.

Later on the mother came to me for six visits, and we discussed the other daughter, whose marriage she was just getting reconciled to. I asked her if she had *misbehaved sufficiently* in that situation to have recovered from it, and she agreed she had. I asked her to write down all the stupid things she had done in her life. She did, and we laughed about those things, particularly the instances when she should have enjoyed herself and didn't. She went off to visit her married daughter and enjoyed the visit.

In this case Erickson illustrates his view of how parents should allow children to lead their own lives, and also his approach to a problem when the social situation makes a problem necessary. The girl was letting herself be used in her parents' struggle with each other and with other parents, even to the point of being physically incapacitated, rather than looking critically at the situation and moving out of it into a life of her own. The therapy encouraged the girl toward a life she wanted while also weaning her parents from their involvement with her.

In other cases where a young person is becoming disengaged from his parents, Erickson might work through the parents and hardly deal with the child. A situation in which the parents were overprotective and indulgent was dealt with by Erickson in a markedly different manner. He reports:

A young lady came to me very much alarmed about her parents. She had two possessive, oversolicitous parents. When the girl went to college, her mother did all her laundry, did all her sewing, and supervised her weekends. However, what was most upsetting to the girl was that as part of her high-school graduation present her parents built rooms onto their house so that when she married she could live there. The girl said she didn't know what to do about this addition to the house, because they expected her to live with them and she didn't wish to. Yet they had invested all this money and were being so kind. The girl had the feeling that she was being trapped by her parents and could never be independent of them even if she married.

There are different ways a therapist might view this problem and choose to intervene. He might intervene through the girl and help her to rebel against the parents, with a possible disruption of the family. The addition to the house would then remain as a symbol of the bad feeling between parents and child. Or he might intervene through the parents by advising them that they were treating their daughter as a helpless appendage with no rights and privileges and were dictating her entire future. This might or might not free the girl, but it would leave the addition to the house as a monument to their being bad parents. Erickson approached the problem through the parents but in a special way. First of all, he advised the girl to go along with what was happening and leave her parents to him, which is typical of his willingness to assume the responsibility for doing something about a problem.

I saw the parents together and we had a pleasant series of talks. I congratulated them on their concern for their daughter's welfare. They had anticipated the daughter's future, so I anticipated her falling in love, getting engaged, getting married, becoming pregnant, and delivering a child. In this discussion I emphasized how much more willing they were than other parents to take the consequences of these future events. Most parents, when a daughter is raised, feel their work is over, but these parents could look forward to a continuation of their labors. With their daughter living right there in the addition on the house, they could look forward to the services they could offer her when she had a child. They would be available for baby sitting at any time, unlike most parents who don't like that imposition. They could look forward to a baby crying in the night, but of course they had soundproofed the wall to the additional rooms? It happens they hadn't. So I congratulated them on being willing to put up with the problems of a small baby as they had when they were young and their daughter was a baby. Then we talked about their future grandchild beginning to walk, and of course, living right there, he would be in and out of their house all the time. We recalled what it was like to have a toddler getting into everything, and how all breakable things had to be placed up high and the house rearranged. Other grandparents wouldn't be that willing to sacrifice their ways of living.

The parents began to express some doubt about whether they really wished their daughter to be living that close to them.

To assist this process, I anticipated with the mother how she would have to deal with her husband's lack of understanding of their future grandson. With the husband, I anticipated his wife's lack of understanding of the child when she became a grandmother. Their differences over the daughter were shifted so they could anticipate differences about the grandchild. This would be a problem they could look forward to dealing with continually with the daughter living right there with them. Each of them agreed with me that the other probably wouldn't be as good a grandparent as might be.

After this discussion they decided they really didn't want to have their daughter and her family living with them, and yet they faced a dilemma. That addition to the house had cost so much money that they might *have* to have the daughter living there. Out of the discussion we "spontaneously" came up with a good idea. The additional rooms could be rented out to some mature, quiet person and the rent could be put aside in the bank for their future grandchild's education.

Later on the daughter did get married and lived in a city some distance away, with the full agreement of her parents. When the daughter had a baby, her parents came to me and consulted me about how often the other one was entitled to visit their grandchild. I said to grandpa that grandma ought not to visit more often than one afternoon every six weeks or two months. By a curious coincidence, I thought the same visiting times would be appropriate for grandpa.

When asked about whether the parents would have benefited from some "insight" into how they had been dealing with their daughter, Erickson pointed out the problem of the addition to the house. He said, "You and I can look at the addition to the house and think what an awful thing it was for them to think of that daughter as someone whose future they should dictate in that way. That addition is the tangible evidence of that dictation. Yet the parents don't see it that way. They think of it as a nice source of income for their grandson. Which is better? Is it essential to feel guilt? I don't believe in salvation only through pain and suffering."

Since Erickson thinks of families in terms of different stages of development, he assumes a major shift for parents is to take the next step and become grandparents. Often he uses this shift to free the child at the time when he should leave home.

Sometimes when dealing with overpossessive parents, I introduce a threat—"When your son reaches your age, will he have the same trouble with his children?" I've actually accused them of having a future of being grandparents. When this is done properly, they have to resolve the son's difficulties all the way along the line up to the point of being grandparents.

When you get them thinking about being grandparents, the husband can think, "What kind of grandmother would she make?" She starts thinking the same thing about him. They haven't seen that coming, and you can get them to accept the idea of a change in themselves and to view each other critically. To deal with their competition and conflict at the grandparent level, they have to have Sonny produce a grandchild. Mother can then deal with her husband's deficiencies as a grandparent, and he can deal with hers. In the anticipation of that fight, they can go for a period of years while the child is out and developing.

Since Erickson doesn't believe that merely pointing out to people that they shouldn't behave as they do is often helpful, he usually doesn't advise parents to behave differently, but arranges that they do so. Sometimes he does this by shifting the ground on which the battle takes place. Occasionally when hypnotizing a subject he will say, "Would you rather go into a trance now or later," as a way of presenting an issue of *when* to go into a trance rather than *whether* to. This is similar to his shift of a parental conflict from the question whether people have been good parents to whether they will be good grandparents. In the following case he focused a mother on the problem of becoming a good grandmother.

In a family I'm dealing with there are three boys, age twenty-three, nineteen, and seventeen. The therapy has been centered on getting the older boy out of the home, the second boy out on his own, and the third boy out and living with his oldest brother while going to school. It's a family with a most unfortunate struggle between the parents and a mother who has always run the whole show. The father is an artist who felt he had never managed to have even his own choice of what form of art to work in because his wife took over everything he did.

As I managed to move the sons out and into school away from home, the father became worried about the mother. I concentrated on the mother and pointed out that she was making one of life's most important transitional steps—from being a good wife and mother in the past to being a good grandmother in the future. I emphasized to her that she now occupied the position of *expectant* grandmother; not a wife or mother but someone who is preparing herself for the day when her sons marry and produce children. She began to work on the expectant-grandmother position, attempting to do her best in it, since she is a woman who likes to do things well. Yet it's vaguely defined while being at the same time plausible and real. She began to be less overmothering to her sons, because she was no longer a mother but an expectant grandmother, and she struggled less with her husband, because she had this important task to sustain her.

When a mother is overinvolved with a child and cannot release him, Erickson does not assume that this is a rational matter that can be dealt with rationally by the mother. His approach to resolving it will vary, but when he deals directly with the mother on the issue, rather than with the whole family, he is likely to do so in a characteristic way. Once he was posed the problem of a mother who was holding on to her daughter but did not see it that way. The mother complained of her daughter's being a perpetual burden, while behaving in a way that kept her daughter attached to her. When the girl had made a real move toward independence by going away to college at the age of eighteen, the mother decided to go to college and went there to join her, with her daughter's encouragement. The girl had a schizophrenic episode and was hospitalized. Over the years, with the girl in and out of the hospital, the mother found she could not get with the girl and could not get away from her, but she seemed unaware that she was unable to separate herself from her daughter, even though a number of psychiatrists had pointed this out to her. Commenting on the problem, Erickson said he would never try to make the mother aware that she had difficulty letting her daughter go. He offered other alternatives.

One procedure that I use is to question the overpossessive mother about her daughter's growth and development. I say to the mother, "You want to establish your daughter as an independent creature. You're quite right in wanting that. But there are a number of things that you have to help me understand about what's wrong with the girl that she doesn't seem to be willing to leave. Now, when your daughter grew from a little girl and entered into puberty, what was the first thing about her pubertal changes that she brought to your attention? Did she alter the way she moved her chest as she was developing breasts? Did she bring her pelvis to your attention? Did she manage to take a bath and ask you to bring a towel so she could let you know that she was growing pubic hair? Just what was her attitude toward lipstick? Was she willing to learn from you to utilize to the fullest her lip contour?"

In this way I take the mother systematically through all the changing steps of her daughter's pubertal growth and development, always emphasizing how the daughter is a different person from herself. In this way the mother develops a sense of not belonging in her daughter's generation or class in college. By emphasizing the growth of the daughter, the mother is being established as an adult, mature female. She is thinking of her daughter's development of pubic hair and breasts that are going to be meaningful to another man than father.

To a possessive mother, the entrance of the daughter into puberty is a shocking experience. I wouldn't help the mother become aware that she has difficulty letting the daughter go as she gets older. I would emphasize how the daughter first appealed to a fifteen-year-old boy, then a sixteen-, seventeen-, and eighteen-year-old. The daughter would be defined as not really appealing to mature men, like father, as mother is. Daughter is appealing to immature boys. That emphasizes the mother's superior maturity, and so the mother is differentiating herself. She's being forced to the conclusion that daughter might be fish, but *she* is fowl. Who wants to hang on to a fish when you really are a bird?

Sometimes with an overpossessive mother with a son, I manage to get the son to move outside the family. When mother finds that this has happened, I prevent her from doing something about it. She really wants to get her son back with her. I frustrate her by continuing to see her but flatly and absolutely refusing to discuss her son's living situation. She can't do anything about getting Sonny back home until she first discusses it with me and makes me admit that I was in error.

Actually a son starts to leave his mother when he enters his teens. Up to that point he is her baby, an undifferentiated human being, but at puberty he becomes a male—destined for some other female.

As another approach to encouraging a mother to release her child, Erickson weans her in the following way:

At times you find that a child has reached the age of leaving home, but he cannot. He cannot get away from his parents or get with them. When he moves toward them they push him away, and when he moves away they pull him toward them. What I do in some of these cases is to disorient the parents so that when the child tries to get away they push him away.

In one family I was trying to move a son out of the parental home to live with his older brother. I talked to the overpossessive mother in a special way. Often she would say to me that I didn't understand her. When she said, "But you don't understand," I would immediately mention that as long as her son lived at home she would have an opportunity to understand *him*. I did that over and over again—when she said I *didn't understand* her, I mentioned something about her son living at home. When she said that I *did understand* her in some regard, I would say, "This idea of your son living with his brother. I haven't made up my mind about it." So when I *did understand* her, I was talking about the son moving out. It was finally the mother who insisted that her son should move out and live with his brother. She's glad she thought of that.

Both mother and father have an attachment to a child, but the child also has a function in their marriage relationship. Therefore that relationship must be changed if the child is to be disengaged to have an independent life. Parents usually present the problem as having nothing to do with them or their marriage. Everything is fine except for the boy who is behaving strangely.

"We would be so happy if Sam wasn't sick." Often the child is presented as their *only* bone of contention in the marriage as well as their only frustration in life. By presenting a united front on this issue, the parents have an excuse for all their difficulties. Erickson often shifts the issue to the marriage. One way he does it is to change the pseudo-alliance of the parents.

When a couple comes in with obvious problems with each other, but they only emphasize the problem of the child, you need to deal with the united front the parents are offering. You have to break it up without seeming to do so. One way I approach it is to say to the wife, while the husband smiles smugly to himself, "You know, to explain things to me you really have to make it rather simple. Because, being a man, I can't really understand the subtleties of what you say." What does the woman do? She steps on the other side of the fence right away. She is going to differentiate herself from her husband and me as a female, in contrast to us poor miserable males. Her husband is going to recognize that I'm an intelligent male and that I really understand the masculine side. He steps over and joins me. I've got their united front undone.

To bring the wife on my side, at some point I define myself as no longer the poor, stupid male. I become the interested third party who is not involved in their struggle. Then I'm on both sides of the fence. I'm on his, but also on hers. Being an objective, interested third party, I can really understand a woman's side. That gives the woman the opportunity to feel either way about me. If she wants to view me as a stupid male, then she's going to compensate for that by crediting me with intelligence. Because she just isn't going to waste her time on a completely stupid man. She came to me because I'm an intelligent, objective person. My stupidity gives her the opportunity to reject, and in return she is under obligation to receive.

When a family situation has gone badly, a member of the family is often extruded into a mental hospital. Sometimes this is temporary; often there is a brief hospitalization, then a longer one, and this process repeats itself until the person is established in a career as a chronic hospital patient. Like most psychiatrists, Erickson received his training in the mental-hospital setting. Unlike most psychiatrists, he developed effective ways of dealing with chronic patients. In his experience at Rhode Island State Hospital and Worcester State Hospital and when he was director of psychiatric research and training at Wayne County General Hospital and Infirmary, Erickson innovated a number of ways of approaching "mental patients." Sometimes his goal was to manage a patient into being a more productive person within the hospital, and sometimes his goal was to move him back into the world again.

Often in a mental-hospital situation the patients and the staff became involved in a power struggle that can end with the patient's demeaning or destroying himself as a person. Erickson's approach often is to enter the power struggle but to use it in such a way that the patient is forced to become a productive person. As he puts it, "You always take charge in the form of a joint enterprise, going along with what the person wants." Before describing the next case, where Erickson goes to the mat with a patient and wins what is essentially a death struggle, a comment he has made on the misuse of benevolence might be in order. He said once,

Psychiatrists, and doctors in general, often think they know what is good for the patient. I recall a millionaire in Los Angeles who said to me, "I've waited a long time to meet you and take you out to dinner. I want to buy you the kind of dinner you'll like. The sky's the limit." As we sat in the restaurant and looked over the menu, I saw that they happened to have corned beef and cabbage. It was only a dollar sixty-five, and I ordered it. The man was shocked and said, "You don't want that." He told the waiter to cancel that order and bring two of the twelve-dollar steaks. When the waiter brought them, I said, "They're for that gentleman; he ordered them. Now go and get my corned beef and cabbage." That chap leaned back and said, "Never in my life have I had anybody set me back on my heels like that." I said, "But you told me to order what I really like, and I like corned beef and cabbage. I think I'll enjoy it more than you will those two steaks."

This concern of Erickson's about a person's choosing his own way—and his own food—is demonstrated in a case that shows what can be done if a person is destroying himself by not eating.

A young man—we'll call him Herbert—became acutely depressed and was hospitalized. He had been working at a weight of 240 pounds, but he declined to eat and was down to eighty pounds after six months in the hospital. He spent his time standing upright in a corner, not moving. Although he would talk, he spoke in a sardonic, negativistic way about everything.

It was necessary to tube-feed Herbert since he would not eat, and he expressed a sardonic view of the tube feeding. He insisted he had no insides, no stomach, and therefore when he was tube-fed he said he didn't know where the tube feeding went since he had no insides. He assumed it was a matter of "legerdemain" when it disappeared. It was not in the room, but it was not in him because he had no stomach.

For a week, each time I tube-fed Herbert, I explained to him that I was going to let *him* prove to *me* that he had a stomach. I said he would also prove to himself that he perceived the tube feeding; all the proof would come from him. Each time I fed him I would repeat this. I said he would prove to himself he had a stomach and then acknowledge that proof to me. The proof would come entirely from him. Herbert made rather sacrastic remarks about this. A fellow talking as I did just didn't make sense.

At the end of a week, I put a special mixture into the tube-feeding equipment. I put in eggnog, raw cod-liver oil, baking soda, and vinegar. Ordinarily you keep air out when you administer a tube feeding so that only the first column of air is forced down. But I poured the mixture in small cupfuls, thereby forcing more and more air into his stomach.

I pulled out the tube. "Burp!" went Herbert. I could smell it, the attendant could smell it. Herbert gave proof that the tube feeding went into his stomach, and gave it to himself first. Never after that did he dispute the issue that he had a stomach. However, he would not feed himself because he said he had no means of swallowing.

He gained weight, and I focused on the swallowing issue. For a week, each time I tube-fed him, I told him that he would swallow some liquid the following Monday. I said that next Monday morning there would be a glass of water and a glass of milk on the table in the dining room. He would be the first one in line to get into the dining room when the door was opened so that he could drink down one or the other or both glasses of fluid. He allowed that I didn't have much common sense. He said he had no means of swallowing. However, I had given him that first experience of proof from within himself, and I provided that again.

On Sunday night I gave him a thick and heavy tube feeding with a great deal of table salt in it. I locked him in a room overnight. At five o'clock the next morning, having been thirsty all night long, he tried to rush to the bathrooms to get water, but I had seen that they were all locked. He remembered about the two glasses of fluid in the dining room and was the first in line at the dining-room door. He was the first patient through when it opened, and he drank that water. He told me, "You think you're smart, don't you."

I said to Herbert, "You have a stomach, and you can swallow, so I think you can eat at the table." He protested, "I can't eat solid food." I said, "At least you can eat soup. Whatever solids are in the soup go down with the liquid of the soup."

I sat Herbert at the table and I wouldn't let him get up until his soup plate was empty. He didn't like sitting there, so he would eat it. I added something to encourage him to eat faster. Beside him I placed a patient who wouldn't eat from his own plate but always stole food from the people on each side of him. So he would reach over and put his dirty fingers into the soup Herbert had to eat, taking out what was in it and eating it. Herbert had to eat fast to keep that patient from putting his dirty fingers into that soup. The faster he swallowed, the less dirt. I just kept on increasing the quantity of solids in the soup.

Next I sent Herbert out to work on the farm attached to the hospital. I had him saw logs, of a large diameter, made of hardwood. I told him it was too bad the saw was so darn dull. He worked with a partner, but the fellow would just ride the saw and let Herbert do the work. The weather was cold. You get awfully hungry out in the cold trying to pull a dull saw across hardwood with the other guy not pulling his share. I explained to Herbert that there was a special treat for lunch. He said, "What sort of hellish torture are you cooking up for me now?" I told him it wasn't torture; the cook was celebrating a birthday and he could sit down with her.

I had the cook prepare all her favorite foods and in copious quantities. This cook weighed about three hundred pounds and she enjoyed eating. I had her set up a small table with two settings, and I had Herbert sit watching her eat. Hungry from his outside work, and faced with all that solid food, he said, "This is devilish torture." The cook ate unconcernedly, with the greatest pleasure. Finally Herbert said to her, "Do you mind if I have some?" She said, "Help yourself, have as much as you want." Herbert ate that solid food. Meat, gravy, potatoes. She was an excellent cook. That ended Herbert's eating problems. That approach was based upon the simple idea that everyone has had the experience of watching someone eat and thinking "My, that looks good, I wish I could have some."

Because Herbert had defined himself as incapable of moving, I was able to place him where I wished and he would stay there. I was careful not to change that until later. I used that in having him watch a game of cards.

Herbert had been an incessant gambler before he came to the hospital. Not particularly for money but because he liked to play cards. He knew every kind of card game there was, and he considered himself an expert. Since Herbert wouldn't move, I stood him in a corner and set up a card table in front of him. At the table I placed four patients who were pretty badly deteriorated with paresis. They just didn't know quite what was what. One would be playing poker, another bridge, another pinochle. One would say, "What's wild?" the other would reply, "I'll bet you two trump." They put one card on another with no reference to each other. I said to Herbert, "You know, you really should have some recreation. Sorry you have to stand still, can't turn around, can't play cards. But you can watch this card game." He said, "You always think of a devilish form of torture." I stood him behind each of the players so he could study their play, saying, "You know, there are different points of view about playing cards."

Herbert put up with that chaotic card game for several evenings, and then he capitulated. "If you will get three good card-players who know what they're talking about, I'll play cards." He couldn't tolerate that insult to a good cardplayer—having to watch people play stupidly.

Herbert and I had a number of battles like that, and each time he lost a battle it built up his realization that I definitely knew what I was talking about. He lost often enough to feel quite agreeable about leaving the hospital and making it on his own.

When Erickson left his hospital position in the late 1940s, he entered private practice and dealt with psychotic people in his office in a similar way. Although he began in involve the family more, his approach to pecular behavior continued to be an acceptance of it in such a way that it changed. In a recent conversation he was asked about his general approach.

INTERVIEWER: To get back to adolescent schizophrenia. Suppose someone called you and said there was a kid, nineteen or twenty years old, who has been a very good boy, but all of a sudden this week he started walking around the neighborhood carrying a large cross. The neighbors are upset and the family's upset, and would you do something about it. How would you think about that as a problem? Some kind of bizarre behavior like that.

ERICKSON: Well, if the kid came in to see me, the first thing I would do would be to want to examine the cross. And I would want to improve it in a very minor way. As soon as I got the slightest minor change in it, the way would be open for a larger change. And pretty soon I could deal with the advantages of a different cross—he ought to have at least two. He ought to have at least three so he could make a choice each day of which one. It's pretty hard to express a psychotic pattern of behavior over an ever increasing number of crosses.

INTERVIEWER: Would you assume that this was some sort of expression that indicated a crazy kind of family?

ERICKSON: I would take it as a helpless declaration that "the family is driving me nuts; they're a cross I cannot bear."

INTERVIEWER: But even given that premise, you would go right to the cross—not immediately to the family.

ERICKSON: No, because the family is going to defend their boy and they will descend harder on him. And that kid is lonesome enough. He's got an unbearable cross to bear. He's all alone with his cross and he's announcing it publicly. And the entire neighborhood is also rejecting him. He's very much alone. What he needs is an improvement of his cross.

INTERVIEWER: You'd start by seeing him and not the parents.

ERICKSON: Much later I might bring the parents in.

INTERVIEWER: But the parents are going to react to a proliferation of crosses, aren't they?

ERICKSON: Oh, yes, they will. But, you know, my office is a very nice place to keep his crosses.

INTERVIEWER: Most people who assume that a boy like that is representing a crazy family would go immediately to the family and assume that he would change as whatever was going on in the family changed.

ERICKSON: Perhaps I can give you an example. Someone summons you for help and you find that there are a whole lot of big stones on the highway. You see a detour with only one stone on it. You take the detour, because you are summoned by society and you have to do something right away. The pile of big stones is the family, and the detour with one stone is the psychotic kid. You give him an area in which he can feel free to be himself, and one where his abnormalities are not rejected but treated respectfully. They deserve good attention, not destructive attention, and you give that and then deal with the family.

When there is a failure of disengagement from the family, the child can continue to be involved with his parents as he grows older. Men and women in their forties and fifties can be as entangled with their parents as can teen-agers if the disengagement process has gone badly. Sometimes they intermittently avoid their families and function as social isolates with bizarre ideas. At other times they stay literally entangled with parents and neither parent nor child can get free of each other.

Once one views the weaning process as reciprocal, it is clear that not only do parents benevolently and helpfully hold on to a child, but the child also clings to the parents. The system functions as if separation would be disastrous. These pathetic relationships can continue to quite an advanced age for all participants. An example illustrates a way Erickson intervened to bring about at least a partial disengagement between a mother and a lifelong problem son.

I had been working with a seventy-year-old mother and her fifty-year-old schizophrenic son. She was a forceful woman and dragged him in to see me, literally. She and her son could not manage independent activity and were together constantly. The mother told me she would like to spend the day in the library reading, but she was not able to because she must be with her son. He moaned and groaned if she left him even for a little while.

In the son's presence, I told the mother to obtain a library book and then take a drive with her son out into the desert. She was to dump him out of the car and drive three miles down the deserted road. Then she was to sit there and enjoy reading until he had walked up and joined her. The mother objected to this idea when I suggested it. She thought it was too hard for her son to walk in the desert in that hot sun. I persuaded her to try it. I told her, "Now listen, your son is going to fall down, he's going to crawl on his hands and knees, he's going to wait out there helplessly to stir up your sympathies. But on that road there will be no passers-by, and the only way he can reach you is by walking. He might try to punish you by making you sit there and wait for five hours. But remember, you have a good book, and he's out on that ground for that length of time. He'll get hungry."

The mother obeyed my instructions. The son tried everything, but he ended up having to walk the three miles. His mother said, "You know, I'm getting to like this reading out in the open." Her son began to walk more and more briskly so that she didn't have quite so long to read. I suggested that when he volunteered to walk, she could cut the distance down to a mile. He volunteered and so only had to walk one mile instead of three.

His mother was astonished at his improvement. She had wanted to put him in a hospital, and had come to see me to see if that could be avoided. Now she began to see some hope for him. Next she wondered if he could start bowling. She began to think of helping him, but not in the old, soft, maternal way.

I knew the son should exercise. As soon as I started him walking, I knew he was going to find some other exercise that he would prefer. He liked the idea of bowling and began to do that. I don't care if he walks or if he bowls, but I'm leading him toward doing what he wants to do. With this kind of directive, you establish a class of things for someone to do, such as the class of "exercising." Then you provide one item in that class such as a walk in the hot desert, which is something he isn't going to be very happy to do. You want him to "spontaneously" find another item in that class. The population of patients tend not to be people who do things that are good for them; that they enjoy and succeed at. They fight against that sort of thing. Therefore you inspire them.

When one examines the ways Erickson deals with the problem of weaning parents and children from each other, it would appear that he sees therapy at this stage as an "initiation ceremony." Most cultures have such ceremonies, and they function not only to allow the young person to shift to the status of an adult but also to require his parents to deal with him as an adult. The culture provides ways to help families through this stage. If a culture lacks such a ceremony—and America appears to—then an intervention by a therapist becomes the ritual that disengages child from parent. Erickson's model for dealing with this stage of family life is not a simple one. He sees the problem of weaning parents from children as a process not merely of disengagement but also of re-engagement in new ways. The parents are not giving up a child but gaining a grandchild, and the child is not losing his parents but remaining involved with them in a way different from that of the past. It is not a simple matter of dependence versus independence but of getting past a stage that is necessary in family life. By taking the dilemma of both child and parents into account, Erickson avoids the errors of Mesmer, Freud, and others who saw the problem as one of a divided camp where the therapist must choose which side to be on in the attempt to help the child achieve "independence." Siding with the young person against the parents at this stage can lead to peculiar and strange young people who lose continuity with their families. The parents, too, lose the continuity through the child that is their immortality.

To illustrate the importance of helping a young adult and his parents successfully to become disengaged and re-engaged, an example can be given of a procedure in India, where the problem is taken so seriously that many years of preparation are involved.

Though natural and sincere, this powerful bond between mother and child, in a country where the mother's existence is built with a religious exclusiveness upon this bond and little else, holds the danger of a profound and almost insoluble crisis for mother as well as son. The threat of the crisis can poison the relationship between mother and son and the son's whole life. But the natural, painful and necessary release of the son from the mother, her giving of her fruit (*phala*) as a gift (*dāna*) to the world, is made possible by the observance (*vrata*) of the giving of the fruit (*phala-dāna-vrata*).

She who would make so great a sacrifice must begin with little things, and through them prepare for the great sacrifice. The time for the beginning of this observance is indefinite; it is somewhere around the son's fifth year but it may be later. The observance continues for an indeterminate number of years and takes up one month each year. The house Brahman and spiritual director of the family (*guru*) supervises it and determines its course; it is he who decides when the mother is ready for termination; that is, at what point, after what preliminary sacrifices, she is prepared for the actual sacrifice of her son. The woman begins with the sacrifice of little fruits of which she is very fond. . . . On each of his visits the guru tells the mother a mythical tale of a woman who sacrificed everything and thence derived the strength to accomplish all things; silent and attentive, holding holy grass in her folded hands, the woman listens, takes in his words and turns them over in her heart.

Each year a new and more precious fruit serves as the symbol at the center of this observance. The sacrifice advances from fruits to metals, from iron to copper, bronze and finally to gold. These are the metals of which a woman's ornaments are fashioned. . . . The last, extreme stage of the sacrifice is a total fast. . . . Brahmans, relatives and household attend this ceremony, representing the world, to which the son must be given. . . . A relative of the male line must also attend to represent the aspect of the world which is most involved in the mother's sacrifice of her son. . . . In this observance, myth and rite combine to effect the necessary transformation in the mother: to release her from the beloved son, whose bond with her she is keenly aware of and would like to maintain forever.*

* Heinrich Zimmer, "On the Significance of the Indian Tantric Yoga," in *Spiritual Disciplines*, edited by Joseph Campbell, Vol. IV, Bollingen series (New Brunswick, N. J.: Princeton University Press, 1960), pp. 4–5.

Although American mothers and sons might not be quite so overinvolved as in this example from India, the bond is deep and disengagement is never a simple process. Over the years Erickson has experimented with a variety of procedures for helping families past this stage of development. Typically, he proceeds by dealing with both child and parents. By using himself as a bridge between the generations, he shifts the parents into an acceptance of the inevitable growth of the young adult and he helps the child into an involvement with peers outside the family.

According to Erikson, just moving the child out of the parental home and resolving the parental difficulties might in some cases not be enough. For a period of time the child can have difficulty getting integrated into a network outside the family, particularly if the family has had rules against intimacy with outsiders. In such cases the young person can be living by himself but subjectively still not functioning like an autonomous person—"I've been away from home seventy-two days and twenty-three hours." Usually a courtship process gets him involved with his peers. Sometimes there is a pre-courtship phase when the child first begins to respond to someone else besides his parents. Erickson gives a procedure for starting the child into a different life.

When you help the child move away from his parents, you also start the process of having him identify people in his new environment. For example, I finally managed to have the daughter of a family I have been dealing with move out of the parental home into her own apartment. Yet she goes to sleep in that apartment with the idea, the feeling, she's still at home and Papa and Mama are in the next room asleep. She said it was so unreal and yet so real. She could almost hear her parents snore or hear them turn over in bed. She hadn't really left her parents.

I posed the girl the problem of finding out in how many ways that landlady and landlord were different from her father and mother. She began to report that the landlady and landlord were crude people, they talk with poor English. They're grasping and not generous. "They aren't thoughtful." Soon she brought in the concept, "But they *do* leave me alone." At that point I had the opening wedge inserted and the young person was starting to identify other people. It's a simple problem of identification of two specimens of the human race. The landlady was so tall, and she weighed so much, and the landlord had a mustache. In time the girl began to look at them as not just physical objects but living human beings.

The first thing they know, they have built up some relationships with other people. The more relationships a young person builds up with other people, the more the relationship with father and mother is adulterated. If at the same time the father and mother are occupied with their own interests, the young person is less intensely involved with them.

IX

THE PAIN OF OLD AGE

Although many people cope with old age gracefully and meet death with dignity, this is not always so. Problems that arise at this stage can be the most difficult for a therapist. One cannot engender hope for the future as leverage for change but must work for acceptance of the inevitable. When the culture puts great value on youth and little value on old age, the problems of the elderly increase. Instead of being considered assets because their longer life has given them wisdom, the elderly can feel that in this time of rapid change they are out of date and superfluous. Often, too, the family problems and symptoms that were tolerable become more intolerable with age.

Before proceeding to some of the ways Erickson deals with grim problems of pain and death, let us examine a more amusing case showing the cure of a symptom that had been a lifelong problem but that became severe with old age. An elderly gentleman came to Erickson to recover from a fear of elevators that had been with him all his life. For many years he had worked on the top floor of a particular building, and he had always walked up the stairs. Now that he was getting old, the climb was too difficult and he wished to recover from his fear.

Erickson has typically used hypnosis when working with such symptoms. If a person can experience an elevator ride without fear, he will often recover and be able to ride in them from that point on. A routine Erickson procedure when using hypnosis is to give a posthypnotic suggestion that will distract the patient from being afraid in an elevator. For example, he will give a person the suggestion that he will be excessively preoccupied with the sensations in the soles of his feet on the way to a certain address. The address will be an office in a high building, and the man must ride in an elevator to reach it. Because of his preoccupation with the sensations in his feet as the elevator lifts, the person will be distracted and ride in the elevator without fear, and once he has successfully experienced the elevator ride, he can ride in them in the future.

With this elderly gentleman Erickson did not use hypnosis. Instead, he used a social situation to distract the man just as he might have used a posthypnotic situation to do so. The old gentleman was a very proper, prudish man who was married to a proper and prudish wife. It was his overconcern with propriety that determined Erickson's strategy. He reports:

> When the old gentleman asked if he could be helped for his fear of riding in an elevator, I told him I could probably scare the pants off him in *another* direction. He told me that nothing could be worse than his fear of an elevator.
>
> The elevators in that particular building were operated by young girls, and I made special arrangements with one in advance. She agreed to cooperate and thought it would be fun. I went with the gentleman to the elevator. He wasn't afraid of walking *into* an elevator, but when it started to move it became an unbearable experience. So I chose an unbusy time and I had him walk in and out of the elevator, back in and out. Then at a point when we walked in, I told the girl to close the door and said, "Let's go up." She went up one story and stopped in between floors. The gentleman started to yell, "What's wrong!" I said, "The elevator operator wants to *kiss* you." Shocked, the gentleman said, "But I'm a married man!" The girl said, "I don't mind that." She walked toward him, and he stepped back and said, "You start the elevator." So she started it. She went up to about the fourth floor and stopped it again between floors. She said, "I just have a craving for a kiss." He said, "You go about your business." He wanted that elevator moving, not standing still. She replied, "Well, let's go down and

start all over again," and she began to take the elevator down. He said, "Not down, up!" since he didn't want to go through *that* all over again. She started up and then stopped the elevator between floors and said, "Do you promise you'll ride down in my elevator with me when you're through work?" He said, "I'll promise anything if you promise not to kiss me." He went up in the elevator, relieved and without fear—of the elevator—and could ride one from then on.

One of Erickson's specialties has been his use of hypnosis in his work with pain. Often he has been called upon to provide relief for someone in the last stages of a painful terminal illness. In such cases a person can die in terrible pain, or when he is so full of medication to prevent the pain that he is out of contact with life long before he dies. A routine method Erickson uses in his approach to this difficult problem is described in the following case.

A woman was dying with cancer of the uterus and was kept in a narcotic semistupor as a way of controlling her pain so that she could sleep and eat without extensive nausea and vomiting. She resented her inability to spend the remaining weeks of her life in contact with her family, and the family physician decided to try hypnosis. Erickson was called, and he arranged that narcotics be omitted on the day he was to see her. He makes this arrangement so that the drugs will not interfere with his work and the patient will be highly motivated to respond to him.

I worked with the patient four continuous hours, systematically teaching her, despite her attacks of pain, to go into a trance, to develop a numbness of her body, to absorb herself in a state of profound fatigue so that she could have physiological sleep despite the pain, and to enjoy food without gastric distress. Her desperate situation motivated her to a ready acceptance of suggestions without questioning doubts. I also trained her to respond hypnotically to her husband, her oldest daughter, and her family physician so that hypnosis could be reinforced in the event of any new development when I was not there. Only this one long hypnotic session was required. She could discontinue her medication except for one heavy hypodermic administered late on a Thursday evening, which gave her additional relief and allowed her to be in full contact with her family in a rested state on the weekends. She also shared in the family evening activities during the week. Six weeks after her first trance, while talking to her daughter, she suddenly lapsed into a coma. She died two days later without recovering consciousness.

This kind of approach is often reported by Erickson, sometimes with variations. He will teach the subject how to develop numbness in the body, or he will add to this a suggestion that the patient feel detached and dissociated from the body. Sometimes he will include a change in the person's concept of time. For example, with an older man in the terminal stages of a carcinomatous illness he proceeded in this way:

> The patient had a complaint of a constant heavy, dull, throbbing ache, as well as sharp agonizing pains that came about ten minutes apart. I suggested that his body would feel tremendously heavy, like a dull, leaden weight. It would feel as if sodden with sleep and incapable of sensing anything except heavy tiredness. As he experienced this dull, heavy tiredness of his body, it would go to sleep while his mind remained awake. To deal with the recurrent sharp pains, I had him fix his eyes on the clock and await the next sharp pain. The several minutes of waiting in dread seemed hours long to the patient, and it became a relief from this dreaded waiting to actually feel the next sharp pain. In this way the anticipation and the pain were differentiated for him as separate experiences. I was then able to teach him hypnotic time distortion so that he could learn to subjectively lengthen time by feeling that a longer time had passed than really had by the clock. He could lengthen the time between pains and so have longer periods free of pain, and he could shorten the time he actually felt the pain. At the same time I taught him amnesia for a pain, so that he would not look back with distress upon the previous one or look forward to the next one with dread and fear. Each sharp pain he experienced he would immediately forget, so that the next one would occur as an unexpected experience. Because the pain was not anticipated or remembered, it became a transient experience as a flash of sensation. The patient reported that hypnosis had freed him almost completely of pains, that he felt heavy, weak, and dull physically, and that not over twice a day did any pain "break through." Some weeks later he lapsed into a coma and died.

A unique approach to a similar problem was the case of a man called Joe. He was a florist who grew the flowers he sold and was an enthusiastic businessman, respected by family and friends. He developed a growth on the side of his face, and when the surgeon removed it there was found to be a malignancy. Joe was informed he had about a month to live, became unhappy and distressed, and developed extremely severe pain. Narcotics were giving him little relief, and a relative asked Erickson to try hypnosis. Erickson agreed reluctantly to see him, doubting whether he could do much in this situation. There were toxic reactions from excessive medication, and Joe disliked even the mention of the word hypnosis. In addition, one of his children was a resident in psychiatry who had been taught that hypnosis was of no value.

I was introduced to Joe, who acknowledged the introduction in a courteous and friendly fashion. I doubt if he knew why I was there. Upon inspecting him, I noted that much of the side of his face and neck was missing because of surgery, ulceration, maceration, and necrosis. A tracheotomy had been performed on him and he could not talk. He communicated with pencil and paper. He slept little and had special nurses constantly at hand, yet he was constantly hopping out of bed, writing innumerable notes about his business and his family. Severe pain distressed him continuously, and he could not understand why the doctors could not handle their business as efficiently and competently as he did his floral business.

After the introduction, Joe wrote, "What do you want?" Despite my doubts about being able to help him, I felt that if I was genuinely interested in him and desired to help him, this would be some comfort both to him and to the family members within listening distance in the side room. I began an approach to hypnosis which I call the interspersal technique. It is a way of talking as if in a casual conversation, but certain words and phrases are given special emphasis so they will be effective suggestions. (They are italicized in the following discourse.) I said, "Joe, I would like to talk to you. I know you are a florist, that you grow flowers, and I grew up on a farm in Wisconsin and I liked growing flowers. I still do. So I would like to have you take a seat in that easy chair as I talk to you. I'm going to say a lot of things to you, but it won't be about flowers because you know more than I do about flowers. *That isn't what you want.* Now, as I talk, and I can do so *comfortably*, I wish that you would *listen to me comfortably* as I talk about a tomato plant. That is an odd thing to talk about. It makes one *curious. Why talk about a tomato plant?* One puts a tomato seed in the ground. One can *feel hope* that it will grow into a tomato plant that *will bring satisfaction* by the fruit it has. The seed soaks up water, *not very much difficulty* in doing that because of the rains that *bring peace and comfort* and the joy of growing to flowers and tomatoes. That little seed, Joe, slowly swells and sends out a little rootlet with cilia on it. Now, you may not know what cilia are, but cilia are *things that work* to help the tomato seed grow, to push up above the ground as a sprouting plant, and *you can listen to me, Joe*, so I will keep on talking and *you can keep on listening, wondering, just wondering what you can really learn*, and here is your pencil and your pad, but speaking of the tomato plant, it grows so slowly. *You cannot see* it grow, *you cannot hear* it grow, but grow it does—the first little leaflike things on the stalk, the fine little hairs on the stem. Those hairs are on the leaves too, like the cilia on the roots; they must make the tomato plant *feel very good, very comfortable* if you can think of a plant as feeling, and then, *you can't see* it growing, *you can't feel* it growing, but another leaf appears on that little tomato stalk and then another. Maybe—and this is talking like a child—maybe the tomato plant does *feel comfortable and peaceful* as it grows. Each day it grows and grows and grows, *it's so comfortable, Joe*, to watch a plant grow and *not see* its growth, *not feel* it, but just know that *all is getting better* for that little tomato plant that is adding yet another leaf and still another and a branch, and it is *growing comfortably* in all directions." (Much of the above by this time had been repeated many times, sometimes just phrases, sometimes sentences. Care was taken to vary the wording and also to repeat the hypnotic suggestions. Quite some time later, Joe's wife came tiptoeing into the room carrying a sheet of paper on which was written the question, "When are you going to start the hypnosis?" I failed to cooperate with her by looking at the paper, and it was necessary for her to thrust the sheet of paper in front of me and therefore in front of Joe. I was continuing the description of the tomato plant uninterruptedly, and Joe's wife, as she looked at Joe, saw that he was not seeing her, did not know that she was there, that he was in a somnambulistic trance. She withdrew at once.) "And soon the tomato plant will have a bud form somewhere, on one branch or another, but it makes no difference because all the branches, the whole tomato plant will soon have those nice little buds. I wonder if the tomato plant can, *Joe, feel, really feel, a kind of comfort*. You know, Joe, a plant is a wonderful thing, and *it is so nice, so pleasing* just to be able to think about a plant as if it were a man. Would such a plant *have nice feelings, a sense of comfort* as the tiny little tomatoes begin to form, so tiny, yet so *full of promise to give you the desire to eat* a luscious tomato, sun-ripened, it's so *nice to have food in one's stomach*, that wonderful feeling a child, a thirsty child has and can *want a drink. Joe*, is that the way the tomato plant feels when the rain falls and washes everything so that *all feels well?*" (Pause.) "*You know, Joe, a* tomato plant just flourishes each day *just a day at a time*. I like to think the tomato plant can *know the fullness of comfort each day. You know, Joe, just one day at a time* for the tomato plant. That's the way for all tomato plants." (Joe suddenly came out of the trance, appeared disoriented, hopped up on the bed, and waved his arms, and his behavior was highly suggestive of the sudden surges of toxicity one sees in patients who have reacted unfavorably to barbiturates. Joe did not seem to hear or see me until he hopped off the bed and had walked toward me. I took a firm grip on Joe's arm and then immediately loosened it. The nurse was summoned. She mopped perspiration from his forehead, changed his surgical dressings, and gave him, by tube, some ice water. Joe then let me lead him back to his chair. After my pretense of being curious about Joe's forearm, Joe seized his pencil and paper and wrote, "Talk, talk.") "Oh, yes, Joe, I grew up on a farm, I think a tomato seed is a wonderful thing; *think, Joe, think*, in that little seed there does *sleep so restfully, so comfortably* a beautiful plant yet to be grown that will bear such interesting leaves and branches. The leaves, the branches look so beautiful, that beautiful rich color, *you can really feel happy* looking at a tomato seed, thinking about the wonderful plant it contains *asleep, resting, comfortable, Joe*. I'm soon going to leave for lunch and I'll be back and I will talk some more."

Despite his toxic state, spasmodically evident, Joe was definitely accessible. Moreover, he learned rapidly despite my absurdly amateurish rhapsody about a tomato seed and plant. Joe had no real interest in pointless remarks about a tomato plant. Joe wanted freedom from pain, he wanted comfort, sleep. This was what was uppermost in Joe's mind, foremost in his emotional desires, and he would have a compelling need to try to find something of value to him in my babbling. That desired value was there, so spoken that Joe could literally receive it without realizing it. Joe's arousal from the trance was only some minutes after I had said so seemingly innocuously, "Want a drink, Joe?" Nor was the re-induction of the trance difficult, achieved by two brief phrases, "Think, Joe, think" and "Sleep so restfully, so comfortably," embedded in a rather meaningless sequence of ideas. But what Joe wanted and needed was in that otherwise meaningless narration, and he promptly accepted it.

During lunchtime, Joe was first restful and then slowly restless; another toxic episode occurred, as was reported by the nurse. By the time I returned, Joe was waiting impatiently for me. Joe wanted to communicate by writing notes. Some were illegible because of his extreme impatience in writing. He would irritably rewrite them. A relative helped me read these notes. They concerned things about

Joe his past history, his business, his family, and "last week terrible," "yesterday was terrible." There were no complaints, no demands, but there were some requests for information about me. After a fashion we had a satisfying conversation, as was judged by an increasing loss of his restlessness. When I suggested that he cease walking around and sit in the chair used earlier, he did so readily and looked expectantly at me.

"You know, Joe, I could talk to you some more about the tomato plant, and if I did you would probably go to sleep—in fact, a good sound sleep." (This opening statement has every earmark of being no more than a casual, commonplace utterance. If the patient responds hypnotically, as Joe promptly did, all is well. If the patient does not respond, all you have said was just a commonplace remark, not at all noteworthy. Had Joe not gone into a trance immediately, there could have been a variation such as, "But instead, let's talk about the tomato flower. You have seen movies of flowers slowly, slowly opening, giving one a sense of peace, a sense of comfort as you watch the unfolding. So beautiful, so restful to watch. One can feel such infinite comfort watching such a movie.")

Joe's response that afternoon was excellent despite several intervening episodes of toxic behavior and several periods when I deliberately interrupted my work to judge more adequately the degree and amount of Joe's learning.

When I departed that evening, Joe cordially shook my hand. His toxic state was much lessened; he had no complaints, he did not seem to have distressing pain, and he seemed to be pleased and happy.

Relatives were concerned about posthypnotic suggestions, but they were reassured that such had been given. This had been done most gently in describing in so much detail and repetition the growth of the tomato plant and then, with careful emphasis, "You know, Joe, know the fullness of comfort each day," and "You know, Joe, just one day at a time."

About a month later, around the middle of November, I asked to see Joe again. Upon arriving at Joe's home, I was told a rather regrettable but not actually unhappy story. Joe had continued his excellent response after I departed on that first occasion, but hospital gossip had spread the story of Joe's hypnosis, and interns, residents, and staff men came in to take advantage of Joe's capacity to be a good subject. They made all the errors possible for uninformed amateurs with superstitious misconceptions of hypnosis. Their behavior infuriated Joe, who knew that I had done none of the offensive things they were doing. This was a fortunate realization, since it permitted Joe to keep all the benefits acquired from me without letting his hostilities toward hypnosis interfere. After several days of annoyance, Joe left the hospital and went home, keeping one nurse in constant attendance, but her duties were relatively few.

During that month at home he had actually gained weight and strength. Rarely did a surge of pain occur, and when it did it could be controlled either with aspirin or with 25 milligrams of Demerol. Joe was very happy to be with his family.

Joe's greeting to me on the second visit was one of obvious pleasure. However, I noted that he was keeping a wary eye on me, hence I took great care to be completely casual and to avoid any hand movement that could be remotely misconstrued as a "hypnotic pass" such as the hospital staff had employed.

Framed pictures painted by a highly talented member of his family were proudly displayed. There was much casual conversation about Joe's improvement and his weight gain, and I was repeatedly hard pushed to find simple replies to conceal pertinent suggestions. Joe did volunteer to sit down and let me talk to him. Although I was wholly casual in manner, the situation was thought to be most difficult to handle without arousing Joe's suspicions. Perhaps this was an unfounded concern, but I wished to be most careful. Finally I reminisced about "our visit last October." Joe did not realize how easily this visit could be pleasantly vivified for him by such a simple statement as "I talked about a tomato plant then, and it almost seems as if I could be *talking about a tomato plant right now. It is so enjoyable to talk about a seed, a plant.*" Thus there was, clinically speaking, a re-creation of all of the favorable aspects of that original interview.

Joe was most insistent on supervising my luncheon that day, which was a steak barbecued under Joe's watchful eye in the back yard beside the swimming pool. It was a happy gathering of four people thoroughly enjoying being together, Joe being obviously most happy.

After luncheon, Joe proudly displayed the innumerable plants, many of them rare, that he had personally planted in the large back yard. Joe's wife furnished the Latin and common names for the plants, and Joe was particularly pleased when I recognized and commented on some rare plant. Nor was this a pretense of interest, since I am still interested in growing plants. Joe regarded this interest in common to be a bond of friendship.

During the afternoon, Joe sat down voluntarily, his very manner making evident that I was free to do whatever I wished. I began a long monologue in which were included psychotherapeutic suggestions of continued ease, comfort, freedom from pain, enjoyment of family, good appetite, and a continuing pleased interest in all surroundings. All of these and other similar suggestions were interspersed unnoticeably among many remarks. These covered a multitude of topics to preclude Joe from analyzing or recognizing the interspersing of suggestions. Also, for adequate disguise, I need a variety of topics. Whether or not such care was needed in view of the good rapport is a debatable question, but I preferred to take no risks.

Medically, the malignancy was continuing to progress, but despite this fact, Joe was in much better physical condition than he had been a month previously. When I took my departure, Joe invited me to return again.

Joe knew that I was going on a lecture trip in late November and early December. Quite unexpectedly I received a long-distance telephone call just before departing on this trip. The call was from Joe's wife, who said, "Joe is on the extension line and wants to say 'hello' to you, so listen." Two brief puffs of air were heard. Joe had held the telephone mouthpiece over his tracheotomy tube and had exhaled forcibly twice to simulate "hello." His wife said that both she and Joe extended their best wishes for the trip, and we had a casual friendly conversation, Joe's wife reading Joe's written notes.

I received a Christmas card from Joe and his family. In a separate letter, his wife had said, "The hypnosis is doing well but Joe's condition is failing." Early in January, Joe was weak but comfortable. Finally, in his wife's words, "Joe died quietly January 21," four months after the discovery of his condition.

This "tomato-plant induction" by Erickson is characteristic of his way of working indirectly with people who might resist more direct suggestions.

A much more active indirect approach is illustrated in the following case. Although most hypnosis is conducted in a dyad, this was a situation in which there was a triadic induction.

A woman was referred to me by a doctor in the town of Mesa. She was an intelligent woman with a master's degree in English, and she had published a couple of books of poetry. She developed carcinoma of the uterus, with metastasis in her bones so severe it was inoperable and cobalt therapy gave her no help. She was in great pain, and narcotics did not relieve it. She also didn't believe that hypnosis could help that pain, but her doctor referred her to me to see what could be done.

I went out to her home and introduced myself. The woman was

in bed, and her daughter was there; a very sweet, pretty eighteen-year-old girl who was very much concerned about her mother's welfare. It was October, and the woman had been told she had only months to live. She told me she had only two real desires: she wanted to see her daughter married the following June, and she wanted to see her son graduate from college in June. She said, "I don't know any way I can cooperate with you in being hypnotized. To be honest, I don't believe there is such a thing as hypnosis that can undo pain the way I have it."

I said to her, "You don't believe you can be hypnotized, and the painful results of cancer don't give you grounds for thinking you can be relieved of that type of pain. But you know, there's a lot of talk about "seeing is believing." So suppose you watch your daughter as she sits down in this chair, and don't miss a thing because I want you to see and notice everything. What you'll see you won't like at all, and because you won't like it you're going to believe it. You'll know it's very real if you dislike it so much. Seeing is believing, and seeing this situation will definitely be believing."

Turning to the daughter, I said, "You want to help your mother. Now, I suppose you've never gone into hypnosis before today. I'm perfectly willing for you to take as much time as you want to. But I expect that you'll want your mother to see you go in as rapidly as possible. Be sure to respond to my suggestions carefully and completely, and if you find out that you're not succeeding, just slow up and take your time. Now you just look straight across the room at some one spot in that picture. You just watch it, and you'll notice while you're watching it, without shifting your gaze, that you've altered your rhythm of breathing and that your eyelids are blinking in a different than ordinary rate. I can see from the pulse at your ankle that your heart rate is decreased. Your eyelids are closing slowly, shortly they'll be shut and remain shut. As you know, they have closed and are staying closed; you feel a compelling need to take a deep breath and go deeply asleep. Then you will take another deep breath to enjoy being deeply asleep. Then take another deep breath and enjoy knowing that you are here alone with me, and that you feel comfortable and at ease, even though you do not seem to be able to move except in the matter of a careful, slow breathing and perhaps an awareness of your heartbeat and an awareness that you're no longer swallowing. Now you're beginning to lose all feeling throughout your body. Your entire body is losing all sense of feeling, and you'll be as completely unaware of stimuli—physical stimuli—to your body as you are to the sensations of the bedclothes at night, or your clothes in the daytime. Then all sensation will disappear completely and you'll have no more feeling than a sculptured marble figure would have. Even though I told you we were alone in this room, if I happen to turn my head away from you and direct my speech to another area, you will not hear it. "And now, mother—I want you to watch this very carefully." I moved the girl's skirt up to the upper third of her thighs. The mother suddenly thought I was making advances to her girl, and *she didn't like it.* I had told her she could see it and she would believe it and she wouldn't like it. Then I raised my hand and brought it down in an awfully hard slap on the girl's thigh. Mother watched the girl's face and there was not the slightest evidence of any response. I said to the mother, "This is rather incredible, isn't it? Let's try the arm." I slapped the arm. Mother said, "Did you feel that?" The girl didn't answer. I said, "Mother, when I'm talking to you, she can't even hear *me.*"

I turned to the girl and said, "We are alone in this bedroom. You nod your head signifying your answer." She nodded, and I turned back to the mother and said, "We can repeat that until you're really sure that you believe what you see. You know that's so, and you realize that seeing is believing." Again I slapped the girl's thighs hard. The mother watched the girl's face. The sound of that slap was nasty. It was hard. I said to the girl, "When you open your eyes, what do you see?" She opened them and said, "You." "Are we alone here?" "Yes." "Now, you can look at your hand?" "Yes." "All right, look at your hand now. Look down toward the bottom, and as your eyes move downward tell me what you see." "My blouse, my skirt, and my thighs, and my knees, and my feet."

I said, "Would you like to see something you would enjoy?" I gave her another hard slap on the thigh, and she said, "I didn't feel that, is there something wrong?" I said, "No, but you saw what I did. Do you believe it? You know you didn't feel it, so after you are awake, I want you to explain to your mother that you're comfortable, that you're ready to go into a trance. Then I want you to notice your lap. You'll notice something there that will distress you, but you won't be able to do anything about it. You'll find you'll have to ask me to do it for you."

I awakened the girl, and she told her mother she was ready to go into a trance and then said, "My skirt is up, I can't pull it down, I don't know how. Will you pull it down? I don't want my legs uncovered."

I said, "Your mother has seen an astonishing thing, because seeing is believing. You know, I don't think there is any feeling in your thighs." She said, "How did my skirt get up? You must have hypnotized me and anesthetized my legs. I can't move my hand. I just don't understand." I said, "You can't feel it when I slap your thighs; tell your mother." She said, "I don't know how it was done, but you sure slapped my thighs hard and I didn't feel it, and, Mother, I do wish you'd tell me that you believe it, because I'd like to pull my skirt down." The mother said, "But I *do* believe it!" So I pulled the skirt down and I said, "Just close your eyes a moment. When you open them, you won't remember what has been going on. Your mother will try to tell you something but you won't believe her. Take a few deep breaths and wake up." Her mother said, "How did you not feel those slaps on your bare thighs when he slapped you like that?" The daughter said, "He didn't slap me on my bare thighs." The mother saw the redness of her face and heard the tone of her voice. Hearing is believing too, just as feeling is believing.

I used less than four hours on that first visit. The next step was to have the girl see herself in a chair on the other side of the room, and then to experience herself as being over there. So I would turn my back to her and talk to her facing that direction. Then she could hear me. But she could not hear me when I faced toward where she was actually sitting, and the mother could see that. Then I had her hallucinate the slapping of her bare legs. I explained that she could question me about things that happened to her. She said, "I heard you talking to me. I heard the sound of you slapping my thighs. But I couldn't feel any pain." I said, "That's right. Any time I want to take the feeling out of your body and put it on the other side of the room, is that permissible? If you can teach your mother? All right, I'm going to take the feeling out of your back right now and put it over on the other side of the room." She tried to push her back against the chair, but she couldn't locate it somatically. "Then should I reach behind you and test you, or should I just tell your joints to loosen so you can lean against the back of the chair?" An innocent, intelligent, naïve girl. So I had taken the feeling out of her back. I said, "Suppose I bring the feeling back to your body and you think you're wide awake, so you can understand the experience when you are awake and when you're in a trance also. You can understand best in a trance. Then you can remember when you are awake and can talk to me and ask me questions. Now suppose I took all the body except your head and neck and shoulders and arms, and put all that lower part of your body over on the other side of the room on the bed there. Now suppose I put your head and shoulders in a wheel chair so that you can start wheeling the chair out into the living room." So we put her shoulders and arms in the wheel chair and the rest of her body on the bed. "Your mother's been watching this, she understands. Ask her if she understands." The mother said, "I understand."

The mother learned that all the painful feelings could go with her body when she put it in bed. She could get in her wheel chair with her head and shoulders and neck, and go out in the living room and watch a TV program.

I came in one morning and there was a new night nurse who told me the woman was sleeping well at night. "But," she said, "she will go and watch a TV program, and every time I try to talk to her she says, 'Hush.'"

I said to the woman, "Would you mind telling your nurse that you left your body in the bed on medical orders and put your head and shoulders in a wheel chair and went into the living room to watch TV? Tell her it's in accordance with my medical orders." The woman did, and the nurse looked at me and said, "What does that mean?" I said, "It means she's in a profound hypnotic trance and is feeling relief from the pain and enjoying the TV program—without any commercials."

In July she was visiting with friends in the living room (as far as she was concerned) and enjoying the conversation. They were actually beside her bed. She suddenly went into a coma and two hours later was dead. She had her two wishes that June. She had seen her son graduate—by hallucinating the graduation scene. Her daughter had been married in the bedroom in her presence.

Besides helping someone die gracefully, Erickson considers it his task also to help someone live out his later years functioning as fully as possible. Sometimes he achieves this goal with gentle hypnotic efforts and at other times he attacks the problem forcefully. Erickson considers his approach to the following case unorthodox, and it seems appropriate to end this work with a description of an unusual therapeutic strategy. He reports:

A woman in California wrote to me that her husband was totally paralyzed as the result of a stroke and could not talk. She asked if she could bring him to me. It was such a pitiful letter that I agreed, thinking that I might be able to comfort the woman enough to allow her to accept her difficult situation.

She brought her husband to Phoenix, registered at a motel, and came with him to see me. I had my two sons carry the man into the house, and I took the woman into my office and talked with her alone. She said that her husband, a man in his fifties, had this stroke a year previously, and for that year he had been lying helpless in a ward bed in the hospital of a university. The staff would point out to students, in his presence, that he was a terminal case, completely paralyzed, unable to talk, and all that could be done was to maintain his health until he eventually died.

The woman said to me, "Now, my husband is a Prussian German, a very proud man. He built up a business by himself. He's always been an active man and an omnivorous reader. All his life he's been an extremely domineering man. Now I've had to see him lying there helpless for a year, being fed, being washed, being talked about like a child. Every time I visited him at the hospital I'd see the hurt and utterly furious look in his eyes. They told me he was a terminal case, and I asked my husband if they had told him that, and he blinked his eyes affirmatively. That's the only means of communication he has."

As she talked, I realized that I need not merely comfort the woman; something might be done with the man. As I thought it over, here was a Prussian, short-tempered, domineering, highly intelligent, very competent. He had stayed alive with a furious anger for a year. His wife had, with extraordinary labor, managed to load him into a car, drive clear from California, drag him out of the car and put him into a motel, then take him out and put him into the car to drive to my house. My two sons had difficulty carrying him into the house, and yet this woman had moved him across country alone.

So I said to the woman, "You brought your husband to me to be helped. I'm going to do my level best to help him. I want to talk to your husband, and I want you to be present, but I can't have you interfering. You won't understand *what* or *why* I'm doing what I'm going to do. But you can understand my statement that you are to sit there quietly with a straight face and say nothing, do nothing, no matter what." She managed to accept that; later, when she wanted to interfere, a deterrent look restrained her.

I sat down in front of the man who was helpless in the chair, unable to move anything but his eyelids. I began to talk to him in roughly the following way. I said, "So you're a Prussian German. The stupid, God damn Nazis! How incredibly stupid, conceited, ignorant, and animal-like Prussian Germans are. They thought they owned the world, they destroyed their own country! What kind of epithets can you apply to those horrible animals. They're really not fit to live! The world would be better off if they were used for fertilizer."

The anger in his eyes was impressive to see. I went on, "You've been lying around on charity, being fed, dressed, cared for, bathed, toenails clipped. Who are you to merit anything? You aren't even the equal of a mentally retarded criminal Jew!"

I continued in that way, saying all the nasty things I could, adding such points as, "You're so God damn lazy you're content to lie in a charity bed." After a while I said, "Well, I haven't had much opportunity or time to think of all the insults you so richly merit. You're going to come back tomorrow. I'll have plenty of time the rest of today to think of all of the things I want to say to you. And you're going to come back, aren't you!" He came back right then with an explosive "No!"

I said, "So, for a year you haven't talked. Now all I had to do was call you a dirty Nazi pig, and you start talking. You're going to come back here tomorrow and get the *real* description of yourself!"

He said, "No, no, no!"

I don't know how he did it, but he managed to get to his feet. He knocked his wife to one side and he staggered out of the office. She started to rush after him, but I stopped her. I said, "Sit down, the worst he can do is crash to the floor. If he can stagger out to the car, that's exactly what you want."

He lurched out of the house, even down the steps, and he managed to crawl into the car. My sons were watching him, ready to run to his aid.

There is nothing quite like a Prussian; they can be so domineering, dictatorial, incredibly sensitive to what they consider insults. I have worked with Prussians. Their demand for respect is so great, their self-image so bloated with self-satisfaction. Here was a man who had been insulted beyond endurance for a whole year in the hospital—then I showed him what insults could really be like and he reacted.

I said to the wife, "Bring him back tomorrow at eleven o'clock in the morning. Drive him to the motel now, and drag him into his room. Put him to bed, following your previous routine of taking care of him. When it's time for him to go to sleep, as you walk out of his bedrom and into your own, tell him he has an appointment with me at eleven o'clock tomorrow. Then keep right on walking out of the room.

"Tomorrow morning feed him his breakfast and dress him. Then at ten-thirty say, 'We've got to leave now for Dr. Erickson's office.' Walk out and get the car, drive it up in front of the door, and race the engine. Wait until you see the doorknob turn. Then you can go and help your husband out and into the car."

The next morning they arrived. He walked, with only her

assistance, into the office and we got him seated in a chair. I simply said, "You know, it was worth going through that hell yesterday to be able to walk out of this office. To be able to say at least one word. Now the problem is, how do I get you to talk and to walk and to enjoy life and to read books. I prefer not to be as drastic again. But you didn't believe in yourself at all. I was sufficiently unpleasant to give you no recourse except to protest. I hope now we can be friends. Let's get started on your restoration to at least some normal activity."

He was very worried in his facial expression. I said, "You realize that I can make you speak by insulting you, but I think you can say 'yes' to a pleasant question. In the light of what we've already accomplished, after your year of terrible helplessness, I think you will want me to continue helping you. You can answer 'yes' or you can answer 'no.' He struggled and got a 'yes' out."

After about two months he was ready to return to California. He limped badly, had circumscribed use of his arm, and some aphasic speech, and he could read books but only if he held the book far to the side. I asked him what he thought had helped him. He said, "My wife brought me to you for hypnosis. I always had the feeling after that first day when you got me angry, you were hypnotizing me and making me do each thing that I succeeded in doing. But I'll take credit myself for walking fifteen miles one day in the Tucson zoo. I was very tired afterwards, but I did it."

He wanted to know if he could return to work, at least part time. I told him he would need to list the most simple things he could do in his place of business and content himself with doing those. He agreed to that.

I received letters from her and from him periodically for nearly seven years. They were happy years. The correspondence came at greater and greater intervals, and finally it ceased. Then about ten years after their visit, his wife wrote that her husband had again had a stroke and he was badly handicapped. Would I be willing to see him again to restore him to physical health?

Considering his age, I didn't think I could possibly take him. I wrote to her and pointed out that he was past the age of sixty, and he had been badly damaged by the first stroke. Now the second one had left him unconscious for several days. He was as helpless as he had been before. I told her I didn't think there was anything more I could do.